Evangelical Convictions

A Theological
Exposition
OF THE
Statement
of Faith
OF THE
Evangelical
Free Church
of America

Free Church Publications, Minneapolis MN

THE STATEMENT OF FAITH OF THE EVANGELICAL FREE CHURCH OF AMERICA

The Evangelical Free Church of America is an association of autonomous churches united around these theological convictions:

God

1. We believe in one God, Creator of all things, holy, infinitely perfect, and eternally existing in a loving unity of three equally divine Persons: the Father, the Son and the Holy Spirit. Having limitless knowledge and sovereign power, God has graciously purposed from eternity to redeem a people for Himself and to make all things new for His own glory.

The Bible

2. We believe that God has spoken in the Scriptures, both Old and New Testaments, through the words of human authors. As the verbally inspired Word of God, the Bible is without error in the original writings, the complete revelation of His will for salvation, and the ultimate authority by which every realm of human knowledge and endeavor should be judged. Therefore, it is to be believed in all that it teaches, obeyed in all that it requires, and trusted in all that it promises.

The Human Condition

3. We believe that God created Adam and Eve in His image, but they sinned when tempted by Satan. In union with Adam, human beings are sinners by nature and by choice, alienated from God, and under His wrath. Only through God's saving work in Jesus Christ can we be rescued, reconciled and renewed.

Jesus Christ

4. We believe that Jesus Christ is God incarnate, fully God and fully man, one Person in two natures. Jesus—Israel's promised Messiah—was conceived through the Holy Spirit and born of the virgin Mary. He lived a sinless life, was crucified under Pontius Pilate, arose bodily from the dead, ascended into heaven and sits at the right hand of God the Father as our High Priest and Advocate.

The Work of Christ

5. We believe that Jesus Christ, as our representative and substitute, shed His blood on the cross as the perfect, all-sufficient sacrifice for our sins. His atoning death and victorious resurrection constitute the only ground for salvation.

The Holy Spirit

6. We believe that the Holy Spirit, in all that He does, glorifies the Lord Jesus Christ. He convicts the world of its guilt. He regenerates sinners, and in Him they are baptized into union with Christ and adopted as heirs in the family of God. He also indwells, illuminates, guides, equips and empowers believers for Christ-like living and service.

The Church

7. We believe that the true church comprises all who have been justified by God's grace through faith alone in Christ alone. They are united by the Holy Spirit in the body of Christ, of which He is the Head. The true church is manifest in local churches, whose membership should be composed only of believers. The Lord Jesus mandated two ordinances, baptism and the Lord's Supper, which visibly and tangibly express the gospel. Though they are not the means of salvation, when celebrated by the church in genuine faith, these ordinances confirm and nourish the believer.

Christian Living

8. We believe that God's justifying grace must not be separated from His sanctifying power and purpose. God commands us to love Him supremely and others sacrificially, and to live out our faith with care for one another, compassion toward the poor and justice for the oppressed. With God's Word, the Spirit's power, and fervent prayer in Christ's name, we are to combat the spiritual forces of evil. In obedience to Christ's commission, we are to make disciples among all people, always bearing witness to the gospel in word and deed.

Christ's Return

9. We believe in the personal, bodily and premillennial return of our Lord Jesus Christ. The coming of Christ, at a time known only to God, demands constant expectancy and, as our blessed hope, motivates the believer to godly living, sacrificial service and energetic mission.

Response and Eternal Destiny

10. We believe that God commands everyone everywhere to believe the gospel by turning to Him in repentance and receiving the Lord Jesus Christ. We believe that God will raise the dead bodily and judge the world, assigning the unbeliever to condemnation and eternal conscious punishment and the believer to eternal blessedness and joy with the Lord in the new heaven and the new earth, to the praise of His glorious grace. Amen.

TABLE OF CONTENTS

EXPANDED TABLE OF CONTENTS

Article 1: God
God's gospel originates in and expresses the wondrous perfections of the eternal, triune God.

Article 2: The Bible
God's gospel is authoritatively revealed in the Scriptures.

Article 3: The Human Condition
God's gospel alone addresses our deepest need.

Article 4: Jesus Christ
God's gospel is made known supremely in the Person of Jesus Christ.

Article 8: Christian Living
God's gospel compels us to Christ-like living and witness to the world.

Article 9: Christ's Return
*God's gospel will be brought to fulfillment by the Lord Himself
at the end of this age.*

Article 10: Response and Eternal Destiny
God's gospel requires a response that has eternal consequences.

FOREWORD

It is a joy to write this foreword to the "theological exposition" of our 2008 Statement of Faith (SOF). For me the passing of the revised SOF was a culmination of a process that began during my ministry as the Executive Vice President to President Paul Cedar (1990-1996) when we initially began discussing the need for and possibility of revising our SOF. On this side of the adoption of that revision, I rejoice.

It will be helpful and important to give a brief overview of our history since the 1950 merger Conference in which the original SOF was adopted. In the late 1970s, questions about certain aspects of our SOF were raised. In particular, some asked about the word "imminent" and the breadth of its meaning. Eventually other questions were raised which led to a proposal in the early to mid 1990s to examine the SOF more closely. The intent was to do this revision in conjunction with the 50th anniversary of the SOF, adopting a revised SOF in 2000. Though the Conference discussed such a possibility, it decided not to pursue it.

In 2003 I revived the Spiritual Heritage Committee (SHC) with a group of pastor-theologians to serve the Board of Directors (BOD). They were tasked to help us remain true to the gospel and to retain our doctrinal fidelity as challenges emerged. In 2004 the possibility of and need for a revision to our SOF was again discussed by the BOD. The Board began with a great appreciation for our 1950 SOF. At this time they raised the question, which was passed on to the SHC, "Are there ways that our Statement could be strengthened, so that it might be refreshed and reaffirmed and thereby continue to be a standard that is truly embraced and not become a historical document that is given mere lip-service, as happens all too frequently in church bodies?"

After presenting three draft revisions of the SOF (December 2005, February 2006 and February 2007), the Board presented a Proposed Revision to the Conference in June 2007. During these years we had numerous public discussions regarding the various revisions. Every district conference and several churches invited members of the SHC to lead sessions where the fine points of the document were discussed. Two Midwinter Ministerial Conferences were dedicated to presentations and discussions regarding the revision, as were sessions at a number of the National Leadership Conferences.

Finally in 2008 the Proposed Revision was before the Conference to be discussed, debated and voted upon. After four amendments to the Revision were defeated, the Proposed Revision was debated. On June 26, 2008, after two days of discussion, 86% of the delegates at the 124th EFCA National Leadership Conference approved the Proposed Revision of the Statement of Faith. This was indeed an historic moment for the EFCA, one in which God's presence was clearly evident.

As I reflect on this whole process, I believe it manifested our congregational polity at its best. Leaders humbly led and listened. Fellow believers, the priesthood of believers, provided invaluable biblical and doctrinal input as we worked through various drafts. Together we adopted a new, strengthened SOF that will serve the EFCA well into the future.

There are many things for which I am thankful:

I am thankful for the wisdom and foresight our Free Church fathers had to adopt a SOF around which we would unite. Through the years since that time, God has used it to protect us from doctrinal aberrations and theological heresies.[1]

I am thankful for the godly leaders the Lord has given to the Free Church. The BOD led remarkably well through this whole process. I specifically mention those who served in leadership roles, who partnered with me closely: Brian Cole (2003-2005), Jimmy Kallam (2005-2007) and Steve Hawn (2007-2009), Chairs of the BOD, and Ron Aucutt, EFCA Moderator.

I am thankful for a Board that had the discernment to say that "where stands it written" is a reference to the Bible as our highest authority, not the SOF. And in light of new theological issues that needed to be addressed, they had the courage, standing on the Scripture, to review and revise our SOF. They also had the foresight to include a BOD policy that recognizes the need for every generation to review and possibly revise our SOF, thus ensuring that the next generation, standing unshakably upon the same inerrant Scripture, may address the new issues of their day.

I am thankful for a group of gifted pastor-theologians, the Spiritual Heritage Committee, who served the BOD so well and led the discussion in the EFCA with grace and truth, evidencing a humble orthodoxy. The SHC was made up of Mike Andrus, Bill Jones, Bill Kynes, David V. Martin, Ruben Martinez, Greg Strand (Chair), and Greg Waybright. These men manifested the fruit of the Spirit in all they did, and they left an aroma of Christ in all their discussions.

---

1 Interestingly, in 1950 a great deal of discussion concerned the need for and use of a SOF. In *This We Believe* (1961), A. T. Olson devoted half of the book to giving a history of Creeds and a defense of their use. Because a SOF has been at the heart of the EFCA since its inception, in our revision process we did not need to defend its use.

I am thankful for the robust theological dialogue that led to the adoption of a new, strengthened SOF. The Bible and doctrinal truth matter to Free Church people. This is a mark of health and vibrancy, and as long as this remains true, there is hope the Lord will continue to use us. Additionally, a biblically-strengthened SOF is especially encouraging in light of the fact that many denominations who are engaged in doctrinal discussions are weakening their commitment to Scripture and moving away from biblical truth.

I am thankful for a SOF that is centered on the gospel, the *evangel*, that focuses on essentials of the faith, and that emphasizes both orthodoxy and orthopraxy. The gospel is at the heart of what it means to be Evangelical, and it is at the heart of what it means to be a part of the Evangelical Free Church of America. The gospel is our reason for being. As a Free Church, we also remain committed to "major on majors and minor on minors." Though our premillennial distinctive remains, this SOF focuses on the essentials of the gospel and provides liberty in non-essential matters. Finally, this SOF emphasizes both the truth of the gospel which we profess and the entailments of the gospel which we live. Gospel truth does have a bearing on our lives. It is not only important to be orthodox but it is critical to declare that sound doctrine is to result in right living. This unique addition in Article 8 may be viewed by EFCA historians as the most important revision in the SOF.

A special word of thanks must be expressed to Greg Strand and Bill Kynes. Their tireless labor of love to produce this important work deserves our appreciation. Understanding and affirming our "evangelical convictions" will bring glory to the Father and will help us maintain the unity of the Spirit in our beloved EFCA. Thank you Greg and Bill for your major contribution to our movement.

It is a joy and privilege to serve as President of the EFCA. Let us pray that our 2008 Statement of Faith will serve this generation as well as the 1950 Statement served previous generations—that it will not only be used to affirm essential doctrinal truth and protect from doctrinal error, but that it will also be used to proclaim the gospel, expanding God's kingdom among all people. May we also pray that this book, *Evangelical Convictions*, will be a vital tool, an invaluable resource in the ongoing efforts to ensure we remain centered in the gospel of Jesus Christ.

Serving with Joy,
William J. Hamel
President EFCA

INTRODUCTION

The Evangelical Free Church of America
is an association of autonomous churches
united around these theological convictions: . . .

(Preamble to the Statement of Faith adopted by the EFCA Conference on June 26, 2008)

A Statement of Faith is more than a mere catalogue of theological propositions; it is an affirmation of convictions. In that sense, it is a confession, a creed (for the Latin word *credo* means "I believe"). As a corporate rather than mere individual expression ("*We* believe . . ."), it unites its adherents in a common faith. Moreover, a Statement of Faith is a declaration of identity. Not only the affirmations made but also the choices of what to include or exclude locate a group on an ecclesiastical grid and define what it considers most important. Our Statement of Faith reveals a great deal about who we are.

Since its inception in 1950, the Evangelical Free Church of America has had a strong Statement of Faith. After an extensive revision process, a new Statement was adopted in 2008 which built on the good work done in 1950. This book, published under the authority of the EFCA Board of Directors,[1] seeks to give clarity to the theological convictions contained in our Statement—spelling out what is affirmed and what is denied (and what is not addressed). Beyond that, it will expound these convictions—helping the reader understand and appreciate the wonderful truth contained in this brief and concise confession.[2] But before proceeding, we offer an introduction to this Statement of Faith and consider what it says about the Evangelical Free Church of America.

---

1 This book was drafted by members of the Spiritual Heritage Committee, but its content was vetted by numerous EFCA pastors and others in various areas of EFCA leadership and ministry, including President William J. Hamel, members of the Board of Ministerial Standing (which includes District Superintendents and the Chair of the Ministerial Association), representatives of ReachGlobal and faculty from Trinity Evangelical Divinity School.

2 This book resembles, in some respects, Arnold T. Olson's *This We Believe: The Background and Exposition of the Doctrinal Statement of The Evangelical Free Church of America* (Minneapolis: Free Church Publications, 1961), which commented on the 1950 EFCA Statement of Faith.

I. This Is an *Evangelical* Statement of Faith

We have titled this book *Evangelical Convictions*, for this Evangelical Free Church Statement of Faith declares our theological identity—we are Evangelicals. As such, it was drafted to reflect our affirmation of the central truths related to the *evangel*, that is, the gospel, as that gospel message has come to us through the biblical and historic stream of Evangelical Christianity.

A. Our Convictions Relate to the *Evangel*

Quite simply, our goal in formulating this Statement was to set forth "sound doctrine that conforms to the glorious gospel of the blessed God," which he has now entrusted to us (1 Tim. 1:10-11[3]). We believe that our essential theological convictions are vitally connected to this gospel.[4]

What is the gospel? The Apostle Paul describes this good news concisely as the declaration that "Christ died for our sins according to the Scriptures, that he was buried, that he was raised on the third day according to the Scriptures" (1 Cor. 15:3-4). This certainly is the heart of the message, but when we proclaim this message, we say much more than this. In a sense, the ten articles of our Statement unpack this simple message of good news by setting forth our central theological convictions in a way that follows the logic of the gospel itself.

First, we recognize this as *God's* gospel,[5] inasmuch as it comes from God and not from any human source. This message begins with God's eternal purpose to redeem a people for himself, a purpose flowing from his own nature. Second, this gospel is "according to the Scriptures," as Paul declares, and it comes to us authoritatively through God's Word in the Bible. Third, because it deals with our sin, God's gospel alone can address our deepest need. In Articles four through six we contend that this gospel is revealed in the Person of Jesus Christ, is accomplished through the work of Christ[6] and becomes effective in and for us through the application of Christ's work by the power of the Holy Spirit.[7] Seventh,

---

3 Biblical citations are taken from the New International Version (1984).

4 The position of premillennialism (in Article 9) is recognized as less central to our understanding of the gospel and is included more as a denominational distinctive. See further discussion of this in the exposition of that Article.

5 For this expression, cf. Rom. 1:1; 15:16; 2 Cor. 11:7; 1 Thess. 2:8-9; 1 Tim. 1:11; 1 Pet. 4:17.

6 Significantly, here at the center of our Statement we have the core of the gospel.

7 In sum, we emphasize the gracious initiative of God the Father in revelation, of God the Son in redemption and of God the Holy Spirit in restoration. Thus, the gospel is thoroughly Trinitarian.

in our union with Christ by the Spirit we are joined to a new community of fellow believers in the body of Christ, the church. As asserted in Article 8, the new life which the gospel imparts to us compels us to live in a new way. We are to love God and our neighbor and bear witness to the gospel in word and deed. This is our calling until God's saving purpose is fulfilled in the glorious return of Christ (Article 9). Finally, in Article 10, we affirm that this coming of Christ will bring with it not only the judgment of the world but also our bodily resurrection and the renewal of all things in the new heaven and the new earth. This is God's gospel, and this good news requires a response. We are to turn to God in repentance and faith, receiving the Lord Jesus Christ as our Savior. Thus, the various topics covered in our Statement—God, the Bible, the Human Condition, the Person of Christ, the Work of Christ, the Holy Spirit, the Church, the Christian Life, the Return of Christ, and the Response and Eternal Destiny—reflect this logical unfolding of the gospel.[8]

Our Statement of Faith is an expanded statement of the gospel. We do not claim that, to be saved, a person must understand and believe all that this Statement contains, but we do believe that it contains the truth that makes our salvation possible and the truth that tells us what our salvation means.

We contend that such a connection to God's saving work in the gospel ought to be the primary means of determining the core doctrines of our faith. Consider the theological controversies of the early church. Questions such as whether the Son of God was of the same or similar substance as the Father or whether Christ was of one or two natures may seem arcane and obscure to us. But these Trinitarian and Christological debates were deemed critical because of their relevance to our salvation.[9] The church determined that the Son of God must be of the same substance as the Father for only a Savior who was truly God *could* save us from our sin. And they determined that Christ must be truly man in every way for only a Savior who was truly human would be *qualified* to save us from our sin. In that sense, such doctrines are essential to the gospel. Thus, the

---

8 In the exposition of the Statement in this book a sub-heading, under the heading of each article, will make this connection with the gospel explicit. These sub-headings, providing a "gospel focus" for the entire Statement, were originally proposed as a part of the Statement itself but were dropped in the revision process. They were, however, retained in the version of the Statement adopted by the Evangelical Free Church of Canada in 2008. That Statement may be read at http://www.efccm.ca/wordpress/?page_id=274.

9 The Niceno-Constantinopolitan Creed (381; often referred to simply as the Nicene Creed) reflects this. Cf. the statement: "who for us men, *and for our salvation*, came down from heaven, and was incarnate by the Holy Ghost of the Virgin Mary, and was made man."

doctrines central to our faith are the doctrines that fit together to form the *evangel*, the message of God's saving work in Jesus Christ.

Because this Statement sets forth the gospel, we determined that it must also include elements of orthopraxy as well as orthodoxy. That is, it seeks to make a connection between what we believe and how we behave. The Bible makes it clear that to live licentiously is to deny the faith (cf., e.g., Jude 4; 1 Cor. 5:1-2; Titus 1:16; 2 Pet. 2:1). Our Article 8 makes this point explicitly, while it appears more indirectly in Articles 2 and 9.

Second, one cannot expound the gospel without also giving praise to God for his glorious grace. Thus, we intend the theology set forth in this Statement to be doxological—that is, it ought to lead us to exalt the greatness of our God. Thus our Statement begins with a focus on God's glory ("for His own glory") and ends with praise for his grace ("to the praise of His glorious grace"). As J. I. Packer observes, "If our theology does not quicken the conscience and soften the heart, it actually hardens both; if it does not encourage the commitment of faith, it reinforces the detachment of unbelief; if it fails to promote humility, it inevitably feeds pride."[10] Our theology ought to exalt our great God!

B. Our Statement Reflects Our Evangelical Heritage

We believe that our Statement of Faith is a true reflection of the teaching of the Bible, but we are not so naïve as to think that we can come to the Bible without preconceptions that influence our interpretation. We believe that the same Spirit who inspired its words will also illuminate our minds so that we might understand the Bible rightly, but one of the ways the Spirit helps us to understand his Word is through the insight and wisdom of believers who have come before us. We stand firmly within the Evangelical tradition,[11] and our understanding of the biblical gospel is informed by historic Evangelical theology.

What do we mean by historical Evangelical theology? First, and foremost, as Evangelicals, we are committed to the Bible as the touchstone of truth. Our Article 2 strongly affirms the Bible's unique and unparalleled authority for all that we believe.

Second, as Evangelicals we have been shaped by the Trinitarian and

---

10 J. I. Packer, *A Quest for Godliness: The Puritan Vision of the Christian Life* (Wheaton: Crossway, 1990), 15.

11 The meaning of Evangelical has been defined historically, experientially and sociologically. As helpful as these definitions are, we understand the term Evangelical first and foremost theologically, viz. by the gospel. As discussed in the previous section, our theology (Evangelical) is defined by and finds its importance in the gospel (the *evangel*).

Christological creeds of the early church, and the language of those creeds is found at a number of places in our Statement.

Third, we have been shaped by the Reformation of the sixteenth century. Those Reformers (who were first called "Evangelicals" before being called "Protestants") rediscovered the core of the gospel, that article on which the church stands or falls, which we call "justification by faith alone."[12] They brought back an emphasis on the Bible as the supreme witness to the gospel, and they gave renewed attention to the all-sufficiency of Christ's atoning death.

Fourth, we have been shaped by the Evangelical Revivals of the eighteenth and nineteenth centuries. Those movements of God highlighted the necessity of the new birth and the ministry of the Holy Spirit, and they laid stress on the need for a personal response of faith to the gospel, resulting in a changed life. The Wesleyan/Arminian elements of Evangelicalism became more prominent during this period.

Fifth, as American Evangelicals we have been shaped by the Modernist/Fundamentalist debates of the late-nineteenth and early-twentieth century. Evangelicals battled theological liberalism and skepticism toward the Bible, and Dispensational theology emerged and became popular in many Evangelical circles.[13]

Finally, the modern Evangelical movement in America took a turn at the mid-point of the twentieth century when people like Carl F. H. Henry called for fundamentalists to move away from separatism and cultural isolation to become unified in an effort to impact the world with the gospel.[14] This new movement was influential in shaping who we are as Evangelicals today.

This Statement of Faith was drafted with an awareness of our place in this biblical, Evangelical tradition, though we are also conscious that we are not bound to our traditions but must be continually reformed by the Word of God. This Statement is not concerned to be inclusive of all who now call themselves Evangelicals but to adhere to the essentials given to us in the Bible and as affirmed in historic Evangelical theology.

---

12 See our explicit inclusion of this doctrine in Article 7.

13 Dispensational theology was fostered through Bible prophecy conferences and the widespread use of the Scofield Reference Bible (published in 1909). On Dispensationalism, see Art. 9, sec. II.C.

14 This was articulated in his book *The Uneasy Conscience of Modern Fundamentalism* (Grand Rapids: Eerdmans, 1947). This vision was shared by the beloved Dean of Trinity Evangelical Divinity School Ken Kantzer, and one which has had a great influence in shaping our vision for ministry in the Evangelical Free Church.

II. This Is an *Evangelical Free Church* Statement of Faith

This Statement of Faith, though broadly Evangelical, also reflects our heritage within the smaller stream of the Evangelical Free Church as it developed in America. With roots in Scandinavia, our Free Church forbears broke away from the state church (hence, the "Free" in our name[15]) and developed a strong conviction that the local church ought to be composed only of believers. At the same time, they had a strong commitment to Evangelical unity in the gospel. They united around the essentials of the gospel and did not want minor issues of doctrine to divide. Hence, they spoke of being a church for "believers only but for all believers" and sought to "major on the majors and minor on the minors." The famous statement attributed to the Lutheran pastor Rupertus Meldenius (1582-1651) expresses their attitude well: "In essentials, unity; in non-essentials, liberty; in all things, charity."

The earlier doctrinal statements reflect this vision.[16] The Swedish Evangelical Free Church, formed in 1884, adopted a statement with only one point: " This organization accepts the Bible, both Old and New Testaments, as the Word of God, containing the Gospel of salvation for all men and the only perfect rule for teaching, faith and life." The Norwegian-Danish Evangelical Free Church Association adopted a very broad Evangelical statement of twelve points in 1912. In preparation for the Free Church merger, the Swedish statement was expanded in 1947 and a subsequent twelve point statement emerged as the basis for the formation of the Evangelical Free Church of America in 1950.

Arnold T. Olson, a preeminent leader in the early days of the EFCA, noted that what was unique about the 1950 EFCA Statement of Faith were the *omissions* when compared with other creeds. He writes, "Once [the early Free Church leaders] began to put in writing what was commonly believed among them, they were *silent* on those doctrines which through the centuries had divided Christians of *equal dedication, Biblical knowledge, spiritual maturity and love for Christ.*"[17] This "significance of silence"[18] reflected our strong concern for Evangelical unity in the

---

15 In our American context, the term "Free" now refers to the autonomy of the local church.

16 See Appendix 1 for the text of these statements.

17 Arnold Theodore Olson, *The Significance of Silence,* Heritage Series 2 (Minneapolis: Free Church Press, 1981), 16 [emphasis not in original].

18 This expression does not mean that we will not discuss and debate these issues but simply that we will not divide over them.

gospel.[19] The Evangelical Free Church is a movement theologically centered on the gospel of Jesus Christ. In a unique way, it seeks to bring together a diverse spectrum of Evangelicals, whose backgrounds may be Lutheran, Reformed, Arminian or Wesleyan, baptists and paedobaptists, Dispensationalists and Covenantalists[20]—united in the essentials to engage the world with the gospel.

III. This Is an Affirmation of Our Central Theological Convictions

The four-year process that resulted in the adoption of a new Statement of Faith in 2008 was an opportunity for those in the EFCA to re-examine and finally to reaffirm our central theological convictions. This Statement of Faith will form the basis for unity at the national and district levels, it will serve as a doctrinal standard for all those who will be credentialed in the EFCA or serving with our international mission, ReachGlobal, and it will be required for all new churches. It will also be used both as a theological norm for professors at our university and seminary[21] and as a basis for instruction in new member classes in local churches.[22] Recognizing that wide range of use, this theological exposition will seek to speak clearly but, as much as possible, without technical theological terms[23] so that it can be profitable for ordinary believers who need to be grounded in the essentials of the faith.

There are dangers inherent in writing creeds. They can become formal, complex, abstract and too detailed. More dangerous still, they can be superimposed over and replace the Bible itself. However, understood and responded to properly, creeds "facilitate public confession, form a succinct basis of teaching, safeguard pure doctrine, and constitute an appropriate focus for the church's fellowship of faith."[24] We trust that ours will be used wisely in that way.

---

19 We acknowledge a significant exception to this principle in the inclusion of premillennialism in the 1950 Statement which has been retained in the current Statement. This is discussed further in Article 9, sec. II.C.2.

20 The distinctive viewpoints of these various groups will be considered in due course in this exposition.

21 Trinity International University, including Trinity Evangelical Divinity School, located in Deerfield, Illinois.

22 Whether affirmation of this Statement of Faith is required for church membership is a matter left to the local church.

23 Or, when theological terms are used, they are explained.

24 Geoffrey W. Bromiley, "Creed, Creeds," *Evangelical Dictionary of Theology*, 2nd ed. (Grand Rapids: Baker Academic, 2001), 307.

Setting forth our central doctrinal convictions is difficult, but it is necessary. Each generation has the responsibility not only to receive what has been passed on, but to own it for ourselves before delivering it to our children. As one writer has put it, "The doctrinal heritage of the past is thus both a gift and a task, an inheritance and a responsibility. What our forebears in the Christian faith passed down to us must be appropriated, in order that we may wrestle with it within our own situation, before passing it on to those whose day has yet to dawn."[25] As Paul instructs Timothy, "What you heard from me, keep as the pattern of sound teaching, with faith and love in Christ Jesus. Guard the good deposit that was entrusted to you—guard it with the help of the Holy Spirit who lives in us" (2 Tim. 1:13-14). May this Statement of Faith be an instrument of the Spirit to help us as the Evangelical Free Church of America to guard, and to bear witness to, the good deposit of the gospel.

---

25 Alister E. McGrath, *The Genesis of Doctrine: A Study in the Foundation of Doctrinal Criticism* (Oxford: Blackwell, 1990; reprinted Grand Rapids: Eerdmans, 1997), 200 .

Evangelical Convictions

A Theological Exposition of the Statement of Faith of the Evangelical Free Church of America

Article 1

GOD

1. We believe in one God, Creator of all things, holy, infinitely perfect, and eternally existing in a loving unity of three equally divine Persons: the Father, the Son and the Holy Spirit. Having limitless knowledge and sovereign power, God has graciously purposed from eternity to redeem a people for Himself and to make all things new for His own glory.

God's gospel originates in and expresses the wondrous perfections of the eternal, triune God.

If you were talking to someone who knew nothing about the gospel, and you wanted to explain who Jesus was and what he did, where would you begin? You might begin with the commencement of Jesus' public ministry, when he came to John the Baptist to be baptized, the voice from heaven addressed him and the Spirit descended on him like a dove. That's where the gospel writer Mark begins his story. He opens with the words, "The beginning of the gospel about Jesus Christ, the Son of God" (Mark 1:1), and then he immediately launches into the ministry of John and his baptism of Jesus.

But we who celebrate Christmas know that the gospel story begins well before Jesus' baptism. We might choose to begin the story of Jesus at his birth and even at his conception in the womb of a virgin mother. That's where both Matthew and Luke begin their account of the gospel—with the angelic messengers addressing Mary and Joseph (Matt. 1:20-21; Luke 1:26-37[1]).

But if you thought about it a little more, you might realize that Jesus spoke of being "*sent into the world by the Father*" (cf. John 3:17; 10:36). Sent from where? That language suggests that the story of Jesus Christ didn't just begin in *this* world at all. He somehow existed before he came into this world—he had a heavenly origin, a heavenly home, from which he was sent to live among us. And that eternal starting point is where John takes us in his account of the gospel: "In the beginning was the Word, and the Word was with God, and the Word was God. He was with God in the beginning" (John 1:1). John continues in v. 14: this "Word became flesh and made his dwelling among us. We have seen his glory, the glory of the One and Only, who came from the Father, full of grace and truth." According to John, the gospel, the story of God's saving work in Jesus Christ, really begins in the beginning, the very beginning, in the eternity of God himself. In our EFCA Statement of Faith, we have chosen to follow John's lead. God's gospel begins with God and his eternal purposes.

"In the beginning, God . . ." (Gen. 1:1). So begins the Bible, and so, too,

---

1 Luke's birth narrative actually begins even earlier with the birth of John the Baptist.

begins our statement of central theological convictions that expound the gospel of Jesus Christ. Many historic confessions start with a statement on the Bible,[2] and that is entirely appropriate, for our knowledge of God comes most clearly from that written Word of God. But we have chosen to speak of God before speaking of the Bible,[3] even though what we say about him is based on the Scriptures. The Bible is the story of God's work in creation, redemption and restoration, and it is a story that has its center in his revelation in Christ. The structure of our Statement of Faith reflects the flow of this biblical story. The eternal God acts, and he acts by speaking—calling creation into being and, later, revealing his actions and his own character in human words which now come to us in the Bible. It all begins with God.

This starting point is also appropriate because any statement about the Bible as the Word of God must assume that there is a God who can speak. Moreover, our trust in the truthfulness of that Word must be based on a confidence in the character of the God who speaks. Though one can make a case for beginning a Statement of Faith at either point, with God or with the Bible, we have chosen to begin with God as the ultimate starting point for everything else, including our own knowledge of God himself.

Beginning with a statement on God is also significant in that it emphasizes that the gospel itself begins with God. In the gospel we are recipients of God's grace, a grace that comes at his initiative, not ours. The gospel is God's saving work from first to last; it flows from within himself as the expression of his essential character. His actions always conform perfectly with his own nature. In other words, God does what he does because he is who he is. Thus, God's gospel originates in and expresses the wondrous perfections of the eternal triune God.

I. The Gospel is the Expression of God's Essential Nature

As fallen creatures we are shot through with contradictions and inconsistencies and often suffer internal conflicts. We may say one thing and do another, making promises we never keep. God never does. He is

---

2 These include the Westminster Confession (Reformed), the Savoy Declaration (Congregationalist Reformed), and the New Hampshire Baptist Confession (largely Reformed).

3 Historic confessions that begin with God include the Augsburg Confession (Lutheran), the Belgic Confession (Reformed), and the Thirty-Nine Articles (Anglican), in addition to the Methodist Articles of Religion (John Wesley's confession).

always perfectly consistent with himself. He is always faithful and true. The first article sets forth essential aspects of the character of the God which provide the fountainhead of all that he does.

A. We Believe in One God

"Hear, O Israel, the Lord our God, the Lord is one" (Deut. 6:4). This creedal statement, which became known by the Jews as the *Shema* (from the Hebrew word for "hear"), was affirmed by Jesus (Mark 12:29) as a fundamental truth about the God we worship. He is a unity and is unique—he alone is God (Ps. 86:10). He has no parts, [4] and he has no rival. He is one.

The God who revealed himself as Yahweh, the God of Abraham, Isaac and Jacob, in the Old Testament is the very same God who is now revealed in Jesus Christ and manifested by the Holy Spirit in the New Testament. He is the God of the whole world, and for that reason his people have a responsibility to make him known to all people. Our monotheism calls for mission, for though other religions may have some elements of truth, a person who does not know this God, the God of the Bible, does not know God at all. As we read in the prophecy of Isaiah, the Lord says, "I am God and there is no other; I am God, and there is none like me" (Isa. 46:9).

B. God Is the Creator of All Things

"In the beginning, God created the heavens and the earth" (Gen. 1:1). From Genesis to Revelation, the Bible affirms this divine act of creation. The various categories of Scripture—the Law, the Psalms, the Prophets, the Gospels and the Epistles—all speak with one voice: "You alone are the LORD. You made the heavens, even the highest heavens and all their starry host, the earth and all that is on it, the seas and all that is in them" (Neh. 9:6). Or as the Apostle Paul put it in speaking to the philosophers of Athens: "The God who made the world and everything in it is the Lord of heaven and earth . . . in him we live and move and have our being" (Acts 17:24,28). God created all things outside of himself, a notion expressed in the theological term *ex nihilo*—"out of nothing."

God's work as the Creator is a divinely revealed truth and, hence,

---

4 This is often referred to as God's "simplicity," that is, he is perfectly integrated in himself such that God in his entirety is always completely present in all his attributes and in all his actions. Thus, for example, God's holiness is always loving and his love is always holy.

an article of faith, for, as the writer to the Hebrews affirms, "By faith we understand that the world was created by the word of God so that what is seen was made out of things which do not appear" (Heb. 11:3). This doctrine is not the conclusion of a scientific inquiry, nor could it be, for it transcends the sphere in which science commonly operates, that is, a closed system of natural cause and effect which assumes that the forces that we see at work in the world today have always operated in just the same way at all times. Since science deals with causal relationships *within* the created order, the existence of creation itself must be a philosophical or theological question. Thus, the fact that God is the Creator of all things is beyond the realm of scientific discovery. At the same time, however, the Christian doctrine of creation provides the foundation for all the known laws of nature, for God's creation is orderly and its clear patterns can be investigated and understood.

Though all Evangelical Christians are united in the conviction that God is the Creator of all things,[5] they have been divided over *how* God created—how long it took and what process he may have used. What is the nature of the "days" of Genesis 1? Most through church history have taken these "days" in a straightforward, literal way and have affirmed a creation in six twenty-four hour periods. Others contend that "day" in Scripture can refer to a longer period of time,[6] and that geologic ages can be subsumed in the word. Still others believe that in using this literary form, the biblical author was not intending to give a description of the mechanics of creation at all. The creation week of Genesis 1 is a literary device which itself makes important points but does not connect much with extra-textual historical referents—that is, it is not intended to provide a guide for scientific accounts of cosmic development.[7] One

---

5 This biblical truth was affirmed in the early creeds of the church, e.g. The Apostles' Creed ("I believe in God the Father Almighty, Maker of heaven and earth") and the Nicene Creed ("I believe in one God, the Father Almighty, Maker of heaven and earth, and of all things visible and invisible").

6 Cf., e.g., 2 Pet. 3:8—"But do not forget this one thing, dear friends: With the Lord a day is like a thousand years, and a thousand years are like a day."

7 Since this view is not as familiar, some explanation is in order here. It is commonly agreed that the Genesis account of creation differs significantly from the mythical accounts of other ancient Near Eastern cultures, but the biblical account is not a strict prose narrative either. It lacks the rhythm of Hebrew poetry, but its use of such literary devices as repetition and certain symbolic numbers like 10, 7, and 3 gives it an exalted, semi-poetic style, almost like a hymn. The pattern of six-plus-one is especially significant in that it recurs repeatedly in the Book of Revelation. This view that the seven days of Genesis 1 provides a "framework" for expressing the truth of God's creative work can be traced at least to the time of Augustine (*On the Literal Interpretation of Genesis* [408]).

form of this approach contends that God's six days of work followed by a day of rest offer an *analogy* to a human week of work rather than a literal *identity*. In support they point to the endless duration of the seventh "day," which provides the rationale for the command of the Sabbath (cf. Exod. 20:8-11).[8]

To be sure, Genesis 1 expresses truth about God as Creator and his creation, but because of the uncertainty regarding the meaning and literary form of this text and the lack of Evangelical consensus on this issue, our Statement does not require a particular position on the mechanics of creation. However, to be within the doctrinal parameters of the EFCA, any understanding of the process of creation must affirm:

1. that God is the Creator of all things out of nothing (*ex nihilo*),
2. that he pronounced his creation "very good,"
3. that God created with order and purpose,
4. that God is the sovereign ruler over all creation which, by his personal and particular providence, he sustains,[9]
5. that God created the first human beings—the historical Adam and Eve—uniquely in his image,
6. and that through their sin all humanity along with this created order is now fallen (as articulated in our Article 3).[10]

1. God Alone Is the Creator

Regardless of differences on the process of creation among Evangelicals, all affirm three things about the biblical teaching of creation. First, God and God alone is the Creator of all things. The Genesis account is at pains to distinguish itself from the pagan world. As one writer put it, there is "a conscious and deliberate anti-mythical polemic"[11] in this first chapter of Genesis. No sun gods, or gods of the sea

---

8 Proponents of this view also point to the analogy of God as gardener (Gen. 2:8-9) which provides the pattern for human beings, as the image of God, to follow (Gen. 2:15-16). This "analogical day" view often puts more emphasis on the chronological development of the creative work of God than the general "literary framework" position.

9 We deny the notion that God is simply the Creator of the universe but is no longer active in it, as is espoused by deism.

10 This Statement does not speak to the precise process of creation or to the age of the universe. To be acceptable within the EFCA any views on these specifics must completely affirm this Statement of Faith and align within these essential parameters.

11 A. Heidel, *The Babylonian Genesis*, 2nd ed. (Chicago: University Press, 1954), 91, cited in Gordon J. Wenham, *Genesis 1-15*, Word Biblical Commentary, Vol. 1 (Waco, Texas: Word Books, 1987), 9. Cf. also Gerhard F. Hasel, "The Polemical Nature of the Genesis Cosmology,"

here—God alone is the Creator.

With this understanding, the Christian view of creation stands in opposition to all forms of polytheism. There is one God, and he has no rivals. There is no power in the universe that can threaten his supreme rule—either spiritual or material. Everything else has only the status of creature before the God who has created all. Therefore, to worship anything else is nothing but idolatry.

The Christian doctrine of creation also rules out every form of pantheism—the idea that the world itself is God or that God is the world. The identity of God and the world is a philosophy of the East which is increasingly common in the West through the influence of Hinduism, Buddhism and New Age thinking. It views the world as an extension of the being of God. Genesis 1:1 says "no" to that understanding.[12] The sun, moon and stars reflect the glory of God, but they are not gods, nor are they God. He created the world apart from himself, *ex nihilo*— "out of nothing."[13] And though God has created human beings in his own image, neither are we gods.

Our doctrine of creation also means that we are not materialists or philosophical naturalists. We cannot believe that "The Cosmos is all that is or ever was or ever will be."[14] Before the world came into being, God forever was, and he now sustains all that exists by his powerful word (Heb. 1:3). In an act of freedom, God spoke, and it came to be. The implications of this are clear. To use the biblical image, he is the potter and we are the clay. The Lord God sits above the universe on his throne as the eternal King, and we are accountable to him. We were made by God and for God, and insofar as we ignore this, we are defying God, the source of all life. We *owe* him; failure to see and delight in this is idolatry. The first responsibility of sentient moral creatures is to acknowledge their creatureliness.

2. God's Creation Is Ordered and Purposeful

A second aspect of the biblical narrative of creation is that God's

---

EQ 46 (1974): 81–102.

12 Cf. also Heb. 11:3.

13 We also deny that the cosmos is somehow "within God" as is affirmed in a system known as panentheism or process theology.

14 To quote the well known opening words of Carl Sagan's book, *Cosmos* (New York: Random House, 1980), 1.

creation is ordered and purposeful. The universe comes from the mind of God—it is a cosmos, rather than chaos.

The narrative form of Genesis 1, with its careful literary design, reinforces this notion of order and purpose. The progression of days clearly demonstrates the unfolding of the divine purpose and points to the increasing complexity of the cosmos. The Lord prepares the habitation, and then he populates it with its inhabitants. The creation week builds to its crowning act in the creation of man,[15] as male and female, in the image of God. It then concludes with the seventh day, which, as the Sabbath rest of God, is the goal of creation.[16] That day points to the supreme purpose of all creation—loving God and enjoying him forever. Entering into God's Sabbath rest is what we are ultimately made for (Heb. 4:6-11).

We are not the result of a blind process of chance. However the world has been shaped into its present form, even if through means that may seem to be random and unpredictable to us with no discernible pattern, it is more than a mindless process. God himself has revealed to us that this world is the result of a divine design with a divine purpose.

Science searches for that divinely-given order, described in what we call the laws of nature, which are simply labels we give to the rational, and even mathematical, patterns built into creation by God. Great scientific minds of the past recognized this. Isaac Newton, for example, saw his work of scientific investigation as "thinking God's thoughts after him." The order of our world reflects the character of its Creator: "The heavens declare the glory of God; the skies proclaim the work of his hands" (Ps. 19:1).

We as human beings are not the authors of creation, able to impose our own order onto this world. There is a divine given-ness to creation, with various categories built into it even before we arrived on the scene. Wise living in God's world means living in accordance with the order God has established.[17]

---

15 This use of the generic masculine is helpful here to reflect the use of the Hebrew (*haadam*), which in Gen. 1:27 moves from the collective singular to the plural ("in the image of God he created him; male and female he created them." Cf. also Gen. 5:1-2). This emphasizes both the corporate and individual nature of humanity.

16 Nothing is said in Genesis about the seventh day ever coming to an end, and in Jewish thought God enjoys an eternal Sabbath rest. Jesus picks up this thought to justify his own healing work on the Sabbath in John 5:17: "My Father is always at his work to this very day, and I, too, am working."

17 Much of the book of Proverbs reflects this truth. Also, Paul in Rom. 1:18-32 speaks of the rebellion of humanity against God and his created order, resulting in the exchange of "natural

3. God's Creation Is Good

A third emphasis in the Genesis account of creation is this: God's creation is good. Five times we read that "God saw that what he had created was good,"[18] and after the sixth day we are told that "God saw all that he had made, and it was very good" (Gen. 1:31). This affirmation is fundamental to a distinctively Christian view of the world.[19]

On the one hand, we affirm that, as the good creation of God, the material world is not to be rejected. Through the centuries some have considered our space-time existence as essentially worthless.[20] They ascribed no value to the ordinary activities of human life—music and art, social or political work, manufacturing, sports, business or scientific research. Some have considered human sexuality as something inherently sinful. They reject these things simply because they are part of this physical, material world. But such a denial of the material world reflects a failure to recognize God as the Creator. As C.S. Lewis put it so simply, "[God] likes matter. He invented it."[21]

A proper understanding of God as the Creator changes our understanding of what it means to be spiritual, and it leads us away from an other-worldly asceticism that somehow denigrates our physical existence in this world. It tells us that salvation and spirituality are to be found not by fleeing from or avoiding the material realm, but by sanctifying it. God made us as embodied souls, living in a material world. We cannot escape that fact, nor should we try to. There is nothing

---

relations for unnatural ones" (v. 26).

18 "A sixth occurrence is found in 1:4 when God pronounces the creation of light as "good."

19 The first deviation from this occurs in Gen. 2:18, when God declares that "It is *not good* for the man to be alone." This declaration reflects not only the essential relational nature of human beings created in his image (cf. Gen. 1:27 [for further implications, see Art. 3, sec. I.B]), but also the ethical implication that God alone is the One who determines what is "good" and what is "not good," what is right and what is wrong.

20 One example is Gnosticism, which became popular from the second century A.D. It was a mixture of pantheistic ideas from the East, the dualism of Plato, and the mystery religions of the Roman world. Though there was great variety, Gnostics generally believed that this world was created not by the supreme God, the eternal Father, who is the ineffable "All in All," but by a lesser god, the god revealed in the Old Testament. Through some sort of primeval catastrophe, some human spirits entered into the poverty and humiliation of this material world and became imprisoned in the fleshly garments of human bodies. Through the revelation of special knowledge (*gnōsis* in Greek) these spirits could discover their origin and return to their true home in the spiritual kingdom of light.

21 *Mere Christianity* (New York: Macmillan, 1952), 65.

evil about the material world in itself, for God's purpose is to redeem and restore his creation, not to destroy it.

This world that God has created is not to be rejected. In fact, it is to be enjoyed as a gift from God (1 Tim. 6:17). We should be thankful for God's creation. We should delight in creation. We should appreciate natural beauty. We should look at it with wonder as it reveals the greatness and goodness of our God. "For everything God created is good, and nothing is to be rejected if it is received with thanksgiving" (1 Tim. 4:4).

This marvelous creation, however, has been spoiled by sin. God purposes to restore it, but creation is not God; therefore, it must not be idolized. Instead, we should act responsibly toward the natural world as good stewards of what God has given to us, neither worshipping it nor exploiting it, but respecting it as a precious gift from the hand of God.

God the Creator is alone worthy of our worship. Our response to him ought to be like that of the heavenly throng pictured in Revelation 4:11: "Worthy are you, our Lord and God, to receive glory and honor and power, for you created all things, and by your will they existed and were created."

C. God Is Holy

Nothing more clearly captures the revelation of God in the Old Testament than the word "holy." In Isaiah's vision of God's glory, the angelic beings call out to one another, "Holy, holy, holy is the LORD Almighty; the whole earth is full of his glory" (Isa. 6:3). The prescribed rituals of worship, and even the design of the temple itself with its most guarded space, the Holy of Holies, were all meant to impress this central truth into the minds and hearts of the people of Israel—the Lord God is holy.

The Old Testament law had this quality of God as its central focus. The Lord says to Israel, "You must distinguish between the holy and the profane, between the unclean and the clean" (Lev. 10:10). The death penalty was regularly prescribed for any act that would disregard or desecrate the holiness of God (cf., e.g., Exod. 31:14). In entering the tent of meeting, the priests were to wear the proper clothes and observe the proper washing, so that they would not die (Exod. 28:43; 30:21). "Among those who approach me I will show myself holy; in the sight of all the people I will be honored," says the LORD (Lev. 10:3). The Israelites were to come before their holy Lord in humble reverence: "Who among the gods is like you, O LORD? Who is like you—majestic in holiness, awesome in glory, working wonders?" (Exod. 15:11).

God's holiness expresses the central notion that God is separate from us. He is separate in that he is transcendent, above us and beyond us, as we have previously described. But more importantly, God's holiness speaks of his separateness from us morally. He is separate from all evil, and he is perfectly righteous in all that he is and does: "the LORD Almighty will be exalted by his justice, and the holy God will show himself holy by his righteousness" (Isa. 5:16).

Neither arbitrary nor capricious, God's wrath is his righteous repulsion against all that is contrary to his holy nature. Like the fire that came from the presence of the Lord and consumed Aaron's sons Nadab and Abihu (Lev. 10:1-3), so God's holiness consumes all evil that enters its presence (cf. Heb. 12:29). Consequently, sinful human beings are disqualified from coming before him. "Your eyes are too pure to look on evil; you cannot tolerate wrong," says the prophet Habakkuk (Hab. 1:13), and we should be led to ask with the men of Beth Shemesh, "Who can stand in the presence of the LORD, this holy God?" (1 Sam. 6:20; cf. also Rev. 6:17). Isaiah experienced this fear in the presence of God's holiness and cried out, "Woe to me! I am ruined!" (Isa. 6:5). Only God's mercy, in atoning for his sin and taking away his guilt, saved the prophet from certain death (6:6-7).

It is perhaps this notion of God's awesome holiness, and his wrath that flows from it, that we most need to grasp in our world today. Without it the gospel makes no sense—we have no conviction of our sin and no need of a Savior. And without it we have no understanding of the new life to which we are called and the final goal of our salvation—that we might share in the character of God himself. For the Lord says, "Be holy because I, the LORD your God, am holy" (Lev. 19:2; 1 Pet. 1:16). Our prayer ought always to be, "Our Father in heaven, may your name be holy."

D. God Is Infinitely Perfect

"Great is the Lord and most worthy of praise; his greatness no one can fathom" (Ps. 145:3). His greatness exceeds our ability to grasp, to conceive or to express in words. When we reflect on the nature of our God, we ought to bow in worship, echoing the words of Paul: "Oh, the depth of the riches of the wisdom and knowledge of God! How unsearchable his judgments, and his paths beyond tracing out!" (Rom. 11:33; cf. Ps. 139:6).

That wonder and awe before the ineffable greatness of God is captured in our apparently redundant affirmation that he is "infinitely perfect."

God's perfection means that he is totally without defect, fault or blemish. The human mind cannot conceive of anything that would exceed our God in goodness and beauty. He himself is the ultimate reality, so he is the foundation of all that is true.

The use of the word "infinite" simply reinforces the notion that there are no limits to his greatness. He is not bound by space and time—"Before the mountains were born or you brought forth the earth and the world, from everlasting to everlasting you are God" (Ps. 90:2; also Gen. 21:33). His power and might, his wisdom and knowledge, his righteousness and goodness are all beyond the ability of our human minds to imagine. There is no deficiency in God; there is no way that God could be better at being God than he is. That is what we mean when we declare him to be "infinitely perfect."

Because God is perfect, he is self-sufficient.[22] As the Lord revealed to Moses, "I am who I am" (Exod. 3:13), or as Jesus declared, God has life "in himself" (John 5:26). God's self-sufficiency provides the answer to that age-old question: "If everything has a cause then what caused God?" Nothing caused God, because God does not need a cause—for there is nothing that stands over God or outside of him to cause him to come into being. He is totally independent in himself, and he causes all things to depend upon him for their existence. He just is, and he must be.[23]

As self-sufficient, God has no needs (cf. Ps. 50:7-14; Acts 17:24-25). "Who has ever given to God, that God should repay him? For from him and through him and to him are all things" (Rom. 11:35-36). Consequently, his love must be a gracious, self-giving love, for he has nothing to gain by it. In his perfection, he is unchangeable in his character, providing a sure foundation for our faith. He is an immovable rock on which to stand.

Also, because God is self-sufficient, he is essentially unknowable, unless he chooses to make himself known. Like the author of a book, God stands outside the story of creation. Nothing in the book can stand over the author as a cause or an explanation or an authority. God is answerable to no one, and everyone is answerable to him. And the characters in the book can know about the author only if the author

22 To describe this perfection of God, theologians use the word "aseity," a Latin term that means that God's being comes from himself.

23 The "ontological argument" for God's existence is based on this notion. It contends that if we can conceive of an all-perfect being, that being must exist.

chooses somehow to reveal himself in the book.

In the same way, we are totally dependent upon God to make himself known to us. He cannot be grasped by scientific investigation, for he stands above our world of cause and effect. His existence and nature cannot be proven by human reason as the conclusion of a philosophical syllogism, for nothing stands behind and apart from God to explain him.[24] He simply is. No wonder Job's friend Zophar can ask,

> Can you fathom the mysteries of God?
> Can you probe the limits of the Almighty?
> They are higher than the heavens—what can you do?
> They are deeper than the depths of the grave—what can you know?
> Their measure is longer than the earth and wider than the sea.
>
> (11:7-9)

E. God Is Loving

Though clearly both Testaments affirm God's holiness and God's love, when we move to the New Testament God's love receives a new place of prominence. John, in his first letter, makes the statement not once but twice: "Whoever does not love does not know God, because *God is love*" (1 John 4:8, also v. 16). Furthermore, these two divine attributes, love and holiness, are not contradictory but complementary. Because God is one, his love is always perfectly holy, and his holiness is always perfectly loving. There are no divisions in the character of God. But the New Testament does give more emphasis to God's love because there God reveals himself in a new way. Instead of viewing God from the outside, in the coming of Jesus Christ we now see God's own inner life as the holy God[25] who is love within himself.

F. The One God Is Triune

Love is a personal quality, for only persons can love. This makes the God of the Bible different from some life-force of science fiction or from the "ground of all Being" found in Hinduism or Buddhism. The God of

---

24 This is not to say that arguments for the existence of God have no value. They make God's existence reasonable but not indubitable.

25 It is important to note that Jesus himself refers to his "holy Father" (John 17: 11; cf. also "*Righteous* Father" [v.25]), and Jesus' concern for the divine holiness is reflected in his frequent references to hell (cf., e.g., Matt. 5:22,29-30; 10:28; 18:9; 23:15,33). On this, see further in Article 10, sec. II.B.1.

the Bible is a personal God who is love.

In fact, the God of the Bible has revealed himself to be so personal, so full of love, that he has personal relationships of love within himself. Though he is one God, he has within himself three Persons,[26] revealed to us as the Father, the Son, and the Holy Spirit.[27] Each of these Persons is equally divine, and these three have forever existed as one God in an eternal union of love. As affirmed in the Council of Nicea (A.D. 325), these three are one in nature and essence—they are of "the same being (*homoousion*)." They are distinct in the relationship they have with one another,[28] for the capacity for relationship is at the heart of the notion of "person" when used of the members of the Trinity.[29]

The term "Trinity" is found nowhere in the Bible, but that term crystallizes the truth found there. God is spoken of as the Father of Jesus Christ, the Son of God (e.g., Rom. 1:7-9).[30] Divine qualities and functions are ascribed to Jesus the Son (e.g., Matt. 10:37; Mark 2:5-7; John 5:18), and he is directly described as God (e.g., John 1:1; 20:28; Rom. 9:5; Col. 2:9). The Holy Spirit, too, is put in the place of God (Acts 5:3,4; John

---

26 The term "person" is difficult for us in this context because we so associate the word with independent and autonomous existence, causing us to think of a person as a separate being. Augustine wrestled with this difficulty and was left with the conclusion that the word "person," though inadequate, may be the best we can do: "Yet, when the question is asked: three what? human language labors altogether under great poverty of speech. The answer, however, is given, three 'persons,' not that it might be [completely] spoken, but that it might not be left [wholly] unspoken" (*On the Trinity*, V.9).

27 Certainly these are not independent Gods, resulting in tri-theism, nor are these simply different forms or "modes" by which the one God appears to us at different times. This view, called "modalism" or "Sabellianism" (after the third-century teacher Sabellius), was deemed inadequate by the early church primarily because it denied real relationships within the Godhead.

28 Theologians through the centuries have spoken of the Father as "unbegotten," the Son as "eternally begotten of the Father," and the Spirit as "proceeding from the Father and the Son." The Scripture affirms that the Spirit proceeds from the Father (John 14:26; 15:26). In the context of the Arian heresy, the church in the West affirmed that the Spirit proceeds from the Son also (cf. John 15:26; 16:7). This resulted in a change in the Niceno-Constantinopolitan Creed at the Third Synod of Toledo (589) with the addition of the so-called *filioque* clause (this Latin term means "and the Son"). This change was never accepted in the Eastern church, and this became a central cause of the Great Schism of 1054.

29 Though equal in all respects, the three Persons have distinct roles in the unfolding of redemption: the Father sends the Son, the Son obeys the Father and the Spirit glorifies the Son and applies his redemptive work (see further in Article 6).

30 In the New Testament the term "God" is primarily used to refer to God the Father. Occasionally the term is applied directly to Jesus (John 1:1; 1:18; 20:28; Acts 20:28; Rom. 9:5; Titus 2:13; Heb. 1:8; 2 Pet. 1:1; 1 John 5:20).

15:26; Mark 3:29). Furthermore, a number of passages speak of the three together, most notably, Jesus' command to baptize "in the name of the Father, the Son and the Holy Spirit" (Matt. 28:19; cf. also Matt. 3:16-17; 2 Cor. 13:14; Eph. 4:4-6; 1 Pet. 1:2). Our God is a triune God—one God in three Persons.

There is one God, but this one God has never been alone. God was love within himself before he ever created a world to love, for within himself the Father loved the Son and the Son loved the Father and the Holy Spirit himself was caught up in this unity of love.[31] God existed eternally in this unity of love, loving himself before he ever loved any of us.

Jesus Christ, the Son of God, speaks of this eternal love in that great prayer of John 17 on the night he was betrayed: "Father, glorify me in your presence with the glory I had with you before the world began . . . the glory you have given me because you loved me before the creation of the world" (17:5,24). "Holy Father, protect them . . . so that they may be one as we are one . . . just as you are in me and I am in you" (17:11,21). Here Jesus points to our participation in this eternal union of love, which is the eternal life he brings (cf. John 17:3).

We confess that this Trinitarian nature of God is a great mystery beyond our understanding, but it is also glorious and beautiful in the way it shows our God to be a God of love—eternally. He is a God of relationships who creates human beings in his image to relate to him and to one another in love.[32]

God is love, and in that love we can, through the Son and by the Spirit, now know him as our Father. But we must notice that in referring to his loving heavenly Father in his prayer in John 17, Jesus refers to him as *Holy* Father" (v. 11; cf. also *Righteous* Father" [v.25]). The God who is love is also the God who is holy; these two must be held together inseparably. As we have said, there is no contradiction in God. His love is a holy love. It is a love that is always and at the same time righteous and just. It is not a sentimental love that pretends that evil things do

---

31 This unity of love is sometimes referred to as *perichoresis*, the doctrine given systematic expression in the work of the eighth-century monk John of Damascus, who taught that the Persons of the Trinity, though distinct, also interpenetrate and mutually indwell one another in an inseparable unity (cf. John 17:21, where Jesus says to the Father: "you are in me and I am in you").

32 The language of "Father" and "Son" to describe the Persons of the Trinity are divinely revealed and are necessary for our understanding. To substitute the unbiblical language of "Parent" and "Child" (or the like) to refer to these Persons is contrary to God's revelation and diminishes our understanding.

not happen. It is not a love that ignores injustice as if it does not matter. His is a love that always loves righteously, and his is a judgment that is always loving.

And if we may anticipate where our exposition of God's gospel will take us, we know that it is on the cross of Christ that God's holy love is most clearly displayed. Understanding God as Trinity is essential to our understanding of the gospel. Paul's affirmation that "*God* demonstrates his own love for us in this: while we were still sinners, Christ died for us" (Rom. 5:8) can only be true if the Christ who dies is also the God who loves. The Trinitarian union of the Father and the Son makes it possible for the Judge who loves sinners to maintain his justice by taking their judgment upon himself in the death of his Son. The action on the cross is truly an action of God upon himself. In a marvelous way, mercy is achieved at the very moment that justice is satisfied. In this glorious gospel, God is holy and God is loving at the same time, magnificently manifesting the wondrous perfections of the eternal triune God. This triune understanding of God is central to our faith, and it is essential to our salvation.

II. The Gospel Is the Outworking of God's Eternal Purpose

We have already asked where you would begin to tell someone about Jesus if that person knew nothing of the gospel. Now we raise a related question: If you were to tell the story of your own life as a Christian, the story of your own spiritual journey, where would you begin?

You might begin with the time of your conversion—that moment when you consciously turned from your sin and trusted Jesus Christ as your Lord and Savior. It may have been a quiet and private moment, or it may have been very dramatic. Perhaps you can't even remember any precise time, though your present spiritual life testifies to such a moment of spiritual birth.

In talking about his own spiritual journey, the Apostle Paul often told the story of his dramatic conversion when the risen Jesus in all his brilliant glory appeared to him on the road to Damascus. He could describe that moment as the beginning of his Christian life.

But as you think about your story and how you came to faith, you might realize that the moment of your conversion was not the beginning of God's work in your life at all. The Lord used many people and events before that point to influence you and to draw you to himself. Often, one of the most important influences is the home in which you were born. From your birth, you could say, God was at work in your life to bring you to himself.

The Apostle Paul says that very thing. In Galatians 1:15, he declares that God set him apart from birth and called him by his grace so that he might preach Christ among the Gentiles.

But when Paul reflected on the story of God's grace in his life, he reached back beyond his conversion, and even beyond his birth. In his letter to the Ephesians, Paul took the story of God's grace in his life back to the very beginning, to the eternal purpose of God himself: "Praise be to the God and Father of our Lord Jesus Christ, . . . For he chose us in him before the creation of the world to be holy and blameless in his sight. In love he predestined us to be adopted as his sons through Jesus Christ, in accordance with his pleasure and will" (Eph. 1:3-5).

A. God Has Purposed from Eternity to Redeem

"God chose us in Christ *before the creation of the world*." And it's not just in Ephesians that Paul speaks like this. In 2 Timothy 1:9, the Apostle confesses that God "has saved us and called us to a holy life—not because of anything we have done but because of his own purpose and grace. This grace was given us in Christ Jesus *before the beginning of time*." Or consider Titus 1:2: "our faith and knowledge rest on the hope of eternal life, which God, who does not lie, promised before the beginning of time, ..."

Even before the first sin spoiled the good world that he had made, God knew what he was going to do. He had created human beings in his own image, so that the eternal Son of God would be able to take humanity into himself and to enter into our world and become incarnate as a human being like us. This was part of God's eternal purpose.

From eternity God purposed more than just the incarnation of Christ. He also willed his death, for the Bible speaks of Christ as "the Lamb who was slain from the creation of the world" (Rev. 13:8). The Lamb was slain to redeem a people who would be God's very own, a people redeemed to know him, to love him and to serve him forever (Titus 2:14; 1 Pet. 2:9; cf. 1 Chron. 17:21).

There is a great mystery here, but the central point of it all must be this: the gospel which has impacted our lives does not begin with us. We are not Christians, we do not share in the very life of God, because of our efforts to seek him out. It is not because of our cleverness or our goodness or our religiosity that we are adopted into God's family. No, the gospel that has come to us and saved us begins with God. He loved us before we ever thought about loving him: "For he chose us in him before the creation of the world to be holy and blameless in his sight" (Eph. 1:4). "This grace was given us in Christ Jesus before the beginning of time" (Titus 1:9). So we believe that God has graciously purposed from eternity to redeem a people for himself (cf. also 2 Tim. 1:9; Eph. 1:11; 3:10; Rom. 8:29-30).

B. God Acts with Limitless Knowledge and Sovereign Power

Certainly, among Evangelicals there are various ways of understanding how this electing purpose of God plays out in human history, and various views, including both the Arminian/Wesleyan and Reformed versions, with their different conceptions of the mysterious interplay of the human and divine wills, are acceptable within the parameters of our EFCA Statement of Faith.[33] While affirming God's sovereignty, we believe that that sovereignty never minimizes human responsibility. And while we are morally responsible creatures, making significant choices to obey, rebel, believe, etc., and are rightly held responsible for our actions, we can never make God absolutely contingent upon our wills.

However we may formulate the notion of human freedom, we affirm that nothing can thwart God's gracious purpose. We believe that God has limitless knowledge and sovereign power, ensuring that he will bring that purpose to fulfillment. His exhaustive foreknowledge includes even the future acts of human beings, even future acts regarded as "free" acts, and his omnipotence entails that nothing is outside his sovereign will.[34] He "works all things in conformity with his will," Paul writes (Eph. 1:11). The Lord himself declares: "I make known the end from the beginning, from ancient times, what is still to come. I say: My purpose will stand, and I will do all that I please" (Isa. 46:10).

This is not a deterministic fatalism of the sort expressed in Islam, but the outworking of the gracious will of a personal God. Our heavenly Father

---

33 On this, see further on Articles 3 and 6.

34 This Statement of Faith is intended to exclude the view commonly known as "open theism." In April, 2001, the EFCA Board of Ministerial Standing determined that it "will not approve credentials for those who deny God's exhaustive foreknowledge, which includes the future free acts of human beings."

is working for the good of those who love him and are called according to his purpose (Rom. 8:28). Our response is not simply submission to an impersonal Power but faith and trust in a loving Father.

C. God Will Redeem a People for Himself

God's redeeming purpose in Christ is not simply to save individual sinners, but to save a people—a community of believers united in Christ. Beginning with his covenant with Abraham, God purposed to bring blessing to all nations (Gen. 18:18: 22:18; 26:4; cf. Ps. 72:17; Isa. 2:2). Now, through the gospel of Jesus Christ, that new people is coming into being (cf. Eph. 2:11-22).

"Here there is no Greek or Jew, circumcised or uncircumcised, barbarian, Scythian, slave or free, but Christ is all, and is in all," Paul writes (Col. 3:11). John pictures this new people in its heavenly glory as "a great multitude that no one could count, from every nation, tribe, people and language, standing before the throne and in front of the Lamb. . . . crying out in a loud voice: 'Salvation belongs to our God, who sits on the throne, and to the Lamb'" (Rev. 7:9-10). The creation of this new people, uniting Jew and Gentile into one new body, is "according to [God's] eternal purpose which he accomplished in Christ Jesus our Lord" (Eph. 3:11). This purpose of God is now ours to embrace as we seek to make disciples among all people. In so doing the church becomes an outpost of that new people God is creating in Christ—a sign to the world anticipating the kingdom[35] that God will finally bring to pass in the new heaven and the new earth.

D. God Will Make All Things New

As the Creator of all things, God's gracious purpose is not only to redeem a people for himself to live in some ethereal and immaterial state. He has revealed his intention to restore his fallen creation, or, to use the language of the Book of Revelation, "to make all things new" (Rev. 21:5). The final, glorious state is described in the final chapters of the Bible as "a new heaven and a new earth" (Rev. 21:1), a place where "there will be no more death or mourning or crying or pain" (21:5). Paul speaks of creation itself waiting in eager expectation for that glorious day when the dead are raised and "the creation itself will be liberated

---

35 Here we understand the kingdom of God as the sphere in which God's righteous rule is manifest and joyfully welcomed.

from its bondage to decay and brought into the glorious freedom of the children of God" (Rom. 8:19-21). There God will dwell with his people forever.

God is great and God is good. In his grace and in his power, he is both willing and able to save what has been lost and to restore what has been spoiled. Through his knowledge of all things, he will act in a way that one day will be understood to be perfect wisdom. We are to pray that his will be done on earth as it is in heaven, and we can be assured that it will be. At the climax of human history as we know it, he will remove the barrier between heaven and earth, and all his creatures will proclaim him the King of all creation.

E. God Will Act For His Own Glory

And to what end does God act? Ultimately all that God does is for his own glory.[36] This is the highest end, the *summum bonum*, the final good, for the glory of God himself is the end for which all things exist. All creation is to display God's power and majesty, and human beings, especially, as those created in his image, redeemed and being conformed into the image of his Son, are to reflect his holy and loving character in the world he has made. As this is done both individually and corporately, it brings God glory!

We must never forget that the gospel is finally not about us but about God and his glory. In his wisdom, this gospel is ours by God's grace through faith, not by works, so that no one can boast (Eph. 2:8-9; cf. 1 Cor. 2:28-29), and God alone will receive the praise. One day John's vision will be realized, and "every creature in heaven and on earth and under the earth and on the sea, and all that is in them" will sing: "To him who sits on the throne and to the Lamb be praise and honor and glory and power, forever and ever!" (Rev. 5:13).

---

36 In the language of the Old Testament, God redeems a people for himself "to make a name for himself" (1 Chron. 17:21; cf. also, e.g., Ps. 106:7-8; Isa. 48:9-11; Ezek. 20:14; Eph. 1:4-6).

Article 2

THE BIBLE

2. We believe that God has spoken in the Scriptures, both Old and New Testaments, through the words of human authors. As the verbally inspired Word of God, the Bible is without error in the original writings, the complete revelation of His will for salvation, and the ultimate authority by which every realm of human knowledge and endeavor should be judged. Therefore, it is to be believed in all that it teaches, obeyed in all that it requires, and trusted in all that it promises.

God's gospel is authoritatively revealed in the Scriptures.

Are we as human beings like orphans stranded on a deserted island in the middle of the vast expanse of empty and lifeless space, with nobody even knowing that we are lost? In our postmodern world[1] many think so, and they have given up the quest for some cosmic connection to establish our identity. In desperation, they construct their own narrative to put their lives into some broader context of meaning.

Others still long for some voice from beyond the clouds. Since 1974, SETI, in its Search for Extra-Terrestrial Intelligence, has been spending millions of dollars annually to tune into the heavens. By means of radio telescopes, SETI workers listen to thousands of sun-like stars within two hundred light years of earth for signals that might indicate some intelligent life. As of yet, no communication has been detected.

"The confirmation of the existence of extraterrestrial life is billed as the greatest possible scientific discovery of all time," suggests one science writer.[2] He continues, "Today, however, we are still experiencing the pangs of cosmic loneliness. Never mind not coming for a visit, no extraterrestrial being has even left a calling card or shouted at us from a distance."[3]

But to a world that looks to the heavens and hears nothing, we proclaim that we have received an extra-terrestrial message of greater consequence than anything that could ever come from the Vega system. Our message has its source in heaven itself. The opening words of the Epistle to the Hebrews express this wonderful news: "In the past God spoke to our forefathers through the prophets at many times and in various ways, but in these last days he has spoken to us by his Son" (Heb. 1:1-2).

We are *not* orphans in an empty universe.[4] This cosmos in which we live is *not* silent, for the God who created all things has spoken. The

---

1 The term "postmodernism" describes a general cultural trend emerging in the late-twentieth century which, among other things, rejects a modernist confidence in human reason to discover objective truth and any notion of a grand story that explains human existence.

2 David Hughes, cited in David Wilkerson, *Alone in the Universe?* (Downers Grove: InterVarsity, 1997), 138.

3 Ibid.

4 In fact, as we will discuss in Article 6, through faith in Christ we are now "adopted as heirs in the family of God."

gospel message we proclaim is "according to the Scriptures," Paul says (1 Cor. 15:3-4). It has been revealed to us authoritatively by God himself.

I. God Has Spoken

The God we worship is a God who speaks. In fact, his first act recorded in the Bible was a speech act: "God said, 'Let there be light,' and there was light" (Gen. 1:3). The Creator continues to speak through his creation, as "the heavens declare the glory of God; . . . Day after day they pour forth speech" (Ps. 19:1-2; cf. Rom. 1:20).

God spoke to create, but from the beginning God also spoke personally to communicate with those creatures uniquely created in his image. He blessed the first human beings in the good world he had made, appointing them as his vice-regents to rule over his creation (Gen. 1:28-30). He commanded them not to eat from the tree of the knowledge of good and evil, and when they did, he spoke a word of judgment, casting them from the garden. As a result, free and direct communication with God ceased. Henceforth, God spoke most often through the prophets, his ordained "spokesmen."

Through the prophets God spoke words of judgment and of grace to his people. Some of those words were preserved in writings ("Scriptures") that we now know as the Old Testament. But in Jesus Christ that prophetic word took a new turn. The Word of God became flesh! God spoke in the most personal way possible—in the person of his Son dwelling among us.

God's gospel is the good news of his saving work in Jesus Christ. That message was entrusted to the apostles of Christ,[5] and through them it has come to us in the New Testament. This apostolic witness provides a sure foundation for the church (Eph. 2:20) and cannot be surpassed, for it unerringly testifies to God's ultimate speech act, Jesus Christ.

II. God has spoken in the Scriptures

A. The Bible Consists of Both Old and New Testaments

God's Word to us comprises the sixty-six books of the Bible—both Old and New Testaments. This collection constitutes the canon of

---

5 The apostles were not only commissioned by Jesus to serve as his witnesses (Acts 1:2,8), they were also promised the Holy Spirit's power to guide their preaching and teaching (John 14:26; 15:26-27; 16:13-14).

Scripture—those books recognized as having divine authority by Jesus and by the early church.

The books of the Old Testament were categorized by Jesus as the Law of Moses, the Prophets and the Psalms (Luke 24:44), and all were authoritative for him. There seems to have been little dispute about which books constituted the Old Testament canon among the Jews of Jesus' day, and they commonly held the conviction that God's speaking through the prophets had ceased after the time of Haggai, Zechariah and Malachi.[6] One study found 350 New Testament citations of the Old Testament, covering 24 of its 36 books.[7] Many of these passages explicitly call the cited text "Scripture," something that does not occur in New Testament citations of Apocryphal writings[8] and other sources.[9]

The canon of the New Testament developed over time as the early church came to recognize the unique authority of those writings which came from the apostles (or those closely associated with the apostles), conformed in teaching to the established "Rule of Faith"[10] and were used widely in the churches in the context of worship.[11] Already in his second epistle, Peter designates letters of Paul as Scripture (2 Pet. 3:15-16), and within the first two centuries a high level of agreement was reached concerning most of the New Testament books, despite the great cultural and geographical diversity of the scattered congregations from Britain to Mesopotamia.

As the church faced the challenge of heretical views such as Gnosticism,[12] rival revelations such as the prophecies of the Montanists,[13]

---

6 See, e.g., Josephus, *Against Apion* 1.41; Babylonian Talmud, Yomah 9b.

7 See the "Index of Quotations" in Barbara Aland, et al. eds., *The Greek New Testament, Fourth Revised Edition* (Stuttgart, Germany: Deutsche Bibelgesellschaft, 1993).

8 These include 1 and 2 Esdras, Tobit, Judith, the Rest of Esther, the Wisdom of Solomon, Ecclesiasticus, Baruch (including the Epistle of Jeremiah), the Song of the Three Holy Children, Susanna, Bel and the Dragon, the Prayer of Manasseh and 1 and 2 Maccabees. These writings, though not part of the Hebrew Bible, were often included in the Greek translation of the Hebrew Bible, the Septuagint (LXX), which was commonly used in the early church.

9 Extrabiblical citations in the New Testament include the *Book of Enoch* in Jude 14-15 and Aratus's *Phaenomena* in Acts 17:28b.

10 This expression refers to the somewhat flexible summary of Christian doctrine used widely in the early church which is reflected in what we know as the Apostles' Creed.

11 These are sometimes referred to as the criteria or tests of canonicity, the chief of which is apostolic authority.

12 On Gnosticism, see Article 1, n. 20.

13 Montanism was a prophetic movement of Phrygian origin which arose around A.D. 170 under the leadership of Montanus who was joined by two prophetesses Priscilla and Maximilla.

competing lists of authoritative books such as that of Marcion,[14] and persecution in which protecting sacred books could result in martyrdom, it became necessary to delineate more clearly what books were considered "Scripture." The first list of the canonical books of the Bible naming the 27 books of the present New Testament came from Bishop Athanasius of Alexandria in his Thirty-Ninth Festal Epistle of A.D. 367. This list was nearly universally accepted.

It would be wrong to assert that the authority of the church stands over the canon of Scripture, as if the church "created" the Bible. The second generation of church leaders recognized that the Word of God came to them through the apostolic witnesses whose authority exceeded their own. As one expert on this process describes it:

> During the second and succeeding centuries, this authoritative word was found, not in the utterances of contemporary leaders and teachers, but in the apostolic testimony contained within certain early Christian writings. From this point of view the Church did not create the canon, but came to recognize, accept, affirm, and confirm the self-authenticating quality of certain documents that imposed themselves as such upon the Church. If this fact is obscured, one comes into serious conflict not with dogma but with history.[15]

Thus we affirm that the 66 books of the Old and New Testaments are the Scriptures through which God has spoken to us.

B. God Has Spoken Through the Words of Human Authors

Though we understand the Bible to be the Word of God, we also affirm that God speaks "through the words of human authors." This is important for our hermeneutical method, for it means that in

They claimed to be the last in a series of prophets that included the daughters of Philip mentioned in Acts 21:8-9. Montanism was condemned by synods of bishops in Asia and elsewhere.

14 The Gnostic Marcion (d. ca. A.D.. 160) made a list of authoritative books which included only an altered version of Luke's gospel and Paul's letters. He was expelled from the church in Rome in A.D. 144.

15 Bruce M. Metzger, *The Canon of the New Testament: Its Origin, Development, and Significance* (Oxford: Clarendon Press, 1987), 287.

interpreting the Bible we seek the intent of the human authors as the primary means by which to discover the meaning God intends for us in the biblical text.[16]

Focusing on the author's intent is often referred to as the grammatical-historical method of interpretation. We ask, what did the writer mean when he wrote these words? In seeking the original intent of the human author, we must take into account the entire range of the historical, cultural, religious, linguistic, and literary factors that help us arrive at that intention.

Do we interpret the Bible literally? Yes, if that term is rightly understood. Literal interpretation, or *sensus literalis* as it has been called since the Reformation, involves a determination of the meaning of the text as the author intended it,[17] taking into account all the factors just mentioned. In this sense, the literal meaning must be determined *literarily*, and an appreciation of genre is important in interpretation. In poetic passages, words are often used metaphorically. Apocalyptic passages are filled with symbols and vivid imagery. Sometimes the authors speak ironically or even sarcastically (cf., e.g., Paul in 1 Cor. 4:8). Our interpretation must wrestle with the way words are used in the literary context in which they are found.

The meaning of the Bible for today must begin with *and be controlled by* the meaning intended by those who wrote it.[18] This is where the objectivity of biblical interpretation must be found. Here we simply affirm that, as with any text, we must respect the intention of the author. The "Golden Rule" demands as much: Isn't that how we wish our own writings to be treated?

While affirming that the Bible is a human book, requiring grammatical-historical interpretation, we must remember, however, that the Bible is also a divine book. As a book fully inspired by the Holy Spirit (which we discuss below), the various biblical books all reflect one

---

16 This is in contrast to a postmodern trend which focuses on the *reader* rather than the author as the locus of authority in determining the "meaning" of a text.

17 The place of the divine Author must also be taken into account in interpretation (see below), which is a justification, for example, of typological interpretation which sees God's hand at work in history prefiguring later events in earlier events, institutions and characters (cf. e.g., Matt. 2:15, citing Hos. 11:1: cf. also Exod. 4:22-23).

18 This is not to deny that the divine Author may intend more in a passage than the human author understood at the time (often referred to as *sensus plenior*, or "fuller meaning"). We respect some disagreement on the extent to which the divine intention may exceed that of the human author.

divine mind and the history it recounts is guided by one divine hand. Therefore, we must assume that the truth the Bible teaches and that the story it tells is united and harmonious within itself. As a consequence, Scripture is its own best interpreter.[19]

This principle of the unity of Scripture has been applied in two ways. First, "the analogy of Scripture" affirms that Scripture must be interpreted in the light of other Scripture. The Holy Spirit who inspired all Scripture does not contradict himself. Though sometimes harmony is difficult to discern, this principle of the ultimate consistency of the Biblical message is important if we are to understand the Bible rightly.

Second, "the analogy of faith" affirms that since Scripture has a unified message, captured in what we call "the faith"—that is, the central "gospel truths" of our faith, then individual passages should be interpreted in a way that is harmonious with that faith.[20]

The early church's summary of the message of Scripture, the "Rule of Faith," played an important role in hermeneutics. The second-century Bishop Irenaeus referred to this using an analogy from the world of art. In those days mosaics were shipped unassembled, but included with them was a plan or key which showed the recipient how the tiles were to be put together. The church's Rule of Faith, Irenaeus said, is like that key. Whereas the heretics arranged the Scriptures wrongly to form the picture of a dog, the church's Rule of Faith explains how the Scriptures are to be arranged to render the portrait of the King.[21]

Certainly, we must be careful that our human description of "the faith"—that is, our theological synthesis of the Bible's message—not take preeminence over the Bible itself. It must be tested by the Bible in a dynamic relationship such that our exegetical work interacts with our theological formulations. This interaction may at times force us to make adjustments to those formulations if the exegetical results are strong enough.[22] But the analogy of faith is still a helpful approach as a general principle of hermeneutics.

We believe that the gospel is God's good news, and to be good news it must be intelligible. The very notion of the gospel requires the

19 As the Westminster Confession states it: "The infallible rule of interpretation of scripture is the scripture itself; and therefore, when there is a question about the true and full sense of any scripture, it must be searched and known by other places that speak more clearly" (I.ix).

20 Jude speaks of "the faith that was once for all entrusted to the saints" (v. 3).

21 *Against Heresies*, 1.8.1; 1.9.4.

22 Hence, the church and its confessions are always to be reformed by the Word of God.

possibility of communication. This undergirds the Reformers' insistence on the doctrine of the perspicuity or clarity of Scripture. God has good news to communicate with his people, and the Bible communicates this "word of truth" (Eph. 1:13; Col. 1:5) in a way that his people can understand. Therefore, though there is much that is not clear, we believe God's saving message of the gospel recorded in the Bible can be grasped by believers.[23]

C. The Bible Is the Verbally Inspired Word of God

What do we mean when we speak of the Bible as the "Word of God"? In a central passage on this theme, the Apostle Paul declares that "all Scripture is God-breathed" (2 Tim. 3:16). From this we speak of the Bible as "inspired" by God. Understood in the light of Paul's statement, however, the emphasis is not so much on the inspiration of the writers as it is on the divine source of what is actually written. The focus is not on the process but on the product. All Scripture comes as if breathed out from the mouth of God.[24]

With this understanding, divine inspiration does not imply that the Bible was given to us by divine dictation, as is claimed for the Koran or the Book of Mormon, though in some parts God did communicate in a direct way to the biblical writers. Instead, divine inspiration allows for the full engagement of all the faculties of the human authors. Luke, for example, begins his Gospel by referring to his careful investigation of the facts which he intended to set forth in his book. When we say that the Bible is a "verbally inspired" book, we mean that God has worked by his Holy Spirit through the instrumentality of the whole personality, life experiences and literary talents of its human authors to produce *the very words* that God desired to be written to reveal himself and his purposes to human beings. Peter describes this process as men speaking from God "as they were carried along by the Holy Spirit" (2 Pet. 1:20-21; Heb. 3:7; cf. Jesus' reference to David "speaking by the Holy Spirit" in Psalm 110 [Mark 12:36]). Apart from Peter's description, we have no way of grasping the mysterious concurrence of God's will working through the human will in producing this divine/ human Word.

---

23 On the role of the Holy Spirit in our understanding of the message of the Bible, see our discussion of Article 6. This statement does not minimize the importance of understanding the Bible with the help of and respect for the Christian community, both past and present.

24 Paul refers to "all" Scripture. We affirm what is often referred to as the *plenary* inspiration of Scripture—it applies to each and every part.

The Bible has its source in God, and for that reason we can conclude that what the Bible says, God says. This is certainly the way Jesus treated the Scriptures in his day. In quoting a passage from the book of Genesis that in its context was a statement of the human author, Jesus spoke of it as something *God* said (Matt. 19:4-5, citing Gen. 2:24). Equally, Paul declares that what the Scripture said to Pharaoh was what God said (Rom. 9:17; cf. also Gal. 3:8,22). In Hebrews we read that "[God] spoke through David" in the words of Ps. 95 (Heb. 4:7). Throughout the New Testament, Scripture is cited as a divine authority. In the Bible God has spoken.[25]

As its ultimate Author, God speaks to us in the Scriptures. We *receive* God's revelation, we do not create it. In that sense we are hermeneutical realists. There is an objective meaning in the Bible to be discovered that is independent of the interpreter's interpretation.

Further, as the verbally inspired Word of God, we affirm three essential qualities of the Bible—that it is true, it is complete, and it is authoritative.

1. The Bible Is Without Error

God is a God of truth. God is both all-knowing and all-good. He is free from all ignorance and all deceit. He never lies; he is completely reliable in all that he says and does (cf. Num. 23:19; 1 Sam. 15:29; Isa. 45:19; Titus 1:2; Heb. 6:18). Because the Bible is the Word of such a God, we affirm that the Bible is wholly true and without error. It can be trusted in all that it teaches.

The basis for our confidence in the truthfulness of the Scriptures lies supremely in the authority of Jesus himself. Jesus' life was shaped by the Scriptures and is inexplicable without it. He came not to abolish but to fulfill the Law and the Prophets (Matt. 5:17). The Scriptures were the basis of his teaching (cf., e.g., Matt. 9:12-13—"But go and learn what this means . . . ," citing Hos. 6:6). They provided a source of authority in his controversies with the Jewish leaders ("Have you not read . . ." Matt. 12:1-8; Matt. 19:3-6; Matt. 22:23-32). The Scriptures as the Word of God were to stand over all human traditions (Matt. 15:1-6). The Word of God "cannot be broken" (John 10:34-35). "Your word is truth," Jesus says to his Father (John 17:17). And as the Word of God, what Jesus says ought to apply to the Bible also. If such is our Lord's view of the Scriptures,

---

25 The Scriptures entrusted to the Jews are described by Paul as the very "oracles of God" (Rom. 3:2).

then ours must be no different, for "a student is not above his teacher, nor a servant above his master. . . . It is enough for the student to be like his teacher" (Matt. 10:24-25). Our commitment to Christ as "Lord" is manifest in our submission to the Scriptures.

But isn't the Bible also the product of human authors? Isn't error inextricably bound up with humanity? We contend that just as Jesus was fully human and yet was without sin, so the Scriptures can be a fully human product yet still be a fully divine product, kept from all error. In a mysterious yet wonderful way, the Bible is God's Word expressed in and through the words of human authors.

This view of the Bible has been the orthodox position of the church through the ages. Among the early church fathers, Irenaeus in the late second century wrote, "The Scriptures are perfect, seeing that they are spoken by God's Word and His Spirit."[26] Augustine in the early fifth century affirmed, when referring to the canonical Scriptures in a letter to Jerome, "[O]f these alone do I most firmly believe that the authors were completely free from error. And if in these writings I am perplexed by anything which appears to me opposed to truth, I do not hesitate to suppose that either the manuscript is faulty, or the translator has not caught the meaning of what was said, or I myself have failed to understand it."[27]

During the sixteenth-century Reformation, Martin Luther adopted the view of Augustine, adding that since the books of Scripture are to be assigned to the Holy Spirit, they cannot err.[28] John Calvin agreed, "For our wisdom ought to consist in embracing with gentle docility and without any exceptions, all that is delivered in the sacred Scriptures."[29] Eighteenth-century revivalist John Wesley put it even more strongly: "If there be any mistakes in the Bible, there may well be a thousand. If there be one falsehood in that book, it did not come from the God of truth."[30] The New Hampshire Baptist Confession (1833) states that the Bible "has God for its author, salvation for its end, and truth without any admixture of error for its matter." Our own Free Church statements also reflect this

---

26 *Against Heresies*, II.28.

27 *Letter 82.3.*

28 *Works* [St. Louis ed.] xix, 305.

29 *Institutes* I.xviii.4.

30 *Works*, 4:82. From Wesley's journal dated July 24, 1776.

view.[31] The inerrancy of the Bible, even when that term was not explicitly used, is the historical understanding of the church.[32]

a. Two Qualifications

Affirming that the Bible is without error must be done carefully lest it be misunderstood. Two qualifications must be kept in mind. First, we maintain that though the Bible is without error, we can know its truth only when it is properly interpreted in accordance with the purpose for which it was written. As discussed earlier,[33] the Bible must be understood in its intended sense. That is, the Bible is without error in all that the writers intend to affirm as true.[34]

In this regard, we must have an appreciation for the way the writers use language. Were they writing poetry, prose, prophecy, proverbs, parables or something else? Did they use metaphor, simile or hyperbole? We must seek to understand the literary conventions of the writers themselves.

Furthermore, the inerrancy of the Bible does not mean that the Bible always speaks with the precision that we might expect. We are tempted to decide what truthfulness must mean by our own modern standards for accuracy and then impose those standards onto the Bible. For example, did the Gospel writers intend to record the precise words of Jesus, like stenographers in a court room? The fact that Jesus probably spoke Aramaic and the Gospels were written in Greek suggests otherwise. We believe that the Evangelists give us precisely the words God wanted

---

31 Cf. the 1884 Swedish Evangelical Free Church statement ("This organization accepts the Bible, both Old and New Testaments, as the Word of God, containing the Gospel of salvation for all men and the only perfect rule for teaching, faith and life."), the 1912 Norwegian-Danish Evangelical Free Church Association statement (Article 1: "We believe, that the Bible, the Old and New Testament, is the Word of God and is the only infallible rule and guide for faith, life, and doctrine."), and the 1950 EFCA statement (Article 1: "The Scriptures, both Old and New Testaments, to be the inspired Word of God, without error in the original writings, the complete revelation of His will for the salvation of men, and the Divine and final authority for Christian faith and life."). See also the Chicago Statement on Biblical Inerrancy (1978).

32 On this, see further, John Woodbridge, *Biblical Authority: A Critique of the Rogers/McKim Proposal* (Grand Rapids: Zondervan, 1982).

33 See Sec. II.B above.

34 A distinction can be made between the Bible's historical or descriptive authority and its normative authority. The Bible may accurately record things that are false (e.g., the false statements of Satan) without approving them or intending to affirm them as true.

us to have to understand the true message of Jesus.[35] Consequently, variations in the way those words are recounted ought not to disturb us, for imprecise citation was conventional and violated no expectations.[36]

In addition, to affirm that the Bible is without error does not require that the Bible is precisely accurate in all its measurements. Imprecision is not the same thing as error if the intent of the author is to give approximations or to use round numbers. Sometimes the biblical writers may present events or sayings topically, rather than following a strict chronology. They may speak in the language of appearances rather than in strict scientific description, as when declaring that "the sun rose" or that "the earth cannot be moved" (Ps. 93:1). The Bible's assertions are fully true, and we know that truth when its words are properly interpreted in accordance with the purpose for which they were written. Literary and historical study are helpful in determining what those purposes might be and the conventions used to communicate them. Our understanding of biblical inerrancy must bear in mind the authors' intent.

The emphasis on the Bible achieving its divine purpose leads to the use of the word "infallible" to describe its nature. God's Word will not fail to bring about its prescribed end. As Jesus affirmed emphatically, "I tell you the truth, until heaven and earth disappear, not the smallest letter, not the least stroke of a pen, will by any means disappear from the Law until everything is accomplished" (Matt. 5:18). God's Word has many purposes—it warns, it encourages, it comforts, it convicts, and it will infallibly accomplish them all. We believe that the Bible is infallible in all that it intends and that when its purpose is to teach,[37] it is without error.[38]

---

35 Scholars often speak of a distinction between the exact words of Jesus (the *ipsissima verba*) and the exact voice or meaning (the *ipsissima vox*). We can observe that the biblical writers appear to be more concerned with the latter than with the former, and this is consistent with the literary conventions of the day.

36 When Jesus is with his disciples in the boat during the storm, the disciples come to him and their words are recorded differently in Matthew (8:25), Mark (4:38) and Luke (8:24). This is Augustine's comment on this discrepancy— "The meaning of those who wake the Lord in their desire to be saved is one and same, and there is no need of inquiring which of these expressions was more probably addressed to Christ. For whether the disciples said any one of these three things, or used other words which no Evangelist has recorded, but which had the same force as regards truth of meaning, what does it matter?" (*De Cons. Evang.* ii.24).

37 We understand the word "teach" here in its broadest sense to include not just theological propositions but all that the biblical writers intend to affirm as true. This includes, for example, historical reports.

38 To clarify, the terms infallible and inerrant are not synonymous and both are important. The Bible's infallibility refers to its unwavering reliability to accomplish its

b. The Bible Is Without Error in the Original Writings

A second qualification of our affirmation of the inerrancy of the Bible limits the complete divine superintending of the process to what the biblical writers actually wrote, and not to the transmission of the text through the centuries. The church has never claimed that the New Testament text has been inerrantly preserved. The Westminster Confession, for example, simply speaks of the "singular care and providence" of God in preserving his Word (I. vii). In the last two centuries through both the discovery of a great number of ancient manuscripts[39] and the careful application of the principles of textual criticism[40] we can speak of that care and providence with even greater confidence.

In fact, we have far better attestation of the Greek New Testament than any other book from the ancient world. Caesar's *Gallic War*, for example, was written about 50 B.C. The earliest manuscript we have of any part of that book dates to about A.D. 900—a span of 950 years after the original, and we only have a total of ten manuscripts. The comparison with the New Testament is telling. Written at the latest by about A.D. 90, the earliest fragment we have from the Gospels dates to about A.D. 125—possibly a span of only 35 years from the time of writing to the first known copy. We have almost all of the New Testament preserved in manuscripts from the second century, and at least 48 manuscripts come from before A.D. 300. Altogether we have over 5,700 Greek manuscripts (and counting). And this does not include the 20,000 ancient manuscripts in other languages, and the hundreds of thousands of Greek citations from the New Testament in early Christian writings. Textual critics of the New Testament have a nearly overwhelming wealth of resources to work with in seeking to recover the original text.

We do not know precisely how many variants have been found in the multitude of manuscripts of the New Testament that we now have. The best estimate is somewhere between three and four hundred thousand. But this should not lessen our confidence in knowing what the biblical writers actually wrote. The more manuscripts that are discovered,

---

divine purpose, and its inerrancy refers to its propositional truth, that is, that it contains no errors in what it affirms.

39 In this context "manuscripts" refer to copies of the Bible written in the original languages.

40 This refers to the study of the transmission of a text over time and the principles used to determine the text most likely to represent what was originally written.

the more the variant readings; but also the higher the likelihood that somewhere among those variant readings one will be able to uncover the original text.

Further, the vast majority of those textual variants are irrelevant. Probably two-thirds of the variations involve either spelling differences— like whether John's name in Greek has one "n" or two—or nonsensical readings that were clearly the result of a scribal copying error.

Another quarter of the variants are minor differences that do not affect translation or that involve synonyms—like replacing a pronoun with a name—or simply a different word order—like "Jesus Christ" or "Christ Jesus."

The next largest collection of variants (perhaps 5-7%) involves differences that affect the meaning of the text but simply cannot reasonably be accepted as a part of the original text. The insertion of the "Trinitarian text" in 1 John 5:6-7 is an example.[41]

Finally, not more than 1% of the variants both affect the meaning of the text and are quite possibly original. But they may affect the meaning only slightly, as in 1 John 1:4, which says, "We write this to make our joy complete." Some manuscripts read *"your joy"*—a difference of one letter, with nothing very significant hanging on that choice. Moreover, regardless of what is the proper reading of this passage, Scripture speaks of the truth of both "our" joy and "your" joy elsewhere. We can say with great certainty that no central Christian truth depends on a passage that is in any way in doubt.

It is true that we cannot claim with absolute certainty that we have the original inerrant text of the Bible. Does this decidedly human process of textual criticism with its still rather small residue of uncertainty invalidate any claims to the divine authority of the Bible? It would if we claimed that the Bible came directly from heaven. But we have already declared that the Bible is a very human book. We must appreciate the very human nature of the Bible's creation, conservation and canonization. God does not normally work apart from human instruments but through them.

It is wrong to think that since it is a human book it cannot also be divinely inspired. The human authors' writing out of their very human experiences, emotions and desires does not exclude the Holy

---

41 The disputed words referring to "the Father, the Word and the Holy Spirit" are found in only one Latin translation and in one Greek manuscript which now appears to have been written in 1520 by a Franciscan friar who himself inserted those words from the Latin into the Greek manuscript he was copying.

Spirit's using those same experiences, emotions and desires to convey divine revelation. This conjunction is at the center of our faith—that the categories of divinity and humanity cannot be so hardened that God could not become man and dwell among us, and so redeem us for himself. God has worked through human means to bring to us his holy Word.[42]

2. The Bible Is Complete

When we speak of the Bible as "the complete revelation of [God's] will for salvation" we are referring to what has traditionally been called the "sufficiency" of Scripture. God has spoken all we need to know for Christian faith and life—for our doctrine and our duty. This understanding flows from the Reformers' formal principle of *sola Scriptura* (Scripture alone). Since Scripture alone is our ultimate authority of truth, all truth necessary for our salvation and spiritual life is taught either explicitly or implicitly in Scripture.

The sufficiency of Scripture is affirmed most clearly in Paul's words to Timothy: "from infancy you have known the holy Scriptures, which are able to make you wise for salvation through faith in Christ Jesus" (2 Tim. 3:15). The saving grace of God is revealed in the Bible. What is written there is able to lead us to salvation. Paul goes on to say that the "God-breathed" Scripture "is useful for teaching, rebuking, correcting and training in righteousness, so that the man of God may be thoroughly equipped for every good work" (2 Tim. 3:16-17). The holy Scriptures are the means God uses to shape our lives. The Apostle here affirms that the Lord will equip us through his Word for whatever "good work" he requires of us (cf. also 2 Pet. 1:3-4). And if Paul speaks in this way of the Old Testament, how much more is this true when we include the clear apostolic testimony found in the New.

In affirming the sufficiency of Scripture, we also deny that the general revelation of God in creation (cf. Rom. 1:20) or in the human conscience (cf. Rom. 2:14-15) is able in itself to bring us to a saving knowledge of God. Far from saving us, such revelation leaves us without excuse when we stand before God as Judge. We need the special revelation of God now given to us in the Bible if we are to know of his mercy and grace

---

42 A further human aspect of biblical transmission is the work of translation from the original languages. Though all translations are subject to correction by the inerrant original text, we believe that sound translations can sufficiently convey God's Word to us.

found in the gospel of Jesus Christ.[43]

The sufficiency of Scripture is illustrated in Jesus' story of the rich man and Lazarus (Luke 16:19-31). The rich man went to hell, and from there he begged Abraham to send Lazarus to his father's house to warn his brothers lest they follow him into that agony. But Abraham replied, "They have Moses and the Prophets; let them listen to them." "'No, father Abraham,' the rich man said, 'but if someone from the dead goes to them, they will repent.' "He said to him, 'If they do not listen to Moses and the Prophets, they will not be convinced even if someone rises from the dead'" (Luke 16:29-31). Jesus affirms that the Scripture is sufficient to meet their need, if they would but listen to it.

The sufficiency of Scripture rests ultimately on the supremacy of Christ—that is, *sola Scriptura* (Scripture alone) follows from *solus Christus* (Christ alone). Nothing can be added to Christ's redemptive work, and nothing can be added to the revelation of that redemptive work found in the Bible. The New Testament is the divinely inspired apostolic witness to the Logos of God, the Word made flesh in Jesus Christ (John 1:1,14), and in Christ, God has revealed himself supremely. "In these last days, God has spoken by his Son" (Heb. 1:2), and "in [Christ] are hidden all the treasures of wisdom and knowledge" (Col. 2:3).

Consider Philip's request of Jesus: "Lord, show us the Father, and we shall be satisfied" (John 14:8), and Jesus' response: "he who has seen me has seen the Father" (John 14:9). In other words, the revelation of Christ is not insufficient or inadequate. It is enough.

Think of Peter's words to Jesus: "To whom else can we go? You have the words of eternal life" (John 6:68). Or the Father's affirmation of the Son on the Mount of Transfiguration: "Listen to him!" (Matt. 17:5). And Jesus' Great Commission: "Go and make disciples of all nations, baptizing them . . . and teaching them to obey everything I have commanded you" (Matt. 28:19-20). This message of Jesus has been delivered to us sufficiently. Hence, the admonition of Jude: "contend for the faith that was *once for all* entrusted to the saints" (Jude 3).

John Calvin writes:

> For it is as if, leading us away from all doctrines of
> men, [God] should conduct us to his Son alone; bid us
> seek all teaching of salvation from him alone; depend

---

43 On this, see further in Article 10, sec. II.

> upon him, cleave to him; in short (...), hearken to his
> voice alone. And what, indeed, ought we now either
> to expect or to hope from man, when the very Word of
> life has intimately and openly disclosed himself to us?
> But the mouths of all men should be closed when once
> he has spoken, in whom the Heavenly Father willed
> all the treasures of knowledge and wisdom to be hid
> [Col. 2:3], and has, indeed, so spoken as befitted the
> wisdom of God (...) and the Messiah (...); that is, after
> himself he left nothing for others to say.[44]

God has spoken, and he has spoken supremely in Jesus Christ, whose apostolic testimony is found in the Scriptures. There we come to know him who is the final Word of God. What more could we possibly need to know?

> How firm a foundation
> Ye saints of the Lord
> Is laid for your faith
> In His excellent Word
> What more can He say
> Than to you He hath said
> To you who for refuge
> To Jesus have fled.[45]

To clarify, it must be said that our understanding of the sufficiency of Scripture does not mean that knowledge found outside the Bible is not helpful to us. Knowledge from other realms can help us live wisely in God's world in all sorts of ways. Specifically, it can help us to understand and apply the Bible's message. We need to know languages, history, and culture as we seek to interpret the Bible rightly. In applying the Bible's message, knowledge of medicine and human bodily functions, for example, can help us in making bio-ethical decisions.

But when we say that the Bible is the complete revelation of God's will for salvation, we affirm that it contains all the *divine words* we need for all of life. Everything required of us to live a godly life is given in the Scripture.

---

44 *Institutes* IV.viii.7.

45 Rippon's *Selection of Hymns*, 1787.

3. The Bible Is Authoritative

A third quality of the Bible as the Word of God, and closely related to its sufficiency, is its authority over us. We affirm that the Scriptures provide "the ultimate authority by which every realm of human knowledge and endeavor should be judged." God's authority is mediated to us through his Word.

In affirming *sola Scriptura*, "Scripture alone," the Reformers were fighting a battle on two fronts. On the one side, the Roman Catholics held church tradition as an authority equal to Scripture. On the other, the "enthusiasts" (the "radical charismatics" of the day) accepted immediate prophetic utterances of the Spirit as messages equal in authority to Scripture. In opposition to both, the Reformers declared that the Bible alone held the position of ultimate authority for the Christian.[46]

The Bible itself supports this view. On the one hand, Jesus condemned the Pharisees for nullifying the Word of God for the sake of their traditions (Matt. 15:6). On the other, the words of a prophet, in both the Old and New Testaments, were always to be judged by the previously revealed Word of God (cf. Deut. 13:1-5) and the authoritative teaching of an apostle (1 Cor. 14:37-38; Gal. 1:8).[47]

The authority of the Bible embraces both belief and behavior. It tells us what we ought to think and how we ought to act. And its authority extends over every realm to which it speaks. That means that all that we teach must be judged by the authority of the Bible itself. Thus, we can never claim that our interpretation of the Bible is inerrant. We are to preach and teach with Bibles open, encouraging people to be like the Bereans of the Book of Acts, who "examined the Scriptures every day to see if what Paul said was true" (Acts 17:11).

To be clear, our statement about the Bible's authority does not mean that there is no knowledge outside the Bible, nor that the Bible must be invoked to justify every aspect of human knowledge and action. The Bible is *authoritative* over every realm of human activity, but, as we have stated, it does not *address* every realm. There is much that is not revealed in Scripture, from atomic physics to the chemical activity of the brain, that can greatly enrich human life. But nothing outside of Scripture comes

---

46 For this reason "Scripture alone" is described as the "formal principle" of the Reformation.

47 The apostolic "tradition" (cf. 2 Thess. 2:15; 1 Cor. 11:2; 15:3) now comes to us in the New Testament Scriptures.

to us with the same universally binding divine authority—not church tradition, not any other religious writings, not prophetic utterances, not inner promptings of the Spirit, not scientific theories, not human reason. All of these can be helpful, and Scripture as our "ultimate authority" does not imply that we should try to understand the world, and even the Bible itself, without using all the resources God has made available to us.[48] Yet we affirm that all knowledge, from whatever source, must be in service of the Word of God, and that Word provides the necessary norms by which to assess all other knowledge. Since what the Bible says, God says, the Scripture remains the ultimate standard of all that is set forth as "truth." It stands over every other claim to truth as the rule to which it must submit.

The Evangelical Free Church began as a reform movement in the state churches of Scandinavia, spawned by a renewed focus on the Bible. Through a network of small Bible studies called the "Readers Revival," these believers developed a strong conviction about the centrality and authority of the Scriptures. "Where stands it written?" became the watchword for all faith and practice. We stand strongly in that tradition.

III. Our Response to God's Word

The Apostle Paul declares that in Christ "are hidden all the treasures of wisdom and knowledge" (Col. 2:3). Christ himself is at the center of the Bible (Luke 24:27,44-45; John 5:39). Christ himself is the means by which God has spoken his ultimate Word to the world (Heb. 1:1-2). Christ himself, in his person and work, is the gospel, and it is the gospel of Jesus Christ that has been authoritatively revealed to us in the Scriptures.

How should we respond to such a revelation? We ought to begin with a humble and awe-filled adoration and gratitude. We do not stand over God's Word as its judge, but under it as those willing to be taught, rebuked, corrected and trained (cf. 2 Tim. 3:17). "This is the one I esteem:" says the Lord, "he who is humble and contrite in spirit, and trembles at my word" (Isa. 66:2). The psalmist of the Old Testament, writing even before the full revelation of the gospel in Christ, extols this Word from God in joyful verse:

---

48 Though the Bible is eternally true, at times what is learned outside the Bible can challenge and even change the way we interpret the Bible. Knowledge of the heliocentric solar system, for example, changed the way that many understood 1 Chron. 16:30; Pss. 93:1; 96:10—"The world is firmly established; it cannot be moved."

> The law of the LORD is perfect,
> reviving the soul.
> The statutes of the LORD are trustworthy,
> making wise the simple.
> The precepts of the LORD are right,
> giving joy to the heart.
> The commands of the LORD are radiant,
> giving light to the eyes.
> The fear of the LORD is pure,
> enduring forever.
> The ordinances of the LORD are sure and altogether righteous.
> They are more precious than gold, than much pure gold;
> they are sweeter than honey, than honey from the comb.
> By them is your servant warned;
> in keeping them there is great reward.
>
> (Ps. 19:7-11)

God has spoken in the Bible. In speaking, God acts, and the "speech acts" in the Bible include not only the revelation of propositional truth about himself and his world, but also words of command and words of promise. Our response ought to reflect the various purposes God intends when he speaks to us through his Word.

All that the Bible teaches us we ought to believe.[49] All that the Bible requires of us, we ought to obey. And all that the Bible promises us, we ought to trust.[50] For what the Bible says, God says, and it is all for our good and for his glory. For in the Scriptures God's gospel of his Son has been authoritatively revealed to us. God has spoken!

---

49 And certainly we ought to deny what the Bible denies.

50 This sentence in our Statement of Faith is adapted from the Chicago Statement on Biblical Inerrancy (1978).

Evangelical Convictions

A Theological Exposition of the Statement of Faith of the Evangelical Free Church of America

Article 3
THE HUMAN CONDITION

3. We believe that God created Adam and Eve in His image, but they sinned when tempted by Satan. In union with Adam, human beings are sinners by nature and by choice, alienated from God, and under His wrath. Only through God's saving work in Jesus Christ can we be rescued, reconciled and renewed.

God's gospel alone addresses our deepest need.

Who are we as human beings? Though our knowledge of the world around us has exploded since the dawn of the scientific age, we remain a mystery to ourselves. The human person continues to perplex and confound. Who is this "I" by which we refer to ourselves? We are more than our bodies, but we seem mysteriously bound to them. We are a part of the natural world as animals among animals, yet instinctively we feel that we are more than that—we are spiritual creatures, conceiving of eternity, longing for immortality. Even those who believe that nothing exists except matter regularly make a telling distinction between what is natural and what is "man-made."

We long for significance, but as mere specks in space and time in the immensity of the cosmos we wonder how we can find it. The Copernican Revolution of the seventeenth century forever wrested from us a place at the center of the solar system, but such a sense of wonder at the vastness of creation was already expressed by the ancient Hebrew psalmist: "When I consider your heavens, the work of your fingers, the moon and the stars, which you have set in place, what is man that you are mindful of him, the son of man that you care for him?" (Ps. 8:3-4).[1]

But the puzzle of humanity also has a moral dimension. We are capable of acts of great compassion and even heroic virtue. Some even sacrifice their lives to rescue others in peril. Yet some deep stain of corruption still plagues human life. Intellectual and technological sophistication seem to have no effect on our proclivity for evil, to which the horrors of the twentieth century attest. All our lofty ideals and utopian dreams eventually flounder on the rocks of reality. The evidences of the darkness of the human heart are pervasive in human history, yet such darkness still surprises us. Somehow we cannot think of it as merely natural and unavoidable. Something seems to have gone dreadfully wrong.

Daniel Migliore sums it up well: "We human beings are a mystery to ourselves. We are rational and irrational, civilized and savage, capable of

---

1 For a modern expression of this, consider Stephen Hawking (Cambridge physicist and author of the best-seller, *A Brief History of Time*), who said, "We are such insignificant creatures on a minor planet of a very average star in the outer suburbs of one of a hundred thousand million galaxies. So it is difficult to believe in a God that would care about us or even notice our existence." (Cited in Kitty Ferguson, *The Fire in the Equations* [Grand Rapids: Eerdmans, 1994], 179).

deep friendship and murderous hostility, free and in bondage, the pinnacle of creation and its greatest danger. We are Rembrandt and Hitler, Mozart and Stalin, Antigone and Lady Macbeth, Ruth and Jezebel."[2]

Or, to put it poetically, our human condition can be expressed in the words of Alexander Pope:

> Created half to rise, and half to fall,
> Great lord of all things, yet a prey to all;
> Sole judge of truth, in endless error hurled;
> The glory, jest and riddle of the world.

Where can we go for help as we wrestle with this riddle? The story is told of Arthur Schopenhauer, the nineteenth-century German philosopher, who was sitting in a park, disheveled and unkempt, as if homeless. A park policeman approached Schopenhauer and asked him who he was. "Would to God I knew the answer to that question!" he replied. In fact, it is to God we *must* go if we are to find the answer to this most baffling riddle.[3] For God our Creator has spoken to us through his Word and has revealed the best and most satisfying answer to be found anywhere. And, as importantly, he has also revealed the one way that human depravity can be destroyed and human dignity can be established through divine redemption.

I. The Source of Human Dignity:
Our Creation in God's Image

The biblical story of creation finds its climax in these words from Genesis 1:

> Then God said, "Let us make man in our image, in
> our likeness, and let them rule over the fish of the sea
> and the birds of the air, over the livestock, over all the
> earth, and over all the creatures that move along the
> ground." So God created man in his own image, in

---

2 Daniel L. Migliore, *Faith Seeking Understanding: An Introduction to Christian Theology*, 2nd ed. (Grand Rapids: Eerdmans, 2004), 139.

3 Cf. Calvin's statement in the *Institutes*: "Again, it is certain that man never achieves a clear knowledge of himself unless he has first looked upon God's face, and then descends from contemplating him to scrutinize himself" (I.1.2).

> the image of God he created him; male and female he
> created them. . . . God saw all that he had made, and it
> was very good.
>
> (Gen. 1:26-27, 31)

Here is the source of all human dignity and significance and the place where the sanctity of human life is rooted. Of all the creatures on the earth, only human beings are created in the image of God. Man is a creature of great majesty, but it is a derived dignity, a God-given greatness. According to the Bible, human beings must be defined in terms of their relation to God—as the image of God.

The more detailed story of the creation of the first man in Genesis 2 makes it clear that human beings are a part of the created order. Adam, the first human, was made from the dust of the earth,[4] just like all the animals (Gen. 2:19). Yet in this one respect he was unique: Though created from the dust of the earth, he was made in the image of God. He was a part of the natural world, yet in some sense above it, transcending it. Part of the riddle of our existence is found in this precarious position; we are suspended between two worlds. But nothing suggests that this amphibian-like nature was a cause of distress, much less of depravity. Our material mode of being was, in God's sight, very good (Gen. 1:31).

A. Human Beings as God's Image

What does it mean to be created in God's image, the *imago Dei*? The Bible does not define that state, so we must draw inferences from elsewhere in Scripture.[5] The combination with the word "likeness" suggests that in some sense human beings were created to "mirror" God, to reflect something of who he is in the world. If the heavens declare the glory of God, how much more the human person?

But what is the nature of this divine reflection? In what ways either *do* or *should* human beings mirror God? Human beings are rational beings, able to think and to seek truth; we are moral beings, able to make judgments about good and evil; we are social beings, able

---

4 The association of the Hebrew word for "human being" or "man" (*adam*) and the word for "dust" (*adamah*) reinforces this connection. Paul refers to all human beings as likewise "made from the dust" (1 Cor. 15:37-38; cf. also 33:6).

5 The fact of our creation in God's image is frequently affirmed. Cf. Gen. 1:26-27; 5:1,3; 9:6; 1 Cor. 11:7; James 3:9. The doctrine is implied in Rom. 8:29; 2 Cor. 3:18; Eph. 4:23-24; Col. 3:10.

to communicate and to love; we are artistic beings, able to create and to appreciate beauty; and we are spiritual beings, able to worship and to pray. All these qualities point to the uniqueness of human beings in creation as persons who think, feel, speak, make free decisions and moral judgments, and who long to know and be known, to love and be loved. In all these ways we somehow transcend our material existence and assume moral responsibility and spiritual apprehension, and reflect the personal nature of God.[6]

As persons we are engaged in relationships, and our creation in God's image suggests relationships in two directions. First, and most obviously, our creation in God's image entails a relationship with God himself. To be a human being is to be directed toward God. We are created by God; we are dependent on God; we are responsible to God. All other relationships are to be dominated and regulated by this one overarching reality—we are made for relationship with God.

In the Genesis text, human beings are the only creatures with whom God engages in personal interaction,[7] and the first word of God to them was a blessing. "God blessed them and said to them, 'Be fruitful and increase in number; fill the earth and subdue it. Rule over the fish of the sea and the birds of the air, and over every living creature that moves on the ground'" (1:28). This was a statement of their privileged position in God's created order.

The next word was a command—"the LORD God commanded the man, 'You are free to eat from any tree in the garden; but you must not eat from the tree of the knowledge of good and evil, for when you eat of it you will surely die'" (2:16-17). We are the only earthly creatures that stand under the moral command of God.[8]

God speaks to us in words of blessing and command. Like a father, God loves us and has authority over us at the same time. We are created by God to receive his love, and we are created by God to submit to his authority. And our response will result in either life or death. This

---

6 We recognize, however, that the Bible's reticence to define the image of God in functional or structural terms should alert us of the danger of denying the true humanity of any who are in any way deficient in normal human functions. For this reason we concur with the judgment of Millard Erickson when he concludes, "The image . . . refers to something a human is rather than something a human has or does. By virtue of being human, one is in the image of God; it is not dependent upon the presence of anything else" (*Christian Theology*, 2nd ed. [Grand Rapids: Baker, 1998], 532).

7 Though God does curse the serpent (Gen. 3:14).

8 The story in Genesis at this point is not concerned with the angelic realm.

vertical dimension must be the starting point for our understanding of ourselves. We are created to live in a relationship with God our Creator. The second dimension of relationship—the horizontal along the human plane—will be addressed below.

Another dimension of this concept emerges when we see that the biblical expression of man's unique created condition could also be translated "*as* God's image" (cf. 1 Cor. 11:7). This suggests that human beings not only *reflect* God in the world, they also *represent* him. Ancient rulers often erected images of themselves in distant parts of their realms. The image stood for the ruler himself; it represented his authority. Whoever possessed that image of the king exercised his royal authority.[9] So, man, too, represents God, almost like an ambassador in a foreign country.

This aspect of the image of God comes out in the command for man to rule over creation (Gen. 1:26) and is illustrated in the task given to Adam of naming the animals in Genesis 2.[10] Human beings are to "subdue" God's creation, in the sense of "having dominion" over it (1:28), and God put Adam in the garden to "work" in it and "to take care of it" (2:15). Nature is not man's slave to be exploited; but man is a steward of the natural world, to govern it as God's vice-regent, ruling it under God's authority. "Nature" can be taken in its broadest context to include all of God's creation, encompassing the human endeavors of science, technology, entertainment, athletics, art and music. We may broaden the command to develop culture in ways in which we use our gifts in all these areas for the good of others and the glory of God (cf. 1 Cor. 10:31).[11]

Because human beings are the image of God, they ought also to be honored appropriately. One honors God by honoring his image. For this reason Jesus links the command to love God with the command to love one's neighbor, who is created in the image of God. Love for one's neighbor demonstrates love for God. In his letter James speaks of the evil inconsistency of the tongue: with it "we praise our Lord and Father, and with it we curse men, who have been made in God's likeness" (3:9).

---

9 Cf. Anthony A. Hoekema, *Created in God's Image* (Grand Rapids: Eerdmans, 1986), 67.

10 This divinely sanctioned authority is "not the content but the consequence" of man being in the divine image (so F. Delitsch, cited in Derek Kidner, *Genesis: An Introduction and Commentary*, The Tyndale Old Testament Commentaries [Downers Grove: InterVarsity,1967], 52).

11 Some refer to this as a "cultural mandate."

The fact that murder is considered to be a capital crime is also grounded in this connection. In Gen. 9:6 we read, "Whoever sheds the blood of man, by man shall his blood be shed; for in the image of God has God made man." We encounter God as we encounter other human beings— "If anyone says, 'I love God,' yet hates his brother, he is a liar. For anyone who does not love his brother, whom he has seen, cannot love God, whom he has not seen" (1 John 4:20). We cannot hate the image and say we love the One it represents.

The Bible affirms that *every* human being is created in the image of God, not just the king, as was believed in many ancient cultures. According to Proverbs 14:31 even the lowly peasant represents God. "He who oppresses the poor shows contempt for their Maker, but whoever is kind to the needy honors God." This is the basis of what we call natural law and universal human rights.

All human life—at whatever stage of development, from conception to death; at whatever socio-economic status; and at whatever level of physical or intellectual capability—is sacred, because all human beings are created in God's image. Even when this image has been corrupted by our sin,[12] every human being is still worthy of honor and respect. There is nothing more valuable in all of creation than a human life.

B. The Significance of Adam and Eve

The Apostle Paul declares in his address to the Athenians that "from one man [God] made every nation of men, that they should inhabit the whole earth" (Acts 17:26). The Genesis story identifies that one man as Adam.[13] As an expression of the incompleteness of creation, God declared that it was not good for Adam to be alone (Gen. 2:18). The first man was joined by the first woman, Eve, and the design of God to create

---

12 This corruption is assumed in the need for the *renewal* of the image (Col. 3:10) and our need to be conformed to the image of Christ (Rom. 8:29; 2 Cor. 3:18) who is the image of God (Col. 2:4). Anthony Hoekema makes the helpful distinction between the structural sense of the image of God, which is retained after the fall, and its functional sense, how it is used, which has been perverted. Hoekema writes, "The image is now malfunctioning—and yet it is still there. The loss of the image in the functional sense presupposes the retention of the image in the structural sense. To be a sinner one must be an image-bearer of God—one must be able to reason, to will, to make decisions; a dog, which does not possess the image of God, cannot sin. Man sins with God-imaging gifts. In fact, the very greatness of man's sin consists in the fact that he is still an image-bearer of God" (*Created in God's Image*, 85).

13 That this name can also be used to refer to all of humanity has a significance we will consider below.

"man" in his own image as male and female was complete (Gen. 1:27).

This "gendered" creation is significant in several ways. First, it points to the essentially relational nature of human existence. As God exists eternally in a Trinitarian union of love of three divine Persons, so human beings created in his image are to share in personal relationships. Adam's solitary life called for a partner—"a helper suitable for him" (Gen. 2:18). To be fully human, we have a need for social interaction with other human beings.

Second, the Genesis account assumes the equal value of men and women. Each is created in God's image. We find no biblical grounds for an oppressive patriarchy.

Third, while affirming the equal significance of man and woman as creatures uniquely created in the image of God, the Bible also affirms their differences. Paul draws on the fact that Adam was created first to ground some instructions regarding behavior in the assembly of the church (cf. 1 Cor. 11:3-10; 1 Tim. 2:8-15).[14]

Fourth, our gendered creation reflects the divine command to "be fruitful and increase in number" (Gen. 1:28), part of God's original blessing of the first human beings. Procreation, in the context of the marriage relationship, is a part of the goodness of God's design for human life.

Finally, the creation of human beings as male and female also reinforces the notion of a created order, particularly as it points us to the marriage relationship. The culmination of the story of Genesis 2 is the explanatory declaration in v. 24: "For this reason a man will leave his father and mother and be united to his wife, and they will become one flesh." Jesus himself points to this passage as the design of the Creator for marriage from the beginning (Matt. 19:3-9).[15] The Apostle Paul also refers to homosexual acts as contrary to this natural order (Rom. 1:26-27). God has created us as male and female, and this difference is significant and ought to be recognized and valued.

There are legitimate differences of opinion about how one understands the nature of the language used in the early chapters of Genesis to describe the actions of God in the world. However, our

---

14 Based on these texts and others, the 1988 General Conference of the EFCA determined that the primary teaching authority in the local church ought to be held by men only and adopted a rule limiting ordination to men. Other ministerial credentials are open to both men and women. On this, see the EFCA booklet, "Steps Toward Credentialing."

15 Male and female relationships are, of course, also significant in discussions of the roles of husbands and wives in the New Testament, though there is no reference to creation in those passages (cf. Eph. 5:22-33; Col. 3:18-19; 1 Pet. 3:1-7) as is the case in discussing certain aspects of the life in the church in 1 Cor. 11:3-10; 1 Tim. 2:8-15.

Statement affirms that Adam and Eve were historical figures[16] in the following sense: 1) From these two all other human beings are descended (Acts 17:26).[17] 2) These two were the first creatures created in God's image such that they were accountable to God as responsible moral agents. And 3) these two rebelled against God, affecting all their progeny.[18]

What is essential to the biblical story-line is that the problem with the world is not ontological—that is, it is not a result of the material nature of creation itself nor is sin an essential part of our humanity.[19] The problem is moral. The first human beings from the very beginning, in a distinct act of rebellion, chose to turn away from God, and this act not only affected all humanity (cf. Rom. 5:12-21), but creation itself (cf. Rom. 8:18-25). This leads us from considering the dignity of humanity to acknowledging our depravity.

II. The Source of Human Depravity: Our Fall into Sin

Mark Twain once said that man is the only creature in all creation that can blush, and he is the only creature that needs to. We are the only creatures who realize that we are not what we should be, and that discrepancy is the cause of great distress. As Blaise Pascal observed: "The greatness of man is great in that he knows himself to be miserable."[20] We are confronted by the moral riddle of human existence: Why do we expect more good out of human beings than is ever realized? Pascal asks, "Who is unhappy at not being a king, except a deposed king?"[21] He concludes, "All these miseries prove man's greatness. They are the miseries of a great lord, of a deposed king."[22] That points us to the answer that we find in the Bible. There human beings are depicted as dethroned

---

16 The historical reality of Adam and Eve has been the traditional position of the church (so Tertullian, Athanasius, Augustine, Calvin) and is supported elsewhere in Scripture. Particularly, Paul compares the "one man" Adam with both Moses and Jesus (cf. Rom. 5:12, 15-19; 1 Cor. 15:20-22). In addition, Luke traces the genealogy of Jesus back to Adam (Luke 3:23-37; cf. also 1 Chron. 1).

17 We take no position on the manner in which the human soul is passed on, either by natural heredity ("traducianism") or by a unique work of God in each life ("creationism").

18 Consequently, no human beings existed prior to these two, and, consequently, no human beings were sinless and without the need of a Savior.

19 This also gives us hope that human beings can be redeemed from sin.

20 *Pensées*, #397.

21 *Pensées*, #409.

22 *Pensées*, #398.

monarchs with a moral memory of their former greatness,[23] a memory which makes them long to regain what is now lost.

Our Statement of Faith follows the biblical story, moving from the glory of Genesis 2 to the guilt of Genesis 3. The man and his wife were both naked, and they felt no shame as they enjoyed the blessing of God in the garden he had created for them. But quite suddenly a new character emerges into this idyllic world—a tempter. Though his existence is real, his origin is unknown; he is depicted simply as a serpent, a snake—a mere creature.

A. Tempted by Satan

But what is the source of this first evil in the cosmos? We are left with a mystery, which reflects the mystery of evil itself. Certainly, this snake, who in the story is the embodiment of Satan himself (cf. Rev. 12:9; 20:2), could not have been created evil, for all that God made was good (Gen. 1:31). Scripture provides hints that may point to a primordial rebellion among the angelic beings that resulted in this evil.[24] But even that does not tell us why evil entered into God's creation in the first place. It just pushes its entrance, and the mystery, still further back. However they originated, the Bible affirms the reality of evil spiritual beings, led by Satan, the tempter and accuser, and a liar and murderer from the beginning (John 8:44). He remains our greatest enemy, though he was defeated by Christ on the cross and will be banished forever when Christ returns in glory, and every enemy is put under his feet and he finally "turns the kingdom over to God" (1 Cor. 15:24).[25]

The tempter simply appears in the garden, and his role in the story emphasizes that there was nothing *in* man himself to prompt him to rebel against God's rule. There was no natural cause of evil within the human race. There was simply freedom, a freedom reflecting God's own freedom.[26] And it was toward this freedom that the tempter directed his efforts.

In his craftiness, the serpent first casts doubt on the word of God,

---

23 Ecclesiastes speaks of God setting "eternity in the hearts of men" (3:11).

24 Cf. Isa. 28; Ezek. 28

25 On the spiritual battle in this present age, see our discussion in Article 8.

26 Some distinction must be made, however, for the first humans were able to sin (*posse peccare*, to use Augustine's expression), which God is not. Augustine expands this to contend that after the fall human beings are captive to sin—not able not to sin (*non posse non peccare*); as redeemed in Christ, they are able not to sin (*posse non peccare*); and in glory they will, like God, not be able to sin (*non posse peccare*).

introducing the first questioning of God's character into the world: "Did God really say, 'You must not eat from any tree in the garden'?" (Gen. 3:1). Through misrepresentation, the serpent creates confusion. He turns the word of God on its head, making it say the opposite of what was intended. God's liberal permission and single prohibition (Gen. 2:16-17) now seem to be restrictive and constraining.

Then the serpent attacks God's truthfulness: "'You will not surely die,' the serpent said to the woman" (3:4), suggesting that sin will not be judged. Once the prospect of judgment is cast away, it is relatively easy to open the floodgates of unbelief.

Finally, in verse 5 he casts doubt on God's goodness in making this prohibition: "For God knows that when you eat of it your eyes will be opened, and you will be like God, knowing good and evil."

The temptation had its intended effect. "When the woman saw that the fruit of the tree was good for food and pleasing to the eye, and also desirable for gaining wisdom, she took some and ate it. She also gave some to her husband, who was with her, and he ate it" (v. 6).[27] We must be clear. The temptation of the serpent was not the cause of Eve's choice, simply the occasion for it.

B. The Nature of Sin

Even with great freedom and dominion over the earth, Adam and Eve were nevertheless God's creatures. The forbidden fruit of this tree of the knowledge of good and evil was a reminder that they were not God, but were responsible to him. The "knowledge" of good and evil refers to deciding or determining what is good and evil, a prerogative that rightfully belongs to God alone. To disobey God and to eat of that tree was a rejection of God's rule and authority. It was nothing less than an act of cosmic treason against the King of the universe.

The New Testament uses a variety of words to express human sin in its various facets.[28] The most common, *hamartia*, suggests that sin is the missing of a target or a failure to reach a goal. Two others, *adikia* ("unrighteousness") and *ponēria* ("wickedness, evil"), depict sin as an

---

27 Strictly speaking, the story only recounts the temptation of Eve, though Adam was with her (Gen. 3:6). However, the parallel that Paul draws between the experience of Adam and of Jesus (Rom. 5:12-21), suggests the appropriateness of ascribing the temptation to both Adam and Eve.

28 On this, see John R. W. Stott, *The Cross of Christ* (Downers Grove: InterVarsity, 1986), 89.

inner corruption of character. Two more active words, *parabasis* and *paraptōma*, speak of sin as a deliberate trespass, a stepping over a known boundary, while still another, *anomia*, is more explicitly the violation of a known law.

But the notion of sin ultimately has a God-ward focus—we sin against *God*.[29] We reject his rightful rule. Thus the essence of sin is rebellion, whether it involves murder or envy, a malicious act or a selfish intention. In the Bible, sin is simply putting oneself at the center of the universe, usurping the place of God. As John Stott puts it: "Sin is the revolt of the self against God, the dethronement of God with a view to the enthronement of oneself. Ultimately, sin is self-deification, the reckless determination to occupy the throne which belongs to God alone."[30] Sin is the attempt to create a *self*-centered universe.

III. The Continuing Effects of Sin: Our Union With Adam

Through human rebellion and disobedience, sin entered into the world, and the effects were immediate. For the first time Adam and Eve experienced shame, and they clothed themselves. In fear they hid from God. The intimate transparency of loving relationships was shattered. When confronted with their sin, they each sought to evade responsibility. But they were responsible, and the Lord cursed them, expressing his judgment upon them for their act which brought about the disruption of all the good relationships that had existed in his good creation—the relationship between God and humanity; the relationship between man and woman; and the relationship between humanity and creation. They were banished from the garden, and the flaming sword which guarded the way back to the tree of life signified their alienation from God and his holy wrath against them (cf. Gen. 3:24). Life in Eden was no more. God's good creation was perverted by sin.

More important still were the continuing effects of sin. The biblical narrative emphasizes this. In humanity's second generation, Cain murdered his brother Abel (Gen. 4), and the moral slide continued. Despite the development of civilization (Gen. 4:17-22), by the middle of Genesis 6, "The Lord saw how great man's wickedness on the earth had become, and every inclination of the thoughts of his heart was only

---

29 Cf. the words of David to the Lord, regarding his acts of adultery and murder— "Against you, you only, have I sinned and done what is evil in your sight" (Ps. 51:4).

30 *Romans: God's Good News for the World* (Downers Grove: InterVarsity, 1994), 100.

evil all the time. The Lord was grieved that he had made man on the earth, and his heart was filled with pain" (Gen. 6:5-6). The account of Adam's line (Gen. 5) is punctuated by the recurring words, "and then he died," tolling like a funeral bell. Death had entered the world, and this genealogy charts its methodical progress.

This is the legacy of the sin of Adam,[31] a legacy which theologians call the fall. The sin of Adam corrupted God's good creation and unleashed the power of sin and death in the world, and this has affected us all. Creation itself has been "subjected to frustration" and is now in "bondage to decay" (Rom. 8:20-21). Moreover, in Genesis 5:3 the writer says that Adam brought forth offspring "in his own image"—his children were like him. They acquired the last name "sinner" the minute they were born, even before they inevitably and not unwillingly display the family likeness. We all now share Adam's image (cf. 1 Cor. 15:49).

In God's design, in a mysterious way we are all linked to Adam. The Apostle Paul most clearly formulates this connection in his letter to the Romans. In chapter 5 he says, "sin entered the world through one man, and death through sin, and in this way death came to all men, because all sinned . . ." (v. 12); "by the trespass of the one man, death reigned through that one man" (v. 17); "through the disobedience of the one man the many were made sinners" (v. 19). That "one man" is Adam (cf. v. 14). Somehow that sin of Adam has affected us all. The corruption of his nature that resulted from his sin is imparted to all his posterity. Our union with Adam is the ultimate source of the universality of sin and death.[32]

---

31 We refer to the sin of *Adam* here (and to our union with *Adam*) without reference to Eve because of the way the Apostle Paul links our condition especially to Adam (cf. Rom. 5:12-21; 1 Cor. 15:21-22). Paul knows that Eve sinned first (2 Cor. 11:3; 1 Tim. 2:14), but he gives Adam a status in salvation history that is not tied to temporal priority.

32 Our union with Adam has been variously explained. Some see our relationship to him as simply biological—he is the first human being to whom all others are genetically related. Others have suggested some "realistic" connection in which Adam embodied the totality of human nature which all human beings now share, such that all humanity somehow participated in Adam's act. This relationship, sometimes called "seminal headship," is comparable to Levi's relationship with Abraham, who is said to have paid a tithe to Melchizedek through Abraham, since "Levi was still in the body of his ancestor" (Heb. 7:10). A third view, sometimes referred to as Adam's "federal headship" of humanity, sees Adam as our appointed head, our representative before God. (It is significant here that his name in Hebrew can also be used generically of the entire race.) Paul's Jewish world of thought and the parallel with Christ in Rom. 5:12-21 support the notion of corporate solidarity reflected in these last two views (cf. 1 Cor. 15:22).

A. Sinful by Nature and By Choice

This corruption of human nature is called original sin. It is original in that it is with us before we are born, and it is the soil out of which all our conscious sins arise. As David lamented, "Surely I was sinful at birth, sinful from the time my mother conceived me" (Ps. 51:5;[33] cf. Ps. 58:3). We do not enter this world with a moral blank slate.[34] Our fallen human nature is with us from before our first breath. Sin's corruption is impressed upon us inescapably, and it will inevitably reveal itself through our own willful acts of sin.[35] We are sinners by the nature we inherit and by the choices we make. Put simply, we sin because we are sinners.

Philip Hughes expresses it this way:

> Original sin, however mysterious its nature may be,
> tells us that the reality of sin is something far deeper
> than the mere outward commission of sinful deeds... It
> tells us that there is an inner root of sinfulness which
> corrupts man's true nature and from which his sinful
> deeds spring. Like a deadly poison, sin has penetrated
> into and infected the very center of man's being...[36]

1. The Breadth of Sin

The Bible affirms that the human culpability in sin is universal, with

---

33 In its context, this verse is not a statement about the act of sex or procreation. Rather, it is a statement about the inherent nature of sin and its perverse and pervasive effects.

34 This excludes any form of Pelagianism, so named after the fourth-century British monk Pelagius who argued that Adam affected us simply by setting a bad example. He contended that our wills are morally neutral and that by nature, though we are able to sin, we also have the power to do all that God requires of us. This Pelagian heresy was condemned at the Council of Carthage in 418 and again at the Council in Ephesus in 431. Both councils affirmed that Adam's corrupt nature was passed on to his descendents such that by nature all human beings are now not able not to sin.

35 Most Evangelicals hold that we not only receive a sinful nature but are, in fact, guilty due to our union with Adam. On the basis of Rom. 5:12-21, Adam's guilt can be said to be *imputed* to us, credited to our account. We sinned in and with him. Some, however, believe that we only become guilty when we inevitably confirm that nature by our own choice. They point to the fact that Scripture relates our ultimate judgment to our own moral acts and not on our union with Adam (cf. Matt. 7:21-27; 13:41; 15:31-46; Luke 3:9; Rom. 2:5-10; Rev. 20:11-14). Both views fall within the parameters of this Statement.

36 "Another Dogma Falls," *Christianity Today* 13/17 (May 23, 1969), 13; cited in Anthony Hoekema, *Created in God's Image*, 154.

the one exception of Jesus Christ. The passages which speak of this all-inclusive reality are many: "If you, O LORD, kept a record of sins, O Lord, who could stand?" (Ps. 130:3); "Do not bring your servant into judgment, for no one living is righteous before you" (Ps. 143:2); "Who can say, 'I have kept my heart pure; I am clean and without sin'?" (Prov. 20:9); "for all have sinned and fall short of the glory of God" (Rom 3:23); "If we claim to be without sin, we deceive ourselves and the truth is not in us" (1 John 1:8). "There is no one righteous, not even one; there is no one who understands, no one who seeks God. All have turned away, . . . there is no one who does good, not even one" (Rom. 3:10-12).

These statements must be allowed to qualify all the references in the Bible to righteous or blameless persons, such as Abraham, Moses, David or Noah.[37] Their righteousness is only relative, in comparison to other people, or limited in reference to certain aspects of the law, for all have sinned before God. Furthermore, throughout the New Testament it is assumed that everyone needs to repent.

But the universality of sin is not just found as a doctrine in the Bible (though that would be enough). The religious experience of mankind attests to it. Religion in all ages and all cultures has wrestled with the question of Job: How shall a man be just before God? Religion reveals the universal consciousness of sin and the need for reconciliation with a Supreme Being. The gods are offended and must be propitiated in some way. Altars reek with the blood of sacrifices, including the sacrifices of children, as mankind seeks to atone for sin or curry divine favor.

There is also the universal voice of conscience speaking to our own hearts. Something inside us testifies against us, and we feel we must do something to make things right. We are all guilty. Sin is universal.

2. The Depth of Sin

The effect of sin upon us is not only broad, it is also deep. It affects our whole person; nothing escapes sin's defilement.

Though the Old Testament generally addresses sins as specific acts rather than as a disposition, Ezekiel and Jeremiah in particular depict sin as a spiritual sickness which afflicts the heart at the deepest level. Our heart is diseased and must be cured. Jeremiah speaks of it this way:

---

37 E.g., Ps. 37:37; Prov. 11:5. These refer to a relationship with God, i.e., covenantal righteousness, civil righteousness, ceremonial righteousness, or the righteousness which is in Christ. Cf. 1:8—but see 14:16-17, where refers to his transgressions.

"The heart is deceitful above all things, and desperately corrupt; who can understand it?" (Jer. 17:9). In fact, Ezekiel says, our hearts of stone must be replaced with a heart of flesh (Ezek. 11:19; cf. Jer. 31:33).

In the New Testament Jesus says our evil deeds flow from an evil heart as surely as rotten fruit grows on a diseased tree (Matt. 12:33-35). Consider Paul's description of the sinfulness of Jews and Gentiles alike with a chain of Old Testament texts using various parts of the body to emphasize the all-pervasive nature of sin's corruption: "Their throats are open graves; their tongues practice deceit. The poison of vipers is on their lips. Their mouths are full of cursing and bitterness. Their feet are swift to shed blood; . . . . There is no fear of God before their eyes" (Rom. 3:13-15,18; illustrating the truth of 3:10-12).

Every part of us, every human faculty, is infected with and affected by this dreadful malady—our mind, our will, our emotions and our conscience. None of them can be trusted as objective guides of truth, because all of them are in collusion against God, caught up in this tangled web of sin. Everything about us that was created to love God and to worship him and bring him glory has now turned against him in sinful rebellion. Sin has affected even our social and political structures, creating injustices and oppression.[38]

This deep pervasiveness of sin that results from the corruption of human nature is what theologians call "total depravity." This doctrine does not mean that every person is as wicked as he or she can possibly be and engages in every possible form of sin. Nor does it mean that the unbeliever is totally insensitive in matters of conscience or never does anything that is good and right before other people, or that sinful human beings cannot be fine citizens with high moral standards. God's common grace is still at work, restraining human sin. Total depravity simply means that everything we are and everything we do is somehow affected by our sin. As J. I. Packer writes: "No one is as bad as he or she might be," though, on the other hand, "no action of ours is as good as it should be."[39] None of our motives is entirely pure, and none of our intentions is entirely praiseworthy. Sin pervades our entire personality.

Consequently, total depravity implies the total inability on the part of the sinner to rescue himself from his sinful condition. Sin is too much

---

38 The prophet Amos, e.g., speaks of this.

39 *Concise Theology: A Guide to Historic Christian Beliefs* (Carol Stream: Tyndale House, 1993), 83-84.

a part of who we are. Paul says that in our natural state we were "dead in our transgressions and sins" (Eph. 2:1). No one can do anything that merits the moral favor of God (Rom. 3:20; cf. John 15:4-5). "For the mind that is set on the flesh is hostile to God; it does not submit to God's law, indeed it cannot; and those who are in the flesh [that is, under the enslavement of sin] cannot please God" (Rom. 8:7-8). "All our righteous acts are as filthy rags," Isaiah says (Isa. 64:6). Evangelical theology, in all its various formulations, has affirmed both our total depravity in sin and our total inability to save ourselves. Without the gracious work of the Holy Spirit enabling a sinful human being to understand and believe the gospel,[40] we are without hope.

This doctrine of original sin, this congenital condition of sinful corruption, is a great mystery, and it remains an offense to the sensibilities of many. But this singular mystery, once accepted, sheds great light on human experience. This Christian doctrine of sin has been described as the only doctrine empirically proven by 5,000 years of recorded human history. How else do we account for this mystifying thing called "human nature"? Why is it that every person ever born, except one, has exhibited this apparently innate human propensity to disobey God? Blaise Pascal put it this way: "Certainly nothing jolts us more rudely than this doctrine [of original sin], and yet, but for this mystery, the most incomprehensible of all, we remain incomprehensible to ourselves."[41]

The Jewish philosopher Martin Buber once lamented, "Is there any force in the world that can change that intractable thing, human nature? There's a tragedy at the heart of things." Yes, there is a tragedy, and we must face it squarely. As J. C. Ryle has observed, "If a man doesn't realize the dangerous nature of his soul's disease, you cannot wonder if he is content with false or imperfect remedies."[42]

---

40 This gracious work of the Holy Spirit can be understood in different ways. Reformed theologians prefer to speak of effectual grace, which they contend only comes to the elect. They believe that God's effectual grace always has the desired effect and those in whom God's Spirit works in this way will repent and believe the gospel. Arminian/Wesleyan theologians prefer to speak of prevenient grace which comes to all. They contend that prevenient grace enables all to respond to the gospel, but only some will. Both views are to be distinguished from Semi-Pelagianism which admits that human moral abilities have been weakened by the fall (in contrast to Pelagianism [see note 34 above]) but denies that human beings have lost all ability to take initial steps toward salvation by their own efforts apart from God's grace. Semi-Pelagianism was condemned at the Council of Orange (529).

41 *Penseés*, #65.

42 *Holiness: It Nature, Hindrances, Difficulties, and Roots*, 2ⁿᵈ ed. (Grand Rapids: Baker, 1979 [originally published in 1883]), 1-2. Jesus made a similar point about our need to understand

B. Alienated from God

Our Statement on humanity not only describes who we are in ourselves but also who we are in relationship with God. From the time of Adam's exclusion from the garden, human beings have existed in a state of alienation from their Creator. Cut off from the real source of life and blessedness, human beings experience a state of spiritual death (Eph. 2:1,5; 4:18). "Once you were alienated from God and were enemies in your minds because of your evil behavior," Paul writes (Col. 1:21; cf. Rom. 5:10). Our sin separates us from a holy God.

C. Under God's Wrath

God's holiness also issues in a righteous rejection of evil which the Bible calls his wrath. God's wrath flows from his Person as much as from his nature. Since God alone is worthy of worship, he is personally jealous for his own honor.[43] To refuse to acknowledge him as God and to give to another the honor rightly due him is idolatry, which is a personal affront to his majesty and glory. "The wrath of God is being revealed from heaven against all the godlessness and wickedness of men who suppress the truth by their wickedness," Paul writes as he begins his exposition of the universal sinfulness of humanity (Rom. 1:18; cf. 1:18-3:20), "For although they knew God, they neither glorified him as God nor gave thanks to him, . . . they became fools and exchanged the glory of the immortal God for images" (Rom. 1:21,23). This is the essence of human sin, and as sinners, Paul declares, we were "by nature objects of wrath" (Eph. 2:3),[44] awaiting a "day of God's wrath, when his righteous judgment will be revealed" (Rom. 2:5; cf. Rev. 6:17). Apart from Christ we stand under God's wrath (Rom. 5:9; 1 Thess. 5:9) facing the prospect of eternal condemnation.[45]

To combat this deadly disease of human depravity and the judgment of God which it rightly deserves we need more than positive thinking. New rules or religious rituals will not suffice; moral maxims are worthless; nor will a self-help manual do us any good. In this tragic condition we need a divine Savior—someone who can save us from God's wrath and renew us in God's image. Nothing less will do.

---

the depth of our sin when he said, "he who has been forgiven little loves little" (Luke 7:47).

43 Cf. Exod. 20:5; 34:14; Deut. 4:24; 5:9; 32:21; Josh. 24:19; Ezek. 16:42; 36:6; Zech. 8:2.

44 God's wrath is poured out on sinful people and not just on sin. Cf. Ps. 5:5—"The arrogant cannot stand in your presence; you hate all who do wrong" (cf. also Ps. 11:5).

45 On this, see further in Article 10.

IV. Our Only Hope: God's Saving Work in Jesus Christ— Rescued, Reconciled and Renewed

For the Christian, the human condition cannot be considered apart from Jesus Christ. Though we will look more extensively at his Person and work in the next two chapters, we must focus our attention here on Jesus as the perfect embodiment of the image of God in humanity.

"He is the image of the invisible God," Paul boldly declares of Jesus (Col. 1:15; cf. also 2 Cor. 4:4). Jesus, in his human nature, is what Adam and Eve were created to be. He revealed God in his incarnation; he lived in relationships of love with his heavenly Father and with his earthly neighbor; and he exercised his rule over the natural world so that even the wind and the seas obeyed him. John tells us, "No one has ever seen God, but God the One and Only, who is at the Father's side, has made him known" (John 1:18). In Hebrews we read, "The Son is the radiance of God's glory and the exact representation of his being" (Heb. 1:3). "Anyone who has seen me has seen the Father," Jesus said (John 14:9).

As the image of God, Jesus reveals God to us; and as the image of God, he shows us what all human beings were meant to be. Jesus is the full expression of the perfection God intended when he created man in his image. In answer to the question, "What is man?," the Bible directs us to Jesus.

Further, as the image of God, Jesus came to undo the sin of Adam. Paul points us to this glorious truth: "For just as through the disobedience of the one man the many were made sinners, so also through the obedience of the one man the many will be made righteous" (Rom. 5:19).

Adam, being made in God's image, longed for equality with God and saw it as something to be snatched. Jesus Christ was equal with God, but he did not see it as something to use for his own advantage (see Phil. 2:5-11). While Adam desired to be great and refused to be God's servant, grasping instead for the likeness of God, Jesus Christ made himself nothing and took on the form of a servant and was made in the likeness of men. Whereas Adam exalted himself and became disobedient unto death, Jesus Christ humbled himself and became obedient unto death. And whereas Adam was condemned and disgraced to the dishonor of God the Father, Jesus Christ was highly exalted and was given the name of Lord, to the glory of God the Father. "Consequently, just as the result of one trespass was condemnation for all men, so also the result of one act of righteousness was justification that brings life for all men"

(Rom. 5:18).

Jesus Christ, "the last Adam" (1 Cor. 15:45), came as God to be what man was meant to be. He came to undo the sin of Adam by his own obedience and to create a new humanity, a people redeemed by his death, who would follow him in their lives. "And just as we have borne the likeness of the earthly man, so shall we bear the likeness of the man from heaven" (1 Cor. 15:49). This is our hope!

And this is our *only* hope. We are either enslaved in the sinfulness of Adam by our natural birth, or we are liberated in the righteousness of Christ by our new birth. Jesus Christ alone can rescue us from the wrath of God that rightly stands over all who are in union with Adam. Jesus Christ alone can reconcile us from the alienation which came when God justly cast Adam from the garden. And Jesus Christ alone can renew that divine image which has been corrupted by Adam's sin.

The good news of the gospel is that this is precisely what he has done! Jesus "rescues us from the coming wrath" (1 Thess. 1:10; 5:9). "There is now no condemnation for those who are in Christ Jesus" (Rom. 8:1). We have been delivered from the condemnation our sins deserve and the moral captivity our sin creates (cf. e.g., Rom. 6:18). Through our Lord Jesus Christ, "we have now received reconciliation" (Rom. 5:11), for "God was reconciling the world to himself in Christ, not counting men's sins against them" (2 Cor. 5:19). We now enjoy peace with God as our Father (Rom. 5:1; 8:16). And in Christ that corrupted image is being renewed into a new humanity, "created to be like God in true righteousness and holiness" (Eph. 4:24; Col. 3:10; 2 Cor. 4:16; cf. Rom. 8:29). Our great hope is that when he appears we shall be like him (1 John 3:2).

The seriousness of our sinful condition demanded nothing less than God's saving work in Jesus Christ. "Salvation is found in no one else, for there is no other name under heaven given to men by which we must be saved" (Acts 4:12). "For there is one God and one mediator between God and men, the man Christ Jesus, who gave himself as a ransom for all men" (1 Tim. 2:5-6). He and his saving work will be the subject of our next two chapters.

Conclusion

Carl Sagan, the Cornell astronomer, once captured the modern problem of understanding what it means to be human: "We humans are like a newborn baby left on a doorstep," he said, "with no note explaining who it is, ..."[46] Thankfully, the Bible gives us that note.

More than that, in Jesus Christ, our God has come personally into this world to adopt us as his own. Our being created by God in his image and then our fall into sin together provide the key to the riddle of the human condition. They explain our origin, illuminate our present tragedy, and point us to our glorious destiny when we as Christians, rescued from God's wrath and reconciled from our alienation with him, shall be fully renewed in the image of Jesus Christ.

---

46 Carl Sagan and Ann Druyan, *Shadows of Forgotten Ancestors* (New York: Random House, 1992), 5.

Evangelical Convictions

A THEOLOGICAL EXPOSITION OF THE STATEMENT OF FAITH
OF THE EVANGELICAL FREE CHURCH OF AMERICA

Article 4

JESUS CHRIST

4. We believe that Jesus Christ is God incarnate, fully God and fully man, one Person in two natures. Jesus—Israel's promised Messiah—was conceived through the Holy Spirit and born of the virgin Mary. He lived a sinless life, was crucified under Pontius Pilate, arose bodily from the dead, ascended into heaven and sits at the right hand of God the Father as our High Priest and Advocate.

God's gospel is made known supremely in the Person of Jesus Christ.

"Who is this man?" No question is more central to the Gospels. After Jesus had declared a paralytic man forgiven, Luke tells us that the Pharisees and the teachers of the law began thinking to themselves, "Who is this fellow who speaks blasphemy?" (Luke 5:21). After Jesus stilled a storm and calmed the waves, Mark recounts that his disciples were terrified and asked each other, "Who is this? Even the wind and the waves obey him!" (Mark 4:41). And Matthew records that in the last week of Jesus' life, when he entered Jerusalem on a donkey, the whole city was stirred and asked, "Who is this?" (Matt. 21:10).

The critical turning point in the Gospel plot hinges on this question. Near Caesarea Philippi, Jesus asked his disciples, "Who do people say I am?" Then he turned and asked, "But what about you? Who do you say I am?" (Matt. 16:15; cf. Mark 8:29; Luke 9:20). From that point on, Jesus began to head toward Jerusalem and his death. John makes answering this question of Jesus' identity his primary concern in writing his Gospel: "[T]hese things were written that you may believe that Jesus is the Christ, the Son of God, and that by believing you may have life in his name" (John 20:31).

Jesus Christ has always been a controversial figure. However, unlike other figures in history, the controversy surrounding Jesus of Nazareth has not focused primarily on his teaching, or even on his actions, but on how these point to his identity. His moral instruction has been widely acclaimed and his religious devotion almost universally admired. But the early Christians were not content with describing Jesus simply as a great moral teacher or even as a prophet of God. His words and actions compelled them to turn to the category of divinity in order to explain him. Nothing less would do. Jesus was God incarnate. In Jesus, divinity took on humanity; he was truly God and truly man. This is more than a theological proposition; it is at the heart of the gospel, for we believe that God's gospel—the good news of God's saving work—is supremely revealed in the Person of Jesus Christ.

I. Jesus' Identity: He Is God Incarnate

Jesus of Nazareth was a man like no other. He preached the Fatherhood of God, but he insisted that he was the Son who stood in a unique relationship with the Father: "All things have been committed to me by my Father. No one knows the Son except the Father, and no one knows the Father except the Son and those to whom the Son chooses to reveal him" (Matt. 11:27). He said to Mary of Magdalene after his resurrection, "I am returning to my Father and your Father, to my God and your God" (John 20:17). Nowhere does Jesus speak of "our Father," including his followers with him. The prayer which begins with those words was for *them* to pray.

Jesus also spoke about the kingdom of God, but he stood in an unparalleled position within that kingdom. It was present through him (Matt. 12:28), and one's entry into it depended on one's response to him (Matt. 25:34-40). "To inherit eternal life" (Mark 10:17-21), to "be saved" (Mark 13:13; John 10:9) and "to enter the kingdom of heaven" were blessings granted only to *his* disciples (Matt. 19:29; 7:21-23).

To the spiritually hungry, Jesus says, "I am the bread of life . . . if anyone eats of this bread, he will live forever" (John 6:35,51). And, "If anyone is thirsty, let him come to me and drink" (John 7:37; cf. John 4:10).

To those groping for illumination in life, Jesus says, "I am the light of the world; he who follows me will not walk in darkness, but will have the light of life" (John 8:12).

To those living under stress and anxiety, he says, "Come to me, all you who are weary and burdened, and I will give you rest" (Matt. 11:28).

To those who feel that they can do nothing of ultimate value, Jesus says, "I am the vine; you are the branches. If a man remains in me and I in him, he will bear much fruit" (John 15:5).

To those who fear death, he says, "I am the resurrection and the life. He who believes in me . . . will never die" (John 11:25-26).

To those looking for spiritual direction and spiritual reality, Jesus says, "I am the way and the truth and the life. No one comes to the Father except through me" (John 14:6).

"I am the good shepherd . . . I am the gate . . . Before Abraham was born, I am . . ." (John 10:11; 10:7; 8:58). As one scholar put it, "His most startling revelation was Himself."[1]

---

1 H.P. Liddon, *The Divinity of Our Lord and Saviour Jesus Christ,* 15th ed. (London: Longmans, Green, and Co., 1891), 5.

Jesus is like no other religious teacher in the world. John Stott presents the contrast: "They are self-effacing; He is self-advancing. They point away from themselves and say, 'That is the truth, so far as I perceive it; follow that.' Jesus says, 'I am the truth; follow Me.' The founder of none of the ethnic religions has dared to say such a thing."[2]

A person's eternal destiny is determined by one's relationship with him— "Whoever acknowledges me before men, I will also acknowledge him before my Father in heaven. But whoever disowns me before men, I will disown him before my Father in heaven" (Matt. 10:32-33).

His demands were unlimited. "Anyone who loves his father or mother more than me is not worthy of me; anyone who loves his son or daughter more than me is not worthy of me;" (Matt. 10:37). Jesus declared that we must be willing even to hate our own life for his sake (Luke 14:26). What kind of man would so audaciously insist upon such absolute allegiance? Whereas the first Christians forbade the worship of men or of angels (Acts 14:13-15; Col. 2:18; Rev. 22:8-9), Jesus commended the worship of himself (John 20:28-29).

Who is this man?

A. Jesus Christ Is Fully God

Jesus put himself in the very place of God, and from the earliest records of the church we find a picture of Jesus as divine. The Apostle Paul spoke of Jesus as the one who was "in very nature God" (Phil. 2:6) and in whom "all the fullness of the Deity lives in bodily form" (Col. 2:9; cf. also 1 Cor. 8:4-6). John's Gospel offers a similar view: "In the beginning was the Word, and the Word was with God, and the Word was God. . . . The Word became flesh and made his dwelling among us. We have seen his glory, the glory of the One and Only, who came from the Father, full of grace and truth" (John 1:1,14; cf. 10:30; 17:5).

The first description of Christian worship from outside the church, written in about A.D. 110 by the Roman governor of Bithynia, Pliny the Younger, to the Emperor Trajan, reinforces this early understanding of Jesus as divine. Speaking of the Christians, he wrote, "They were accustomed to meet on a fixed day before dawn and sing responsively a hymn to Christ as to a god."[3] He also reported that the Christians refused to worship any other god.

2 *Basic Christianity*, 2nd ed. (Grand Rapids: Eerdmans, 1971), 23.

3 *Epistulae* X. 96.

This claim that Jesus was worthy of worship is all the more astounding because it arose within a Jewish context. No group had a more fiercely monotheistic framework, and none would so violently oppose such a practice. Their opposition is seen in the Gospels themselves. When Jesus spoke in exclusive terms about God being his Father, the crowds took up stones to kill him. His words were blasphemous to their ears, for he was "making himself equal with God" (John 5:18; 10:33). This offense was only intensified when the Christians claimed that this one who was divine died the degrading death of a crucified criminal. No wonder the Christian message was "a stumbling block to Jews" (1 Cor. 1:23).

But this message was also foolishness to the Gentiles. Not only was it ludicrous that a Savior could have been crucified, it was inconceivable that God could become incarnate. To the Greek philosophers, God was transcendent and abstract, existing high above the messiness of this material world. To think of God entering into this world of flesh was abhorrent to the Greeks.

In fact, it was from this philosophical perspective that one of the most significant early attacks on Christian teaching arose. Arius, a popular fourth-century pastor in Alexandria, Egypt, gave Jesus as the Son of God an exalted status, even ascribing to him a form of divinity; but he was convinced that Jesus was not truly equal with God. Arius believed that the Son of God had a beginning in time, even if it was at the beginning of time, while God the Father was eternal.[4]

Arius was an engaging speaker who used certain passages of the Bible to support his view,[5] and a fierce conflict ensued. As it developed, the dispute centered on just one letter, an *iota*, the smallest letter in the Greek alphabet. One side argued that the relationship of the Son of God with the Father could be described by the Greek word *homoiousios*, which meant he was of "*like* substance or being" with the Father; that is, he was semi-divine. The opposition, however, insisted that only the word *homoousios* would do, a term which meant that Jesus was of the "*same* substance" with the Father, the very same divine being; that is, he was fully God.

The battle raged in the church for decades.[6] The leading defender

---

4 The well-known Arian slogan referring to the Son of God was, "There was a time when he was not."

5 Most notably, Col. 1:15— "Christ is the firstborn over all creation."

6 The controversy appeared to be settled in A.D. 325 at a council of bishops called by the Roman Emperor Constantine which met in the town of Nicea. There the bishops affirmed that Jesus the Son was truly God—he was of the same divine being as the Father. But that did not

of Jesus' full divinity, Athanasius, was exiled no fewer than five times for holding to his position. But in the end, the truth of his view was recognized, and what we today call the Nicene Creed[7] embodies the conviction that Jesus the Son of God was "very God of very God, begotten not made, of one substance with the Father."[8] This description best captures what is expressed in the words of both Jesus and the New Testament writers.[9]

Why Does It Matter?

But why was the argument over the *iota* so important? Why does it matter if Jesus is truly divine or not? Isn't it enough to speak of Jesus simply as a divinely inspired man, a prophetic figure, almost God-like in his character and teaching?

The church, based on the authority of the Bible, has said, No, it is not enough. First, only if Jesus is divine can he be a full and complete revelation of God. If Jesus is not God, then how can he be God's final word, supremely revealing God to us (Heb. 1:1-2)? As Jesus himself said, "Anyone who has seen me has seen the Father" (John 14:9; cf. 1:18). If Jesus is not God, how can he declare that only those who hear and obey his words will enter the kingdom of God (cf. Matt. 7:21-27)? And if Jesus is not God, then can we truly say, as Paul does, that *God's* love is demonstrated to us when Jesus died on the cross (Rom. 5:8)? Jesus reveals God personally only if he is fully divine.

Second, if Jesus is not God himself come to us, the redemption he brings is powerless to forgive and to save. It is God we have offended; only he can take away our sin. Unless Jesus is divine, his death is irrelevant to our moral status before God. We would be left to ourselves, to justify ourselves. Only God can save us, for the Lord says, "I, even I, am the Lord, and apart from me there is no savior" (Isa. 43:11). Jesus must be a *divine* Savior, or he could not save at all.[10]

Because Jesus Christ is fully God, he deserves our devotion, and he

---

end the matter, and the controversy carried on for another 50 years until in A.D. 381 a second statement was affirmed at the Council of Constantinople.

7 More properly it is the Niceno-Constantinopolitan Creed because the creed of Nicea was revised by the Council of Constantinople.

8 The Arian position can still be found in groups like the Jehovah's Witnesses.

9 Cf. John 1:1; 1:18; 20:28; Acts 20:28; Rom. 9:5; Titus 2:13; Heb. 1:8; 2 Pet. 1:1; 1 John 5:20.

10 The saving work of Christ is discussed more fully in Article 5.

is worthy of our worship. But if he were not divine, then such worship would be nothing less than blasphemous.

B. Jesus Christ Is Fully Man

Jesus Christ is fully God, but we affirm equally that Jesus Christ is also fully man. Though that seems obvious to most, in fact, the first Christological heresy in the early church concerned this very issue. Among a group called the Gnostics[11] some held to a view known as *docetism*—a term derived from the Greek word which means "to seem or appear." In their teaching, Jesus only "seemed" or "appeared" to be human. In one common form of this belief, "the Christ" was a divine person who came upon the man Jesus at his baptism and then left him immediately before the crucifixion.[12] This view was condemned in the New Testament itself, as John writes, "Every spirit that acknowledges that Jesus Christ has come in the flesh is from God, but every spirit that does not acknowledge Jesus is not from God" (1 John 4:2-3).[13]

During the next two centuries the church wrestled with its understanding of how the biblical teaching about Jesus could be rightly understood and articulated. Various views were tested and then rejected. One position proposed by Apollinaris (c. 310-392), the bishop of Laodicea, was that in Jesus Christ, God lived in a human body but without a human nature. In support of this viewpoint, Apollinaris and his followers cited John 1:14: "the Word became flesh." Their narrow interpretation of this text led to the belief that at the incarnation, the divine Word (the Logos) displaced the animating and rational soul of the human Jesus. Only his physical body was human. After substantial debate, the Council of Constantinople in A.D. 381 condemned the Apollinarians. The bishops affirmed, in harmony with the Bible,[14] that Jesus was a human being in a real and complete sense, with all the qualities that constitute true humanity.

---

11 On Gnosticism, see Article 1, n. 20. In the early period, the Christians may have encountered what is referred to as proto-Gnosticism.

12 This view was held by the Gnostic Cerinthus, and something similar is often referred to as "adoptionism" and was championed in the third century by Paul of Samosata

13 John is also at pains to emphasize that the Son of God, the Eternal Word of Life, could be seen, touched and heard (1 John 1:1-3), that is, he was fully human.

14 Cf., e.g., Paul's reference to "the man, Christ Jesus" in 1 Tim. 2:5. The Gospels depict Jesus as one who endured the full range of human experiences—e.g., growth (Luke 2:52), hunger (Matt. 4:2), thirst (John 19:28), fatigue (John 4:6) and grief (John 11:35).

One Person in Two Natures

But how could Jesus Christ be both fully human and fully divine? This is certainly a great mystery. After the rejection of the teaching of Apollinaris, a popular preacher in Antioch and later Archbishop of Constantinople, Nestorius (died c. 451),[15] suggested a model in which Christ the divine Logos was joined to the man Jesus. However, this view seemed to assert that Christ consisted of two persons, instead of just one. Another model, which came to be known as monophysitism,[16] came through Eutyches (d. 454), the spiritual leader of a monastery near Constantinople. Eutyches taught that Christ had only one nature, in which the human appeared completely absorbed by the divine, just "as a drop of honey, which falls into the sea, dissolves in it."[17] This view blurred Jesus' humanity, creating a confused amalgamation of the two.

Through these debates the early church sought to do justice to the picture of Jesus found in the Gospels. Finally, an acceptable formulation emerged from the work of the Council of Chalcedon in 451. The Chalcedonian Creed declared that at the incarnation the eternal Son of God—that divine Person—joined his divine nature with human nature to become the God-man Jesus Christ. Only in the incarnation did the collection of qualities that constitute human nature become realized[18] in this divine Person as Jesus of Nazareth. In the language of the Chalcedonian Creed, "[W]e all with one accord teach men to acknowledge one and the same Son, our Lord Jesus Christ, at once complete in Godhead and complete in manhood, truly God and truly man . . . the distinction of natures being in no way abolished because of the union, but rather the characteristic property of each nature being preserved, and coming together to form one person." Jesus Christ is thus one Person in whom two distinct natures are united.[19]

Jesus Christ is truly God and truly man. He is fully and completely both at the same time, showing us the true nature of each. He is not some

---

15 Followers of Nestorian teaching can be found largely in the Middle East under the name of "Assyrian Christians."

16 A term that means "one nature."

17 This illustration had been used earlier by Gregory of Nyssa in *Against Eunomius*, v, 5.

18 The theological expression used is that human nature found its *subsistence* in the Person of Christ.

19 This is referred to as the Hypostatic Union (the Greek term *hypostasis* means "person").

mixture of humanity and divinity, creating a third kind of being, like a horse and donkey becoming a mule. The Son of God remained God—he never gave up being God,[20] but he added to his divinity real humanity. As God incarnate, the divine subject made real human experience his own, and since the incarnation, the Son of God will forever be human.

Against Arius, the Chalcedonian Creed asserts that Jesus was truly God. Against Apollinaris, it asserts that he was truly man. Against Eutyches, it asserts that Jesus' deity and humanity were not changed into something else. And against Nestorius, the Creed asserts that Jesus was not divided but was one Person and in this one Person are two distinct natures, which are divine and human in all their fullness.[21]

Why Does It Matter?

Why is the true humanity of Jesus so important? Most of all, because our salvation depends upon it—the humanity of Jesus is an essential element of the gospel message. The Epistle to the Hebrews speaks to this issue: "Since the children have flesh and blood, he too shared in their humanity. . . . For this reason he had to be made like his brothers in every way, in order that he might become a merciful and faithful high priest in service to God, and that he might make atonement for the sins of the people" (Heb. 2:14,17). The humanity of Christ is also central to Paul's argument that Jesus has overturned the work of Adam: "For just as through the disobedience of the one man the many were made sinners, so also through the obedience of the one man the many will be made righteous" (Rom. 5:19).

Only as God did Christ have the power to bear our sins and conquer them, but only as man was he qualified to do so. This understanding was the driving theological force which led the early church to press so hard against those like the Docetists and the Apollinarians who denied Christ's full humanity. As the early church father Irenaeus put it, "He became like us so that we might become like him."[22] In Christ, *God* was

---

20 Jesus' self-emptying (or *kenōsis*, from the Greek word for "emptying") referred to in Philippians 2:7 refers to the honor and glory of his status (cf. John 17:5; 2 Cor. 8:9), not to the essential divinity of his being. However one understands the mystery of the human limitations of the Son of God in the Gospels in which he does not display the full measure of his divine nature (cf. e.g., Matt. 24:35), one must affirm that he remains fully God.

21 Cf. Bruce L. Shelley, *Church History in Plain Language*, 2nd ed. (Nashville: Thomas Nelson, 1995), 115.

22 *Against Heresies,* III.10.

acting to reconcile the world to himself (2 Cor. 5:19), and at the same time, as a real human being just like us, Jesus Christ could truly serve as our representative before God. "There is one God and one mediator between God and men—the man Christ Jesus" (1 Tim. 2:5).

C. Conceived Through the Holy Spirit, Born of a Virgin

The divine-human character of Jesus Christ is exhibited from the beginning of his earthly life through his miraculous conception. After the angel Gabriel appeared to Mary to announce that she would bear a son, she asked, "How will this be, since I am a virgin?" The angel replied, "The Holy Spirit will come upon you, and the power of the Most High will overshadow you. So the holy one to be born will be called the Son of God" (Luke 1:34,35; cf. also Matt. 1:18-25). Our Statement affirms this fact of Jesus' birth to a virgin,[23] an affirmation that was embedded in early Christian confessions.

To many in our day, such a miracle of conception is too difficult to accept, but it was scandalous even in the first century, particularly in its Jewish context. The Jews had no sympathy for the myths of the Greeks, nor for the immoral sexual activity of their gods.[24] Moreover, in a culture extremely sensitive to sexual propriety, the virgin birth of Jesus as it is portrayed in the Gospels is simply not the kind of story that the early Christians would have made up. From the earliest days stories were circulating about the illegitimacy of the birth of Jesus,[25] and the Christians would have been foolish to throw fuel on the fire by preserving a story such as this. It was undoubtedly considered true and important in understanding who Jesus was.

Certainly the virgin birth points to Jesus' *origin* as one who comes from God. He is the bread of life that comes down from heaven, the light of God descending into the darkness of this world. Throughout the Gospel accounts we find this emphasis on the divine initiative. Jesus was not the ideal man who reached up to God. He was God incarnate;

---

23 When used to modify Mary, the word "virgin" is not capitalized in our Statement, emphasizing that this is a description of Mary and not a part of a proper name. This follows the practice, for example, of the Lutheran *Book of Concord* (Tappert edition, 1959) in its translations of the Apostles' and Nicene Creeds. Inasmuch as the child born to her was truly divine, Mary can rightly be referred to as *theotokos* (bearer of God), as affirmed at both the Council of Ephesus (431) and Chalcedon (451).

24 Cf. the comments of Trypho in his dialogue with Justin Martyr (chap. LXVII).

25 Cf. John 8:41 and Jewish attacks mentioned in Origen, *Against Celsus* (1.28).

God reaching down to man. God graciously entered into human affairs to accomplish his good purposes. That is the picture the Bible offers us, a picture that the virgin birth vividly displays.

The virgin birth also points to Jesus' conception as a new act of *creation* by God. Unlike pagan stories, the Gospels avoid all sexual imagery; nor do they depict the Holy Spirit as the male partner in some celestial marriage.[26] The picture here is not one of marriage but of creation, for the Holy Spirit who would "overshadow" Mary was the same Holy Spirit who moved over the face of the deep in the Genesis account of the creation of the cosmos (Gen. 1:2). He acted as God's agent when he first made the world. Thus, the virgin birth represents a new act of God within the natural order, creating nothing less than a new Adam, one untainted by sin (1 Cor. 15:47).

Jesus was not, however, the creation from another world transplanted into ours. The virgin birth speaks of a new creation within a human womb. Jesus experienced all of human existence from conception to death, from life's beginning to its end. Jesus' origin was with God, but the virgin birth speaks of his coming as a new creation within the order of this world, as God creates afresh the image of God in man.

Finally, the virgin birth points us ultimately to Jesus' identity as the divine Son of God. Jesus did not become God's Son simply because he was born without a human father.[27] The divine Person who became Jesus of Nazareth existed in relationship with God the Father from all eternity. He was God's own Son who became Immanuel, God with us: The Creator became a creature; the Word became flesh; the Judge became the one who is judged, thus reconciling humanity to himself.

D. Jesus Is Israel's Promised Messiah

Just as a word finds its meaning only in the context of a sentence and then a paragraph, so a human life finds its meaning only within the context of the social and historical setting in which it is lived. For Jesus that setting was clearly first-century Palestinian Judaism and the biblical

---

26 In our Statement we have chosen to say that Jesus was conceived "through" rather than "of" the Holy Spirit because this helps to emphasize that the Holy Spirit does not simply play the role of the "father" in this conception. In this we have sought to reflect the language of Matt. 1:18 (which uses the preposition *ek* [reflected in the wording of the Niceno-Constantinopolitan Creed]).

27 Nor is the mere absence of a human father the means by which he can be born "sinless."

story of the nation of Israel. For the God who is incarnate in Jesus Christ is the God of Abraham, Isaac, and Jacob.

From the early second century onwards, attempts have been made to sever Jesus from his Jewish roots. The Gnostic Marcion, for example, who came to Rome in A.D. 140, embraced Jesus but rejected the Old Testament. Marcion claimed that Jesus had abolished the Law and the prophets. He recognized only Paul's epistles and an edited version of Luke's Gospel as authoritative Scripture. This foreign context in which to understand Jesus, including his distinction between the "inferior God" of the Old Testament and the "unknown God and Father of Christ," led to a gross distortion of the gospel, and the Marcionites were rejected as heretical.[28]

In the infancy narrative of Luke's Gospel, the angel described the Son who was to be born of Mary in terms of the Old Testament promises: "The Lord God will give him the throne of his father David, and he will reign over the house of Jacob forever" (Luke 1:32-33). Mary's song of praise exalted the Lord who had brought about this upcoming birth, saying, "He has helped his servant Israel, remembering to be merciful to Abraham and his descendants forever, even as he said to our fathers" (Luke 1:54-55).

Matthew connects Jesus to the story of Israel most clearly of all the Gospel writers. His opening genealogy begins with Abraham, the father of Israel, and emphasizes Israel's greatest leader, King David, and the most tragic event of Israel's history, the exile to Babylon (Matt. 1:1,6,11). This national history finds its culmination in the birth of Jesus (1:17). Mary's husband Joseph is described as a "son of David" (1:20), and the Magi declare Jesus to be "king of the Jews" (2:2). Matthew repeatedly shows how the events in Jesus' life took place "to fulfill what the Lord has said through the prophets."[29] Most notably, Matthew uses a passage from Hosea that originally referred to the nation of Israel (Hosea 11:1— "out of Egypt I called my son") to point to Jesus (Matt. 2:15). Jesus, in going to Egypt and then returning to Galilee, was recapitulating the experience of the nation. This theme is picked up again in the temptation narrative of Matthew 4. Jesus as the Son of God (cf. 3:17) is faithful when tested in the

---

28 Those who pit the God of the Old Testament against the God of the New fall into this Marcionite error today.

29 Matthew includes eleven of these "fulfillment citations"—Matt. 1:22; 2:5-6; 2:17; 2:23; 3:3; 4:14; 8:17; 12:17; 13:35; 21:4; 27:9.

wilderness, whereas Israel was not.[30] Matthew's Gospel affirms that Jesus did not come to abolish the Law and the prophets, but to fulfill them (5:17). And when Jesus dies, it is as the King of the Jews (27:29,37,42).

Paul also understood Jesus as heir to the promises of the Old Testament. In introducing Jesus in his opening words in his letter to the Romans, Paul speaks of him as one "who as to his human nature was a descendant of David" (1:3). The Apostle's central gospel message of Jesus' death and resurrection was "according to the Scriptures" (1 Cor. 15:3-4). He taught that the promise to Abraham to bring blessing through his descendants to all nations was now fulfilled in Christ. "If you belong to Christ," Paul wrote to the Galatians, "then you are Abraham's seed, and heirs according to the promise" (Gal. 3:29). "For no matter how many promises God has made, they are 'Yes' in Christ," he declared (2 Cor. 1:20). Jesus' life and ministry cannot be understood rightly apart from the Old Testament story, and particularly the promises of God to his people Israel. "Salvation is from the Jews," Jesus said (John 4:22), and from the one faithful Jew, Jesus the Messiah of Israel, that salvation goes out to the whole world (Rom. 1:5-6; 1 Tim. 2:3-5; 1 John 2:2; Matt. 28:19).

The first followers of Jesus understood him in the light of the Old Testament story, but it is equally true that they could not understand that Old Testament story rightly apart from him. Certainly difficult issues remained regarding the continuity and discontinuity of God's purposes for Israel moving into the church age, but the first Christians understood the life and ministry of Jesus Christ to be the hermeneutical key, the lens of understanding, through which to view the whole Bible.

The Epistle to the Hebrews is an extended exposition of this theme. After the coming of the Messiah, the message of the Old Testament was seen in terms of its fulfillment in Christ. Through Jesus the various institutions of Israel—the priesthood, the temple, the sacrifices—take on new meaning, pointing forward to Christ. All are seen as only a shadow of the good things to come, not the realities themselves (Heb. 8:5; 10:1), a conviction expressed also by Paul (Col. 2:17). Even the law itself had a prophetic function, pointing to the filial relationship of faithful love now embodied in Jesus (cf. Matt. 11:13; 5:17). He is the one "in whom is hidden all the treasures of wisdom and knowledge" (Col. 2:3).

What was the source of this hermeneutical revolution in the early

---

30 Jesus' citation of passages from Deut. 6:13,16; 8:3 (cf. Matt. 4:10,7,4), all of which concerned Israel's experience in the wilderness, reinforces this connection.

disciples' understanding of the Scriptures? Who was the creative genius behind this fresh approach? The Gospels point to none other than Jesus himself. During his ministry he declared that Moses wrote about him (John 5:46) and that Abraham longed to see his day (John 8:56). Jesus spoke of himself as the temple, the manna from heaven, the living water, and the true vine—Old Testament images given new meaning in him and by him.[31] And after his resurrection, with the two men on the road to Emmaus, "beginning with Moses and all the Prophets, he explained to them what was said in all the Scriptures concerning himself" (Luke 24:27). To his disciples Jesus said, "Everything must be fulfilled that is written about me in the Law of Moses, the Prophets and the Psalms" (Luke 24:44). Although Christians recognize two Testaments, they embrace one Bible, with Jesus, as Israel's promised Messiah, being the key that holds them together.

II. Jesus' Life

From considering Jesus' identity, we move to a few aspects of his life that are central to the gospel message. The gospel is not a code of ethics or a philosophy of life, much less a myth or legend. The Christian message is essentially a declaration of the saving acts of God in history, as he has come into our world personally in Jesus Christ. Here we highlight four aspects of that historical revelation in Christ, with a fuller exposition of their meaning reserved for Article 5.

A. Jesus Lived Without Sin

In the second half of his prophecy Isaiah speaks in glorious terms of "the servant of the Lord."[32] The first time the expression occurs, the identification with Israel is explicit—"But you, O Israel, my servant, Jacob, whom I have chosen, you descendants of Abraham my friend, I took you from the ends of the earth, from its farthest corners I called you. I said, 'You are my servant'" (Isa. 41:8-9).[33] We learn that the mission of this servant is to bring God's justice to the nations (Isa. 42:1). He is to be a light for the Gentiles, to open blind eyes and to rescue those captive to their oppressors (Isa. 42:6-7). He brings light, liberty and life.

---

31 Cf. John 2:19-22; 8:41; 8:37; 15:1.

32 Isaiah uses the term "servant" 25 times in his book, 19 times in chaps. 40-55.

33 This same connection with Israel occurs in 43:10; 44:1, 21; 45:4; 48:20; 49:3.

But as the prophet unfolds his vision of the Lord's servant, something disturbing emerges. "Who is blind but my servant, and deaf like the messenger I send?" the Lord asks (Isa. 42:19). The servant who was to set forth a vision of God and his glory is himself blind to who God is. The messenger who was to proclaim the word of God is himself deaf to that word. This handicap is not accidental, but intentional, for the servant is not innocent, but culpable. He has seen much, but has closed his eyes to it; he has been told great things, but has stopped his ears to them. The servant himself is blind and deaf to the things of God—he has failed in his mission. And instead of liberating those in bondage, the Israelites were themselves captives:

> But this is a people plundered and looted,
> all of them trapped in pits or hidden away in prisons.
> They have become plunder, with no one to rescue them;
> they have been made loot,
> with no one to say, "Send them back."
>
> (Isa. 42:22)

Israel was called by God to be a blessing to the Gentiles. She was given the law of God and was to display his holiness and righteousness. But in her own sinfulness Israel had become just like all the other nations. She was just as blind and deaf as they were.

This is the paradox, the mystery, of Isaiah's figure of the servant. Though clearly identified with Israel in some places, Israel in its present state was clearly unfit to fulfill the servant's mission. Israel's problem, and the problem of all humanity, was her sin. The prophet's vision of the servant, however, points forward to one who would suffer, not for his own sins but for the sins of his people (Isa. 52:13-53:12).

The New Testament presents Jesus as one perfectly qualified to fulfill this exalted role of the suffering Servant. Jesus is that light of the world who always lived in faithful obedience to his Father. "He committed no sin," Peter affirms of Jesus,[34] enabling him to "die for our sins, once for all, the righteous for the unrighteous" (1 Pet. 3:18). John makes the same connection: "you know that he appeared so that he might take away our sins. And in him is no sin" (1 John 3:5). As does Paul: "God made him

---

34 This may have been a common Christian understanding of Isa. 53:9, coming through the Septuagint (LXX), the Greek translation.

who had no sin to be sin for us, so that in him we might become the righteousness of God" (2 Cor. 5:21). In contrast to the transgression of the first Adam, it was Jesus' act of obedience that enabled many to be made righteous (Rom. 5:19).

The Epistle to the Hebrews speaks of Jesus' sinlessness as his supreme qualification to serve as our great High Priest. "For we do not have a high priest who is unable to sympathize with our weaknesses, but we have one who has been tempted in every way, just as we are—yet was without sin" (Heb. 4:15). His offering of himself to God was "unblemished" (Heb. 9:14), for "unlike the other high priests, [Jesus] does not need to offer sacrifices day after day, first for his own sins, and then for the sins of the people" (Heb. 7:27), for he is "holy, blameless, pure, set apart from sinners" (v. 26). "Here I am," he said. "I have come to do your will" (Heb. 10:9).

Jesus lived a sinless life.[35] As he himself said, "I always do what pleases [the Father]" (John 8:29). As a result, he was perfectly qualified to save us.[36]

B. Jesus Was Crucified Under Pontius Pilate

We will expound the meaning of the crucifixion in the next chapter, but here we emphasize its reality. Contrary to the common understanding of the Quran,[37] Jesus, the Son of God, was crucified and died.[38] This was a real historical event, located in space and time by the reference to Pontius Pilate, who served as the governor of the Roman province of Judea during the reign of Tiberias Caesar (Luke 3:1).[39]

---

35 Could Jesus have sinned? We must affirm what Scripture explicitly affirms—that Jesus was truly tempted, that Jesus never actually sinned, that Jesus was fully God, and that God cannot sin. We conclude that as one who was (and still is) fully God, Jesus could not sin, yet as one who was fully man, he could be tempted to sin.

36 Jesus' life of obedience to the Father is often described as his "active obedience" as opposed to his "passive obedience" in bearing our sin on the cross. Both are necessary to his saving work for us. See further discussion in Article 5.

37 Most Muslims interpret Surah 4:155–159 of the Quran as explicitly ruling out Jesus' death on the cross.

38 From earliest times, the reality of Jesus' death was emphasized through the mention of his burial (cf. 1 Cor. 15:4 and the Apostles' Creed). We do not refer to Jesus' burial, for we did not believe such an emphasis was necessary in our Statement. Not only does crucifixion assume death, but we also refer to Jesus rising "from the dead" in the next phrase; and in Article 5 we speak of Jesus' "atoning death."

39 Tiberias reigned as emperor from A.D. 14-37; Pilate governed in Judea from A.D. 26-36/37. Pilate is mentioned in the historical accounts of the Jewish writer Josephus and by the Roman writer Tacitus, and his name is found on coins and a building inscription from Caesarea.

Why is the fact of Jesus' horrible death given such prominence in a statement of Christian belief? Jesus identified himself as God's Servant, but he also knew that that role entailed suffering. He was to be a suffering Servant, a crucified Messiah (cf., e.g., Matt. 16:21; 20:19; 26:2). To his disciples, this was unthinkable. Peter rebuked him when he first spoke openly of his coming fate (Matt. 16:22). But such a fate was a part of God's perfect plan revealed in his Word. "How foolish you are, and how slow of heart to believe all that the prophets have spoken," Jesus said to the confused men on the road to Emmaus after his resurrection. "Did not the Christ have to suffer these things and then enter his glory?" (Luke 24:25-26). Jesus went to his death in obedience to the will of his Father. Suffering was essential to his role as Messiah. He was, in effect, born to die.

Jesus' death was "according to the Scriptures," Paul declared (1 Cor. 15:3). In proclaiming this, the Apostle claimed that he was "saying nothing beyond what the prophets and Moses said would happen" (Acts 26:22; cf. also 17:2-3). Peter also came to this understanding. He preached on the Day of Pentecost that Jesus was handed over to be killed "by God's set purpose and foreknowledge" (Acts 2:23; cf. also 3:18). Peter believed that the prophets themselves searched intently to understand what the Spirit of Christ in them meant when he predicted the suffering of Christ and the glories that would follow (1 Pet. 1:10-11). In the Epistle to the Hebrews Jesus' suffering unto death is the fitting means to bring many sons to glory, fulfilling the intent of the institution of the temple. It was an offering to God that atoned for the sins of the people (cf., e.g., Heb. 2:17; 9:13-14).

Jesus' death on a cross is not incidental to the Christian message; it is essential. Paul considers it as of "first importance," part of the core of the gospel (1 Cor. 15:1-3). To the Corinthians he said, "I resolved to know nothing while I was with you except Jesus Christ and him crucified" (1 Cor. 2:2). Describing the message he preached to the Galatians, Paul declared, "Before your very eyes, Jesus Christ was clearly portrayed as crucified" (Gal. 3:1). "We preach Christ crucified" (1 Cor. 1:23).

C. Jesus Arose Bodily From the Dead

The crucifixion of Jesus is central to the gospel, but if Jesus had remained in the grave, there would have been no gospel at all. When Jesus was arrested and then executed by the religious and political powers of the day, his disciples fled in fear for their lives. Peter, their bold leader, denied even knowing Jesus to a lowly servant girl (Matt. 26:69-70). After Jesus' execution, his followers were disconcerted, discouraged, and demoralized (cf. Luke 24:17-21). All seemed lost.

But on the third day their despair turned to great joy. Jesus was raised from the grave in an act of divine power, and he appeared to them in bodily form. It was an unusual body, to be sure (cf. Luke 24:30-32,36; John 20:19,26), but he was no ghost (cf. Luke 24:40-43). The tomb was empty. He appeared at various times and places to various people, including a group of over five hundred at one time (1 Cor. 15:5-6), giving "many convincing proofs that he was alive" (Acts 1:3).

The same Jesus who died was raised to new life—a new kind of life. This was no mere resuscitation, leading once more to death, as was the case with Lazarus (John 11). It was resurrection—a life now immune from death. Jesus had conquered death and now existed in a new incorruptible form, a glorified body, never to die again (cf. 1 Cor. 15:53; Phil. 3:21; Heb. 7:24). The Son of God was forever united to humanity in this new bodily form.

The existence of the Christian church is inexplicable apart from the reality of the resurrection of Jesus from the dead. Nothing else can explain the transformation of the disciples and their message of victory over sin and death to be found in Jesus Christ. The resurrection was the divine vindication of the person and work of Jesus as God's Messiah. The verdict of the human court was overturned by a higher authority. As Paul writes, Jesus was "declared with power to be the Son of God[40] by his resurrection from the dead" (Rom. 1:4; cf. Acts 17:31).

Without the resurrection there simply is no "good news." If Christ has not been raised, Paul writes, our preaching is useless, our faith is futile, and we are still in our sins (1 Cor. 15:14,17). But Christ has been raised! The Scriptures had declared that the Messiah had to suffer "and then enter his glory" (Luke 24:26). God's Holy One was not abandoned to the grave (cf. Acts 2:31, where Peter expounds Psalm 16). "Let all Israel be assured of this," Peter declared, "God has made this Jesus, whom you crucified, both Lord and Christ" (Acts 2:36).

D. Jesus Ascended to the Father's Right Hand

The vindication of Jesus did not end with his resurrection from the grave. He was also exalted to the place of highest honor at the right hand

---

40 Or "was declared to be the Son of God in power" (ESV).

of the Father (Acts 2:33).[41] After appearing to his disciples in various contexts over a period of forty days, Jesus was visibly taken from his disciples in a cloud (Acts 1:9)—a symbol of the divine presence—as a dramatic display of his new status and new home. This ascension to heavenly glory is also called Jesus' Session,[42] for, having gone into heaven, Jesus is said to have taken his seat at the Father's right hand (Col. 3:1; Eph. 1:20; Heb. 1:3; 8:1-2; 10:12; 12:2; Rev. 3:21).

Beginning with Peter in his sermon on the Day of Pentecost, the early Christians saw in David's words in Psalm 110:1 a description of Jesus' fate:

> The LORD says to my Lord:
> "Sit at my right hand
> until I make your enemies
> a footstool for your feet."

This psalm became the most frequently quoted Old Testament passage in the New Testament.

Jesus' ascension to the Father's right hand is significant for several reasons. First, it signifies that Jesus shares in the kingly rule of his Father as Lord of heaven and earth, "far above all rule and authority, power and dominion, and every title that can be given, not only in the present age but also in the one to come" (Eph. 1:21). In the words of J. I. Packer, "[H]e sits at the Father's right hand—not to rest but to rule. The picture is not of inactivity but of authority."[43] Jesus has been exalted to the highest place and has been given the name that is above every name—he is Lord (Phil. 2:9-11; cf. Isa. 45:23). As the Lamb upon the throne, he is worthy of all worship (Rev. 5:11-14), and he has been appointed as the Judge of all (Matt. 25:31; Acts 17:31; Rom. 2:16; 2 Cor. 5:10). Whereas angels stand or fall down in worship in God's presence (1 Kings 22:19; Rev. 4:10), the exalted Son sits.

Second, the ascension of Jesus results in his sending the Holy Spirit. On the Day of Pentecost, Peter spoke of this: "Exalted to the right hand

---

41 Several New Testament texts have been interpreted to suggest that Jesus first "descended into hell" before he rose from the grave (cf. Acts 2:27; Rom. 10:6-7; Eph. 4:8-9; 1 Pet. 3:18-20; 4:6), and this view found its way into later versions of the Apostles' Creed. However, this phrase does not occur in the Bible, and the texts used to support the notion are ambiguous at best. It is unwise to make much of this contested theological point.

42 From the Latin *sessio*, which means "sitting."

43 *Concise Theology: A Guide to Historic Christian Beliefs* (Wheaton: Tyndale House Publishers, 1993), 129.

of God, he has received from the Father the promised Holy Spirit and has poured out what you now see and hear" (Acts 2:33). Jesus was going away, but he was not abandoning his disciples. He would be present with them through the Spirit whom he would send from the Father (John 15:26; 16:7).

Finally, as is specifically mentioned in our Statement, Jesus' ascension to the Father's right hand points to his role as our great High Priest. In contrast to the priests of the old covenant, who stood in the temple offering the same sacrifices day after day (and which could never take away sins), Jesus, as our High Priest, offered for all time one sacrifice for sin and *sat down* at the right hand of God (Heb. 10:11-12; also 1:3). He had completed the task; his earthly work was done, for he had offered a sacrifice of permanent efficacy. More than that, he lives forever to be our continual Advocate with the Father, exercising a perpetual priestly role (Heb. 7:23-25; 1 John 2:1). He is at the right hand of God interceding for us (Rom. 8:34). "Therefore, he is able to save completely those who come to God through him" (Heb. 7:25). The heavenly vindication of Jesus at the right hand of the Father will be joined to an earthly recognition of his exalted status when he comes again in glory.

Conclusion

God's gospel is made known supremely in the Person of Jesus Christ. He is the definitive and final revelation of the saving grace of God in the world (cf. Heb. 1:2). Our next chapter concerns the work of Christ, which cannot be separated from his Person. Jesus Christ can do what he does only because he is who he is—God incarnate, fully God and fully man, Israel's promised Messiah.

Evangelical Convictions

A THEOLOGICAL EXPOSITION OF THE STATEMENT OF FAITH
OF THE EVANGELICAL FREE CHURCH OF AMERICA

Article 5

THE WORK OF CHRIST

5. We believe that Jesus Christ, as our representative and substitute, shed His blood on the cross as the perfect, all-sufficient sacrifice for our sins. His atoning death and victorious resurrection constitute the only ground for salvation.

God's gospel is accomplished through the work of Christ.

Our Statement thus far has affirmed truths about the human condition and truths about God that, when viewed together, present an obvious problem. On the one hand, we have declared that human beings are sinners by nature and by choice, alienated from God, and under his wrath (Article 3). We all stand in need of the restoration of our corrupt nature, reconciliation with our estranged Creator, and rescue from the condemnation which our rebellion against God's rule richly deserves.

Yet we have also declared the gracious purpose of God from eternity to redeem a people for himself, allowing them to share in his own triune love (Article 1). That purpose was first glimpsed in God's pledge in the Garden of Eden that from the seed of Eve would come one who would crush the head of the serpent (Gen. 3:15); it was revealed more clearly in God's promise to bless Abraham, and through him to bring blessing to the world (Gen. 12:1-3). The Old Testament story of Israel left little ground for hope, however, for Israel herself had rebelled against God and was in need of a Savior. In the light of our sinful condition, how is this purpose to be accomplished?

Many would simply echo the words of the German poet and skeptic Heinrich Heine, which he spoke as he lay on his deathbed: "God will forgive me. That's his job." Isn't forgiveness God's duty, his obligation? Can't God simply forgive freely?

But the Bible affirms that God is holy and just, which means that he cannot tolerate evil and must condemn all iniquity—"Acquitting the guilty and condemning the innocent—the LORD detests them both" (Prov. 17:15). Because of his very nature, God's role as Judge of all the earth demands the execution of justice. Evil must be seen to be evil, or cosmic justice will have no meaning; and without such a recognition even our human dignity as responsible moral agents will be undermined. Mere forgiveness of sinful human beings apart from the exercise of the judgment due their sin would be in contradiction of God's character.

The resolution of this theological dilemma, and the core of the gospel, is found in the work of Jesus Christ. Especially in the death of Christ on the cross, God's righteousness is revealed—a righteous hatred of sin and a righteous commitment to his covenant promise to bring blessing to the world. There God's wrath is poured out and his love is demonstrated, and he shows himself to be just even while justifying sinners (cf. Rom. 3:25-26).

The institutions of Israel provide the categories by which to understand the work of Christ, as he fulfills the roles of Prophet—revealing the grace and truth of God as his perfect image; of Priest—representing and redeeming a sinful people; and of King—exercising the authority of God in reigning over his creation. Our statement on the work of Christ focuses on his priestly role through which he effects our salvation by his atoning sacrifice on the cross.

I. Of Central Importance: Jesus Christ Shed His Blood on the Cross

The Evangelists, in various ways, present the crucifixion of Jesus in Jerusalem as the focal point of the gospel story. Matthew and Mark follow a similar story line. Matthew first alludes to the violent conflict to come in his narrative of the birth of Jesus when the wicked King Herod seeks to eliminate the one who is born king by murdering infants near Bethlehem (Matt. 2:13-18). Then, as in Mark's Gospel, early in his account of Jesus' ministry in Galilee, Matthew mentions the Pharisees' intention to kill Jesus (12:14; cf. Mark 3:6), setting the stage for what follows. After Peter's confession of Jesus' identity as the Son of God, Jesus explicitly declares that he must go to Jerusalem, where he will be killed (Matt. 16:21; cf. Mark 8:31), a destiny reaffirmed twice (Matt. 17:22-23; 20:18; also 26:2; cf. Mark 9:30-31; 10:33). Indeed, Jesus goes to his death as the fulfillment of the divine purpose revealed in the Scriptures (Matt. 26:24, 54-56).

In Luke, Jesus affirms his determination to face his death (Luke 9:22). Luke further tells us that Jesus "resolutely set out for Jerusalem" (9:51), for "no prophet can die outside of Jerusalem" (13:33). "I have a baptism to undergo," Jesus declares, "and how distressed I am until it is completed!" (12:50).

John emphasizes the centrality of Jesus' death by the repeated reference to Jesus' appointed "hour." Three times we read that Jesus' hour had not yet come (John 2:4; 7:30; 8:20; cf. also 7:6,8). Then, as he enters Jerusalem for the last time and faces his certain death, Jesus declares, "The hour has come for the Son of Man to be glorified" (12:23; cf. also 17:1). Jesus wrestles with the torment which this entails, but faces it faithfully: "Now my heart is troubled, and what shall I say? 'Father, save me from this hour'? No, it was for this very reason I came to this hour" (12:27).

Jesus was born to die. His crucifixion by Pilate was not thrust upon him; he chose it as his divine vocation (John 10:18). He was tempted to turn from such agony, and in the Garden of Gethsemane he prayed, "My Father, if it is possible, may this cup be taken from me" (Matt. 26:39). But it was not possible, and Jesus willingly went to the cross. John records his dying words: "It is finished" (John 19:30). Jesus had accomplished that for which the Father had sent him into the world.

In their accounts of the ministry of Jesus, the Gospel writers emphasize the centrality of the cross,[1] and the teaching of the apostles does the same.[2] But why? What is the meaning of this cruel death? What did it accomplish?

Fundamentally, as Israel's promised Messiah, the story of Jesus in the Gospels is seen as the fulfillment of Israel's story (cf., e.g., Matt. 1:1-17). As such, he is the means by which a sinful Israel can bring blessing to the world. Jesus accomplishes this by taking on the role of Daniel's Son of Man[3] and the suffering Servant described by the prophet Isaiah.[4] He becomes the Righteous One who bears the sins of his people, bringing forgiveness and restoration (Matt. 1:21).

Simply put, the New Testament proclaims that Jesus died "for our sins" (cf., e.g., 1 Cor. 15:3; 1 Pet. 3:18; Rom. 3:25-26; 5:8), implying that Jesus' death provides the means by which our sins are forgiven or taken away (Eph. 1:7). Jesus himself pointed his disciples in this direction when he spoke of his ultimate act of service in terms of "giving his life a ransom for many" (Mark 10:45; Matt. 20:28). This connection was confirmed during the Last Supper. In preparing his disciples for his imminent death, Jesus spoke of the cup as "my blood of the covenant, which is poured out for many for the forgiveness of sins" (Matt. 26:28).

This reference to "blood" signals a sacrificial significance to Jesus' death, especially since it was made at a meal which celebrated the saving work of God through the blood of the Passover lamb sprinkled on the doorposts of the families of Israel. Blood was a central aspect of the sacrifices prescribed in the Old Testament (cf. Heb. 9:22), as it testified

---

1 The Gospel of Mark has been described as a passion narrative with an extended prologue.

2 Cf. e.g., Acts 2:23; 1 Cor. 1:23; 2:2; 15:1-3; Gal. 3:1; 1 Pet. 1:19; 3:18; Heb. 7:27; 10:14. See also our discussion of Jesus' crucifixion in Article 4, sec. II.B.

3 See Daniel 7; cf., e.g., Matt. 26:64.

4 See Isaiah 40-55, esp. 42:1-9; 49:1-6; 50:4-9; and especially 52:13-53:12; cf. e.g., Matt. 8:17; 20:28; John 12:38.

to a life poured out in death (Lev. 17:11).[5] The "blood of Jesus" became a common way of speaking of Jesus' death as a saving, sacrificial act. In Christ, "we have redemption through his blood, the forgiveness of our trespasses," Paul writes (Eph. 1:7; cf. 2:13; Col. 1:20; Rom. 3:25; 5:9). John affirms that "the blood of Jesus his Son cleanses us from all sin" (1 John 1:7; cf. Rev. 1:5; 12:11). And Peter speaks of our being ransomed "with the precious blood of Christ, like that of a lamb without defect or blemish" (1 Pet. 1:19; cf. John 1:29). In Hebrews this theme is expounded in even greater detail (Heb. 9,10; cf. especially 10:19). Jesus' death must be seen as an atoning sacrifice for our sins.

II. Christ's Atoning Death:
The Perfect, All-Sufficient Sacrifice for Our Sins

The New Testament description of Jesus' death as an atoning sacrifice finds its fullest expression in the Epistle to the Hebrews. There the Levitical priesthood and the temple worship provide the paradigm for understanding the work of Jesus. The Old Testament priests offered the same sacrifices year after year for themselves and for the people. The repetition of these offerings, however, bore witness to their ineffectiveness in perfecting the worshippers (Heb. 10:1-3). "But now," we read, "[Jesus] has appeared once for all at the end of the ages to do away with sin by the sacrifice of himself" (9:26). Jesus assumes the roles of both the high priest and the sacrificial offering as he offers himself to God, making perfect those who draw near to God through him (10:14).

Jesus' atoning sacrifice is "perfect" (that is, complete, absolute, optimal, unsurpassed), based on the nature of that sacrifice. If the blood of bulls and goats could effect ceremonial cleansing in the worship of God, how much more can the precious blood of Christ cleanse our hearts so that we might serve the living God (Heb. 9:13-14). It was impossible for the blood of bulls and goats to take away sin; that was but a shadow of the reality to come (10:1,4). But in Jesus that reality has now appeared, and by the sacrifice of himself once for all, "he has made perfect forever those who are being made holy" (10:14). His perfect sacrifice obtains "eternal redemption" (9:12). It was not with perishable things that we were redeemed, "but with the precious blood of Christ, a lamb without blemish or defect" (1 Pet. 1:19).

---

5 Cf. Leon Morris, *Apostolic Preaching of the Cross*, 3rd ed. (Leicester: InterVarsity, 1965), 112-26.

In its perfection, Jesus' atoning sacrifice is also "all-sufficient." Nothing is lacking from it, and we can add nothing to it. It is complete, fully efficacious and all that is required to atone for our sin. It satisfies all the requirements of God's holiness and justice in providing the means of our salvation—in its past, present and future dimensions (cf. 2 Tim. 1:9; 1 Cor. 1:18; 1 Pet. 1:5). For that reason, Jesus could say, "It is finished" (John 19:30).

A. Biblical Language of the Atonement

Jesus' atoning death on the cross is the means by which God deals with our sin and the corruption, alienation and the wrath of God which that sin engenders. This is the *fact* of the atonement, but how is this atoning work to be understood?

The New Testament writers use rich and evocative language in seeking to expound the saving work of Christ on the cross, with word pictures from various fields of human experience. These are by no means mutually exclusive, and each has something to contribute to our understanding of this profound event.

As we have seen, the sacrificial system of the Old Testament temple provides an essential background for understanding Christ's death. It depicts sin as defilement before God which disqualifies us for worship. Christ's work is a cleansing that expiates, or takes away, our sin, and so makes us acceptable in God's presence.

Another way of understanding the atonement comes from the marketplace, and it pictures our salvation in terms of a redemption in which we are bought out of our slavery to sin.[6] This liberation comes at a great cost. We were captives to sin's power and under its merciless control, but by his death, Jesus ransoms us, buying us back with his precious blood. We have been, at the same time, set free from the devil's power and set under God's rule, for he is now our new Master.

A third approach invokes the image of a battlefield. In the cosmic war for the control of our souls, Jesus as our Champion has defeated the demonic forces of evil and delivered us from their dominion. Jesus spoke of his ministry in terms of binding the strong man so that one can then plunder his possessions (cf. Matt. 12:29). Paul echoes this imagery when he says, "having disarmed the powers and authorities, [Christ] made a

---

6 The language of "redemption" and "ransom" have this background (cf. Matt. 20:28/Mark 10:45; 1 Tim. 2:6; Heb. 9:15; see also 6:22; Ps. 49:8).

public spectacle of them, triumphing over them by the cross" (Col. 2:15). "The reason the Son of God appeared was to destroy the devil's work," John writes (1 John 3:8; cf. also John 12:31; 16:11; Heb. 2:14-15).

Relationships within the family are also significant as a sphere of human experience which sheds light on the saving work of Christ. Jesus' death provides a means of reconciliation between estranged parties, bringing peace between them. Through Christ's death, we who were God's enemies can become adopted into God's family as his children and heirs of all his riches (Rom. 5:10-11; 8:15-17; Gal. 4:4-5; Titus 3:6-7).[7]

Finally, and most fundamentally, the Bible uses the imagery of the law court to picture the accomplishment of the gospel. God is Judge, the final moral authority before whom all must give an account. All sin is ultimately rebellion against his righteous rule, and the penalty of disobedience is death (Gen. 2:16-17; Rom. 6:23). Because he is holy, God's necessary reaction to all that acts contrary to his will is wrath. God's wrath is not a capricious and irrational rage, as is often found in sinful human beings, but the pure and consistent response of a righteous and just God when confronting all that is evil in his creation. He hates sin with a holy hatred. "Your eyes are too pure to look on evil; you cannot tolerate wrong," the prophet Habakkuk declares of him. Or, as we read in Nahum:

> The LORD is a jealous and avenging God;
> the LORD takes vengeance and is filled with wrath.
> The LORD takes vengeance on his foes
> and maintains his wrath against his enemies.
> The LORD is slow to anger and great in power;
> the LORD will not leave the guilty unpunished.
>
> (Nahum 1:2-3)

This response of God to human sin is assumed in the Gospel of John: "Whoever believes in the Son has eternal life, but whoever rejects the Son will not see life, for God's wrath remains on him" (John 3:36).

In his magisterial exposition of the gospel in his letter to the Romans, Paul sets forth the revelation of the wrath of God as the central obstacle to be overcome (1:18; 2:5,8). All humanity stands under the righteous judgment of God (2:2-3; 3:9-20), whose just sentence is death (1:32; 5:12; 6:23). But in Christ, and through his atoning death, we are rescued from

---

7 The notion of adoption is discussed further in Article 6, sec. II.B.3.

that condemnation (3:21-26; 8:1,33-34). God as Judge acts to justify those who believe in Christ. On the basis of their union with Christ, he declares that they are no longer under his judgment and are now righteous in his sight, members in good standing of his people, becoming sons of Abraham by faith. Though "we were by nature objects of [God's] wrath" (Eph. 2:3), Paul argues in his letter to the Thessalonians that "God did not appoint us to suffer wrath but to receive salvation through our Lord Jesus Christ" (1 Thess. 5:9). It is Christ alone who can rescue us from that divine wrath (1 Thess. 1:10).

B. Theological Views of the Atonement

Through history various theological views have been proposed to make sense of these diverse biblical backgrounds. Some have stressed the subjective aspect of the work of Christ—that is, the effect that Christ's death has on our own moral state. The "moral influence" theory contends that Christ's death on the cross is the ultimate expression of God's love for us and that this should move us to respond to him in kind. Names often associated with this view include Pelagius (died c. 424), Peter Abelard (1079-1142) and Faustus Socinus (1539-1604). This theory became popular among liberals in the last century.[8]

Another approach, also with a decidedly subjective dimension, emphasized the way in which God acts in the atonement to safeguard his moral rule of the universe. This "governmental theory" was propounded by the Dutch jurist Hugo Grotius (1583-1645). He contended that the death of Jesus was God's means of demonstrating the seriousness of sin and was appropriate to prevent the corruption of human morals. In this way God upholds the authority of his law through the vicarious death of his Son; but the emphasis is again on the subjective impact of Christ's death on human beings.

A similar emphasis was found in a view of the atonement that was held by one early leader of the Evangelical Free Church, J. G. Princell, a notable teacher in the early Swedish mission movement.[9] Propounded first in Sweden by Paul Peter Waldenström in the late nineteenth century, this view taught that God had no need of reconciliation with man, for human beings were not under his wrath. Atonement was necessary not to appease God

---

8 Cf., e.g, Hastings Rashdall, *The Idea of Atonement* (1915).

9 On this issue, see David M. Gustafson, "J. G. Princell and the Waldenströmian View of the Atonement," *Trinity Journal*, 20.2 NS (1999), 191-214.

but to reconcile man, and only in that sense was Christ's death atoning.

Certainly the death of Christ is the ultimate expression of God's love, and Paul declares it to be such: "God demonstrates his own love for us in this: while we were still sinners, Christ died for us" (Rom. 5:8). Jesus' death shows how much God loved the world (John 3:16). We ought to respond to such love with repentance and faith; a failure to do so shows contempt for God's kindness (Rom. 2:4). Further, the life of Jesus is held up as a moral example to us, particularly as he responds to evil with patience, humility and love (cf. Phil. 2:5-8; 1 Pet. 2:19-23).

While the subjective views of the atonement stress the effect of Christ's work on our moral condition, they fail to account for the depth of human depravity or the reality of God's opposition to sin. They highlight Jesus' role of Prophet, revealing God to us, rather than his role as Priest. And while these perspectives convey truth about the power of the cross to affect us, they are sorely inadequate on their own. There must be a vital connection between the loving sacrifice of Christ's death and the situation of the sinner. Biblical scholar James Denney once observed, in effect, that a man jumping off a pier, yelling, "I love you, world!" before he sinks to the bottom would be considered a misguided madman. But if he jumps off the pier to save someone who is drowning, and gives his life in the process, he becomes a real hero. So Jesus' death must be more than a vague declaration of love; it must be an actual achievement.[10] Thus, in contrast, the "objective" views of the atonement point to a real change in the spiritual realm, including God's posture toward us.

One of the earliest objective perspectives on the atoning death of Christ emphasized Jesus' role as King and described it as a conquest over the powers of evil. Hebrews speaks of Christ sharing in our humanity "so that by his death he might destroy him who holds the power of death—that is, the devil—and free those who all their lives were held in slavery by their fear of death" (Heb. 2:14-15). Though this view seeks to do justice to the New Testament's battlefield imagery to describe the victorious effect of Christ's death and resurrection, it is insufficient as an explanation of his atoning work. It fails to spell out how the power of Satan was defeated (though crude imagery was suggested, with Christ pictured as bait to lure an unsuspecting devil to bite the hook of the cross![11]). Closely associated with this view was the notion of a liberating

---

10 James Denney, *The Death of Christ* (London: Tyndale, 1951), 103.

11 Cf. Gregory of Nyssa (330-c. 395), *Great Catechetical Discourses*, 24.

ransom. That image is graphic, but it is not clear to whom the price of redemption is paid, for certainly Satan has no lawful rights over the human race.

The most prominent and promising understanding of atonement builds upon the Bible's forensic (or legal) language of God as righteous Judge. Though found throughout Christian history,[12] this view was developed most clearly by Anselm of Canterbury (1033-1109) in his book *Why Did God Become Man?* He stressed the ideas of satisfaction and vicarious sacrifice. Essentially Anselm contended that moral offense entails a moral debt which must be paid. Therefore, those who sin against God owe him either their own punishment, or some restitution or satisfaction for their transgression of his law. God's justice demands such payment, but human beings cannot make satisfaction since they are guilty and are deserving of God's punishment. Satisfaction can be made only by one who is innocent, so God himself makes this possible by the incarnation of Jesus Christ. The God-man Jesus Christ is under no obligation to die, since he is sinless, but he willingly offers himself as the satisfaction for human sin. Atonement is thus seen as a payment of human debt to God by a substitute which God himself provides.

Anselm's approach has been subject to criticism, chiefly in the way it seems to reduce God's actions to logic—providing a rationalistic explanation of Christ's atoning work—and in the way he relied upon medieval notions of honor, reflecting the feudal society of his day. However, later proponents of this satisfaction model, including Thomas Aquinas[13] and the sixteenth-century Reformers, modified Anselm's views to meet these objections. Their efforts resulted in an approach that best captures the heart of the biblical teaching of Christ's atonement, while

12 For a helpful compilation of references to early writers, see Steve Jeffery, Michael Ovey, Andrew Sach, *Pierced for Our Transgressions: Rediscovering the Glory of Penal Substitution* (Crossway: Wheaton, IL, 2007): 164-183. Cf. *The Epistle to Diognetus* 9:5 (perhaps A.D. 150-225): "O the sweet exchange, O the incomprehensible work of God, O the unexpected blessings, that the sinfulness of many should be hidden in one righteous person, while the righteousness of one should justify many sinners!" See also Athanasius, *Letter to Marcellinus on the Interpretation of the Psalms*: "For [Christ] did not die as being Himself liable to death: He suffered for us, and bore in Himself the wrath that was the penalty of our transgression" (found in Athanasius, *On the Incarnation*, translated and edited by A Religious of C.S.M.V. [Crestwood, NY: St. Vladimir's Seminary Press, 2003], 101).

13 Cf. *Summa Theologica*, 3a.49,5: "Now by Christ's Passion we have been delivered not only from the common sin of the whole human race, both as to its guilt and as to the debt of punishment, for which he paid the penalty on our behalf, ..." Also, 50,1: "he who bears another's punishment takes such punishment away."

embracing the other views as well: the notion of penal substitution.[14]

1. Jesus, Our Substitute: Penal Substitution

When we refer in our statement to Jesus as our substitute, we have particularly in mind the forensic model of the atonement known as penal[15] substitution: Jesus, the Righteous One, died in our place, paying the penalty that we deserved, thus satisfying God's justice. God's wrath is thereby appeased, reconciling sinners to a holy God, such that his forgiveness does not compromise his holiness. This process is God-initiated, and is, from beginning to end, an expression of God's love and grace.

This view fit well with the renewed interest in the doctrine of justification at the time of the Reformation, particularly as it was understood by Martin Luther from Paul's letter to the Romans. The pressing question in Luther's mind was how a sinner could be made right with God. Paul's words in Romans 1:18-3:20 seemed to leave no doubt that all of humanity lay under the divine wrath. God operates with strict retributive justice, rendering to each person according to what he has done (2:6), with "trouble and distress for every human being who does evil: first for the Jew, then for the Gentile; but glory, honor and peace for everyone who does good: first for the Jew, then for the Gentile" (2:9-10). But because Paul concludes that "all have sinned" (3:23), that "There is no one righteous, not even one" (3:10), and that on the day of judgment "every mouth will be silenced and the whole world held accountable to God" (3:19), whatever answer the gospel gives as a means of escape must somehow deal with the righteous wrath of God which sinful human beings deserve.

For this reason, the critical passage, Romans 3:21-26, was understood among the Reformers to support the notion of "satisfaction," a key element of Anselm's doctrine. God can maintain his own justice in justifying sinners only if that justice is satisfied by the righteous death of another. Thus, in the death of Jesus, God substituted himself, thereby demonstrating his own righteousness. In 3:25, Jesus is the *hilastērion*, the propitiating sacrifice,[16] which turns away the righteous wrath of God

---

14 In affirming the centrality of penal substitution, we do not claim that this view in itself is exhaustive as a way of understanding all that Scripture teaches about the atoning work of Christ.

15 This comes from the Latin word *poena* which means "punishment."

16 See also Heb. 2:17; 1 John 2:2; 4:10, in which a form of this word is found. The New

toward sinners (cf. 5:9), bringing reconciliation (5:1,10). Calvin writes: "If the effect of his shedding of blood is that our sins are not imputed to us, it follows that God's judgment was satisfied by that price."[17]

The notion of penal substitution is found elsewhere in the New Testament as well. Fundamental is the idea that the Righteous One dies in the place of the unrighteous, as expressed by Peter: "For Christ also suffered for sins once for all, the righteous for the unrighteous, in order to bring you to God" (1 Pet. 3:18). Paul expresses this exchange in 2 Corinthians 5:21: "For our sake he made him to be sin who knew no sin, so that in him we might become the righteousness of God."[18] Or, again, in his letter to the Galatians, the Apostle can declare that "Christ redeemed us from the curse of the law by becoming a curse for us" (Gal. 3:13). Jesus acts "for us"—on our behalf and in our place. He is a righteous substitute who bears our penalty.[19]

This conception of the death of Jesus would not have come naturally to the first disciples. At first, when they saw their beloved Master hanging on a Roman cross, they were confused and disheartened. They had thought he was their Messiah, the Anointed One of God, who would lead them into the glory of the Kingdom of God. But on the cross he died as a common criminal, bearing the curse of God. With his resurrection, however, their view of his death changed. In his vindication by God, they realized that Jesus was, in fact, the Christ, and that it was not for his own sin that he had died, but for theirs. The prophet Isaiah had declared it so well:

> Surely he took up our infirmities and carried our sorrows,
> yet we considered him stricken by God,
> smitten by him, and afflicted.
> But he was pierced for our transgressions,

Testament notion of propitiation, however, does not depend on the use of this word alone.

17 *Institutes*, 2.17.4.

18 Theologians use the language of imputation to describe this exchange. Through his substitutionary death on our behalf, he takes our sin, and it is no longer imputed to us, that is, it is not reckoned or charged to our account. In addition, through our union with Christ as our representative, his righteousness is imputed to us. It is, in Paul's words, "a righteousness not my own" (Phil. 3:9; cf. also Rom. 4:3,6). Further, on our union with Christ, see Article 6, sec. II.B.2.

19 While the explicit language of "punishment" and "penalty" is not found in the New Testament (though "curse" comes close [Gal. 3:13; cf. also Isa. 53:5]), the reality it expresses very certainly is. The clear teaching of the Bible is that death, as the expression of God's wrath, is what sin deserves (cf. Gen. 2:16,17; Rom. 6:23). That is its penalty.

> he was crushed for our iniquities;
> the punishment that brought us peace was upon him,
> and by his wounds we are healed.
> We all, like sheep, have gone astray,
> each of us has turned to his own way;
> and the LORD has laid on him the iniquity of us all.

(Isa. 53:4-6)

They understood Jesus' death to be a vicarious sacrifice, a penal substitution, in which "He himself bore our sins in his body on the cross" (1 Pet. 2:24).

This understanding of vicarious suffering was built into the sacrificial system of the Old Testament. Sacrifice was needed in Israel as a remedy for sin (cf. Lev. 5:6). The one bringing the sacrifice was to lay his hands on the animal as a sign of the transfer of sin to the victim so that it might be accepted on his behalf. The animal was then slain, and its blood was sprinkled on the altar. The effect of the offering was the remission of sin and the declaration of forgiveness (cf. Lev. 1:4; 4:20,26,31; 6:7). The offering provided cleansing from sin, but it did so in a way that was based on the propitiation of God's wrath through the vicarious death of another.[20]

Those sacrifices, we are told in Hebrews, have no real efficacy in dealing with sins (Heb. 10:11). They were but a shadow of the reality that was to come. "But now [Christ] has appeared once for all at the end of the ages to do away with sin by the sacrifice of himself" (Heb. 9:26). "Christ was sacrificed once to take away the sins of many people" (Heb. 9:28); and "by one sacrifice he has made perfect forever those who are being made holy" (Heb. 10:14).

One might say that this principle of substitution lies at the heart of both sin and salvation. As John Stott puts it:

> [T]he essence of sin is man substituting himself for
> God, while the essence of salvation is God substituting
> himself for man. Man asserts himself against God
> and puts himself where only God deserves to be; God

---

20 Consider also the Passover, when the Lord was delivering the Israelites from the power of Pharaoh: On the night the angel of death passed through Egypt killing all the firstborn, each Jewish family had to kill a lamb and apply its blood on the doorframe of their house. When the angel saw the blood he would pass over that house and would spare the firstborn. That was a form of substitution—the lamb died in the place of the firstborn.

> sacrifices himself for man and puts himself where only
> man deserves to be. Man claims prerogatives which
> belong to God alone; God accepts penalties which
> belong to man alone.[21]

This doctrine of penal substitution is represented in standard documents of the Reformation. The Lutheran Augsburg Confession (1530) states that Christ "was crucified, died and was buried in order to be a sacrifice not only for original sin but also for all other sins and to propitiate God's wrath" (III.2,3). The Heidelberg Catechism (1563) explains the suffering of Christ in this way:

> ...throughout his life on Earth, but especially at the
> end of it, he bore in body and soul the wrath of God
> against the sin of the whole human race, so that by
> his suffering, as the only expiatory[22] sacrifice, he
> might redeem our body and soul from everlasting
> damnation, and might obtain for us God's grace,
> righteousness, and eternal life (Q. 37).

Article 31 of the Anglican Thirty-Nine Articles (1571) declares: "The offering of Christ once made is the perfect redemption, propitiation, and satisfaction for all the sins of the whole world, both original and actual, and there is no other satisfaction for sin but that alone."

Later doctrinal statements representing various theological traditions also reinforce this understanding of atonement. The Reformed Westminster Confession of Faith (1646) affirms: "The Lord Jesus, by his perfect obedience and sacrifice of himself, which he through the eternal Spirit once offered up unto God, hath fully satisfied the justice of his Father" (VIII.v). This is echoed in the more recent Wesleyan *Confession of Faith* of the Evangelical United Brethren Church (1963): "The offering Christ freely made on the cross is the perfect and sufficient sacrifice for

---

21 *The Cross of Christ* (Downers Grove: InterVarsity, 1986), 160.

22 Penal substitution is often linked with a propitiatory aspect of Christ's atoning death, that is, the atoning work of Christ not only cleanses a person from sin (captured in the word "expiation"), but also appeases the wrath of God (captured in the word "propitiation"). The word used here in the Heidelberg Catechism (*Sühnopfer*) is translated by the word expiation rather than propitiation, but because that expiation takes away the sin that arouses God's wrath, the terms overlap in meaning.

the sins of the whole world, redeeming man from all sin, so that no other satisfaction is required" (Art. VIII).

Penal substitution is not stated explicitly in our Statement of Faith, but it is clearly there. Jesus is declared to be our "substitute" and the "perfect and all-sufficient sacrifice for our sins" on the cross saves us from the wrath of God (see Article 3). While a few may not have held this view at one point in our history, it is certainly embraced by the Free Church today and is considered critical to understanding Christ's atoning work.

Objections to This View

The understanding of the atoning death of Christ in terms of penal substitution has not been without its detractors, both ancient and modern. Frequently, however, objections fail to consider the work of Christ in the light of his Person, either misunderstanding his relationship to God the Father or to humanity.[23] We will consider three common objections, looking first at an obvious complaint that points us to a mystery at the heart of God.

One might ask, is it even coherent to contend that God in his love can satisfy his own wrath against human sin—that he can, as expressed by Augustine, "love us even while he hates us"?[24]

With Calvin, we may recognize this apparent contradiction of God, who in love appeases his own wrath; but we may also affirm with Calvin that this is simply the way Scripture speaks (cf. Rom. 5:10; Gal 3:10,13; Col. 1:21-22). It may be, he suggests, that "Expressions of this sort have been accommodated to our capacity that we may better understand how miserable and ruinous our condition is apart from Christ."[25]

Or, with Augustine, we may understand the wrath and love of God operating at different levels and in different ways: "[God] knew at once both how, in each of us, to hate what we had done [in our sin], and to love what he had done [in his creation]."[26] God's wrath arises from his holiness in response to human rebellion; but his love is from eternity as an intrinsic perfection of his nature and is not caused by the character

---

23 Cf. the perceptive comment by John Stott: "At the root of every caricature of the cross there lies a distorted Christology" (*The Cross of Christ*, 160).

24 *John's Gospel* cx.6. On God's "hatred of the wicked," cf. Pss. 5:5; 11:5.

25 *Institutes*, 2.16.2.

26 *John's Gospel* cx.6.

of the one loved.[27] Thus, these need not be logically incompatible, though their connection may remain a mystery. We are compelled by the teaching of Scripture to hold both of these together.

A second objection to penal substitution questions the goodness of God. In a caricature, God the Father is pictured as the vindictive agent of wrath who must be cajoled into acting graciously toward his human subjects. The Son of God takes the abusive punishment we deserve and so wins the good will of a begrudging God.

Fundamentally, this grotesque representation misunderstands the unity of the triune God. The death of Christ on the cross is not the affliction of punishment by the Father upon the "eternal Son" (that is, apart from his humanity), much less upon a mere human being. Jesus' death on the cross is truly an action of God upon himself. God is both the subject and the object of atonement. That atoning work of God is entirely self-initiated and self-inflicted; it is truly an act of self-substitution. "God was in Christ reconciling the world to himself" (2 Cor. 5:19). This was not an act necessitated by some cosmic logic but freely chosen as an act of holy love.

A proper conception of penal substitution insists that there are not three parties in the atonement; there are but two: God in Christ and humanity. Immediately this separates the atoning death of Jesus from any pagan notion of worshippers offering their own sacrifices to appease an angry god. Here, God himself offers the sacrifice. Moreover, the propitiatory atonement which God offers provides no legitimation for abuse in human relationships, as some accuse. On the cross the triune God acts upon himself. The Father and Son are one in purpose, acting as one divine Subject in this act of divine self-substitution. "God demonstrates his own love for us in this: while we were still sinners, Christ died for us" (Rom. 5:8).

A third common objection to penal substitution questions the

---

27 Cf. D. A. Carson, *The Difficult Doctrine of the Love of God* (Wheaton: Crossway, 2000), 67. In this book, Carson distinguishes various ways in which God's love is manifest—the intra-trinitarian love, the love of the Father for the Son, the love of God for his creation, his redemptive, selective love for the elect, and his conditional love for his children based on their obedience.

morality of such a transaction. How can one person take on the punishment of another? Is this just a "legal fiction"? Here we find an inadequate appreciation of Christ's Person in his identification with humanity. Jesus Christ is not only truly God, he is also truly man. As Paul affirms, "there is one God and one mediator between God and men, the man Christ Jesus, who gave himself as a ransom for all" (1 Tim. 2:5-6). Christ can act as our substitute only because he has first united himself with us as our representative, a subject which merits further attention and to which we now turn.

2. Jesus, Our Representative: Union with Christ[28]

In our modern Western world, we think in individualistic terms which often deny real social solidarities such as nation, tribe and family. Two institutions in Israel demanded such solidarity of the leader as the representative of his people: the role of high priest and of king. These show us how the actions of one can affect the many.

In offering sacrifices on behalf of the nation, for example, the actions of the high priest affected those he represented before God. Hebrews speaks often of Jesus in that position and emphasizes his right to exercise that role: "[H]e had to be made like his brothers in every way, in order that he might become a merciful and faithful high priest in service to God, and that he might make atonement for the sins of the people" (Heb. 2:17). "In bringing many sons to glory" Jesus shares in their suffering. He and they are of the same family, and he is not ashamed to call them brothers (Heb. 2:10-11). Jesus can represent his people such that he may bear their sins in the offering of himself.

Regarding the representative role of kingship in Israel, the law of Moses demanded that the king of Israel be chosen "from among your own brothers" (Deut. 17:15), and that his subjects could be said to "have a share" in him (cf. 2 Sam. 20:1). The king could represent the people, either bringing them God's blessing or involving them in God's curse (cf. 2 Sam. 24:1-25). Jesus as Israel's Messiah identifies himself with his people (cf., e.g., Matt. 3:13-15) and dies as their King (cf. Matt. 27:37). In this way he saves "his people" from their sins (Matt. 1:21).

Finally, just as Paul could speak of our solidarity with Adam as our

---

28 This topic is discussed in a different context relating to the work of the Holy Spirit in Article 6, sec. II.B.2.

representative head, so it is with Christ (cf. Rom. 5:12-21). Each acts in a way that affects those bound up with them. In our union with Adam by nature, his sin brings death to us; in our union with Christ by faith, his obedience brings us righteousness and life. These two are the great representative figures of the human race.[29]

Because of Jesus' union with us in his humanity as the second Adam, as the Messianic King, and as our great High Priest, he is able to represent us before God. He bears our sin, and, in our union with him, we receive his righteousness. As those "in Christ" (*passim* in Paul; e.g., Rom. 6:2-11; Phil. 1:1; Eph. 1:3) we are now children of God and co-heirs with Christ. This is no "legal fiction," for he has effected a real change in our condition before God.

In his atoning death Jesus acts in our stead and on our behalf. As our substitute, he does what we could never do for ourselves—he bears our sin and judgment, and he takes it away. As our representative he acts on our behalf in such a way as to involve us in what he has done. Jesus goes to his death alone, but he calls us to take up our cross and follow him in the new life that is ours by virtue of our union with him. This new life will be discussed further in Article 6 when we consider the work of the Holy Spirit in applying the finished work of Christ to our lives.

III. Christ's Victorious Resurrection: His Victory and Ours

The cross of Christ cannot be considered apart from his resurrection from the dead. In his faithfulness to the will of his Father, Jesus took on the role of the suffering Servant, bearing the sin of his people,[30] and as a consequence of that faithfulness God raised him from the grave and gave him the name above every name (cf. Phil. 2:5-11). Jesus' resurrection both vindicated his work and demonstrated his victory; and as those in union with him by faith, we benefit from that work and that victory becomes ours.

---

29 On our union with Adam, see Article 3, sec. III, and on our union with Christ, see further in Article 6, sec. II.B.2.

30 This Statement of Faith does not state a position on "the extent of the atonement," and both "particular" (or limited) views (affirming that Jesus' death atones only for the sins of those who will be saved, represented by the Reformed tradition) and "universal" (or unlimited) views (affirming that Jesus' death atones for the sins of all, but is effective only for those who are saved, represented by the Arminian/Wesleyan tradition) are acceptable within the EFCA. In both perspectives, those who actually come to faith constitute "Christ's people" who are saved by his death. Universalism, which declares that in the end all humanity will be saved, is precluded by our Article 10.

A. Jesus' Vindication and Victory

In the first public proclamation of Jesus' resurrection, Peter declared to the Pentecost crowd in Jerusalem, "Therefore let all Israel be assured of this: God has made this Jesus, whom you crucified, both Lord and Christ" (Acts 2:36). Jesus had been condemned by the human court—both Jewish and Roman—but by an act of divine power that verdict was overturned. In raising him from the dead, God declared him to be "the Son of God in power" (Rom. 1:4 [NRSV]), exalting him to a position of "all authority" (Matt. 28:18). He was indeed the true King of Israel, and his teaching on the exaltation of the humble in the kingdom of God is realized. In his innocent suffering he entrusted himself to him who judges justly (1 Pet. 2:23), and that faith was honored. God would not abandon his Holy One to the grave (Acts 2:31, citing Ps. 16:10).

But not only did the resurrection of Jesus validate his Person, it also vindicated his work. It demonstrated that it was not for his own sin that he died, but for the sin of his people (as in Isa. 53:4). He had accomplished his mission and God rewarded his vicarious suffering, just as the Scriptures predicted (cf. Isa. 53:11-12; Luke 24:26; Acts 26:22). If Christ has not been raised, Paul says, our faith is futile and we are still in our sins, subject to God's condemnation (1 Cor. 15:17). "But Christ has indeed been raised from the dead" (v. 20). His atoning sacrifice was acceptable to God, and it was effective in taking away our sin. Therefore, Paul can say that Christ "was handed over to death for our trespasses and was raised for [or "because of" (Greek: *dia*)] our justification" (Rom. 4:25).

The cross appeared to signal the victory of evil. The enemies of Jesus mocked this would-be Messiah hanging on a cross like a common criminal. God had come in the flesh to do battle with evil, but it appeared Satan had won. Or had he? The empty tomb turned the tables. What appeared to be total defeat was transformed into a glorious triumph. Jesus' resurrection is the divine testimony to his victory over the forces of evil (Eph. 1:19-22; Phil. 2:9-11; 1 Pet. 3:21-22; Rom. 8:37-39) and over death itself (2 Tim. 1:10). "God raised him up," Peter declared, "having freed him from death, because it was impossible for him to be held in its power" (Acts 2:24). The sting of death is gone, and by the resurrection of Jesus we now have assurance of victory over it (1 Cor. 15:55-56; 1 Cor. 6:14; 2 Cor. 4:14). Christ is victorious over the forces of evil, and that victory has its foundation in his substitutionary death and its proof in his glorious resurrection.

B. Our Great Hope

The meaning of Christ's resurrection cannot be limited to his own experience of vindication and victory. Because we are united with him as our representative head, his resurrection involves us. Paul speaks of Jesus' resurrection as "the first fruits of those who have fallen asleep" (1 Cor. 15:20). He was "the beginning and the firstborn from among the dead" (Col. 1:18; so also Rev. 1:5). Resurrection from the dead, an end-of-the-world event, has broken into the midst of the present age, and Jesus Christ is the first of those who are to follow (Acts 26:23). Though we must wait until the day of his glorious return, we can be assured that when he comes, we shall be like him (1 Cor. 15:23; Phil. 3:20-21; 1 John 3:2). The spoiled image of God in our fallenness will be restored when we are fully conformed to the image of Christ and are finally glorified in our resurrection bodies (Rom. 8:29; Phil. 3:20-21). And even creation itself, which has been "subjected to frustration . . . will be liberated from its bondage to decay and brought into the glorious freedom of the children of God" (Rom. 8:19-22). For this reason, the resurrection of Jesus is our great hope (cf. 1 Pet. 1:3-4).

But his resurrection also has a significant implication for the present. In union with Christ we are already raised with him and seated with him in the heavenly realms (Col. 3:1; Eph. 2:6). His righteousness before God is now ours—reckoned or imputed to us by virtue of our union with Christ (cf., e.g., Phil. 3:9).[31] We are already partakers of his new and risen life (Rom. 6:4; Eph. 2:5; 1 John 5:12), liberated from our captivity to sin (Rom. 6:6-7). And by the Holy Spirit we have, even now, tasted "the powers of the coming age" (Heb. 6:5). The power of the demonic world, whether experienced explicitly or more covertly, has been broken by Jesus' victory (Col. 2:15). He stands as Lord of all.

Christ's glorious resurrection has inaugurated that new age, and we now live in an interim period, experiencing something of its power while still awaiting its fulfillment when Christ returns. This "already" and "not yet" existence means that we have been saved in hope (Rom. 8:24).[32]

---

31 The English Reformer William Tyndale (d. 1536) used the relationship of marriage to illustrate this point: "For as a woman, though she be never so poor, yet when she is married, is as rich as her husband; even so we, when we repent and believe the promises of God in Christ, though we be never so poor sinners, yet are as rich as Christ; all his merits are ours, with all that he hath" (*Doctrinal Treatises*, 254).

32 These two must be held together, for denying either leads to a distorted understanding of our current situation. The New Testament speaks of our salvation in three tenses: we have been

IV. Conclusion: The Only Ground for Salvation

Who can stand before a holy God? Certainly not sinful human beings, corrupted by sin, alienated from God and under his wrath. We are helpless and hopeless apart from the grace of God. But we have a gospel message: "For what I received I passed on to you as of first importance: that Christ died for our sins according to the Scriptures, that he was buried, that he was raised on the third day according to the Scriptures" (1 Cor. 15:3-4). "By this gospel you are saved" (15:2).

In the cross and resurrection of Jesus Christ God has done for us what we could never have done for ourselves. He has accomplished his gracious purpose by entering into our world himself in the Person of his Son, fulfilling his own promise of blessing. He has joined our humanity to himself, so that in Christ the Judge could take the place of those who are judged. On the cross Jesus atoned for our sin, bearing its punishment in our stead. There was displayed all at once the fire of God's holiness, the darkness of our sin, and the depth of God's gracious love. There, in a mysterious way, God's wrath and mercy met, perfectly. And on the third day, when he raised Jesus from the grave, God vindicated his Son and brought victory over sin and death.

God need not have saved anyone; but in his holy love, having purposed from eternity to redeem a people for himself, he determined to save us through the work of his Son. Jesus prayed, "My Father, if it is possible, may this cup be taken from me" (Matt. 26:39). In the wisdom of God, it was not possible any other way. Christ's atoning death and victorious resurrection constitute the only ground for our salvation.

---

saved (Eph. 2:8), we are being saved (1 Cor. 1:18) and we will be saved (Rom. 5:9-10).

Evangelical Convictions

A THEOLOGICAL EXPOSITION OF THE STATEMENT OF FAITH
OF THE EVANGELICAL FREE CHURCH OF AMERICA

Article 6

THE HOLY SPIRIT

6. We believe that the Holy Spirit, in all that He does, glorifies the Lord Jesus Christ. He convicts the world of its guilt. He regenerates sinners, and in Him they are baptized into union with Christ and adopted as heirs in the family of God. He also indwells, illuminates, guides, equips and empowers believers for Christ-like living and service.

God's gospel is applied by the power of the Holy Spirit.

As we have seen, our Christian faith is anchored in history. Reflecting the Apostles' Creed, our Statement declares that Jesus was crucified "under Pontius Pilate" (Article 4). The mention of a first-century Roman governor may seem out of place in a broad statement of Christian truth, but it situates the gospel at a particular place in the chronicle of human events.

A Jewish baby named Jesus was born in a village called Bethlehem some 2000 years ago. This baby grew to be a man, who lived and taught in the regions of Galilee and Judea. He was crucified by the Romans on a real wooden cross, and he rose bodily from the grave—his tomb was actually empty. As Luke tells us, this took place during the reign of Roman Emperor Tiberius Caesar, when Pontius Pilate was governor of Judea, Herod was tetrarch of Galilee, Herod's brother Philip was tetrarch of Iturea and Traconitis, and Lysanias was tetrarch of Abilene, during the priesthood of Annas and Caiaphas (Luke 3:1-2). This is actual history.

In fact, the life, death and resurrection of Jesus is the *center* of history—the most important moment of all. But the question arises: How does all of this relate to us? How could something so far away in space and time affect our lives here and now?

This is far different from the kind of effect that, say, Alexander the Great had through the natural course of human events, for Christians claim that Jesus' death and resurrection accomplished God's saving purpose. Jesus Christ now brings new life to all who trust in him and leads them into an eternal relationship with God. How could what happened in the particularity of this one man in that one historical moment have a significance that transcends space and time?

Jesus himself anticipated that question in his final words with his disciples on the night before he died (see John 14-16). He was departing from them, and in one sense, he would no longer be with them. But he assured them that they would see him again (John 14:19), that he would continue to love them and that they would know that love (14:21). Furthermore, because he lived, they, too, would live (14:19). Those who love him will be loved by the Father, he said, and he and the Father will come to them and make their home with them (14:23). Jesus even said to them, "you are in me and I am in you" (14:20).

What is the nature of the relationship Jesus describes here? How can he be with his disciples even after his death, resurrection and ascension? The answer must be found in Jesus' words of promise: "I will ask the Father, and he will give you another Counselor to be with you forever—the Spirit of truth" (John 14:15-16). This Counselor, this Spirit of truth, is none other than the Holy Spirit (cf. 14:26).

Here Jesus is assuring his disciples that though he will be leaving them physically, he will be forever with them spiritually through the personal presence of the Holy Spirit. The Spirit, this other Counselor, unites us with Jesus the Son and so draws us into a personal relationship with God as our Father. In this way the barriers of space and time are overcome, and the life of the one man, Jesus, touches our lives today. God's gospel is applied by the power of the Holy Spirit.

I. Who Is the Holy Spirit?

The subject of the Holy Spirit has often been shrouded in mystery, and the old translation of the King James version of the Bible as Holy *Ghost* hardly helps.[1] Unlike God the Father or the Son, God the Spirit is hard to imagine in a personal way, and many conceive of the Spirit as some impersonal power at work in the world, not unlike gravity or electricity.

Certainly power is one of the primary characteristics associated with the Holy Spirit. Frequently, we read in the Old Testament of the Spirit of the Lord coming upon a person in power, enabling the fulfillment of some God-given task.[2] The Spirit was active in creation (Gen. 1:2), in the revelation of God's word to the prophets (Ezek. 2:2; cf. 8:3; 11:1,24), and in the empowering for craftsmanship and administration in Israel (Exod. 31:3-5; Zech. 4:6; Num. 11:25; Deut. 34:9). The Old Testament prophets also looked forward to a future age when the ministry of the Spirit would be more complete. That age would be led by one anointed by the Spirit (Isa. 11:1-5; 42:1-4; 61:1-3) who would usher in a new covenant in which the Spirit would be poured out on all God's people (Ezek. 36:25-27 [cf. Jer. 31:31-34]; Joel 2:28-32).

This emphasis on the power of the Holy Spirit continues in the New Testament. Jesus' conception in the womb of a virgin is attributed to the Spirit's power (Luke 1:35), and at his baptism by John, the Spirit visibly

---

1 To be fair, in its own time, this translation need not have caused confusion.

2 Cf., e.g., Judges 14:6,19; 15:14; 1 Sam. 10:10; 11:6; 16:13.

descended upon him, empowering him in his ministry (Luke 4:14; Acts 10:38). Jesus announced himself as one "anointed by the Spirit" (Luke 4:17-21, citing Isa. 61:1-2). It was "by the Spirit of God" that Jesus drove out demons (Matt. 12:28). In a final act, the Spirit's power raised him from the dead (Rom. 1:4).

Before his ascension to the Father, Jesus promised his disciples, "you will receive power when the Holy Spirit comes on you; and you will be my witnesses" (Acts 1:8). On the Day of Pentecost the Spirit did come in power, and the apostles performed many miraculous deeds. All believers were promised the Spirit's power at work within them (Eph. 3:16; Rom. 8:11; 15:13).

The Holy Spirit is powerful, but it is important to recognize that the Spirit is also personal. In his farewell discourse (John 14-16), Jesus refers to the Holy Spirit as the "Counselor." The Greek word *paraklētos* used here refers to one who comes alongside another to act on his behalf. However the word is translated, it refers to a person and not a thing, one providing personal services. A *paraklētos* helps, guides, advises, encourages.

The personhood of the Spirit is reinforced when Jesus speaks of giving his disciples "*another* Counselor" to be with them (John 14:16). As Alice observed at the Mad Hatter's Tea Party, you cannot be offered *more* tea unless you have drunk some already. So Jesus' promise implies that his disciples already had a Counselor, and the assumption is that Jesus himself is that Counselor.[3] The Spirit is as personal as Jesus, and the Holy Spirit was personal in Christian experience. Elsewhere in the New Testament, the Spirit acts in very personal ways: he can be grieved (Eph. 4:30), he acts with volition (1 Cor. 12:11) and he has affections (Acts 15:28). This Counselor, the Holy Spirit, is not an impersonal force but a person.[4]

In fact, the Holy Spirit is a *divine* Person. Several lines of evidence support this. First, references to the Holy Spirit are sometimes interchangeable with references to God. Most notably, in Acts 5:3-4, Peter accuses Ananias of lying to the Holy Spirit, and then, in repeating that

---

3 This assumption is confirmed by 1 John 2:1, which makes that identification explicit.

4 As additional support for the personal nature of the Spirit it is frequently argued that though the Greek word "spirit" (*pneuma*) is grammatically neuter in gender, in presenting Jesus' words in John 16 the Evangelist has used a masculine pronoun to refer to that term (John 16:13-14). However, it is also possible that the pronoun refers to the masculine noun *paraklētos* earlier in v. 7 (cf. also the use of the same pronoun in v. 8).

accusation, he says that Ananias has not lied to men but to God.[5] The Holy Spirit also possesses the attributes of God, such as omniscience (1 Cor. 2:10-11; cf. John 16:13) and eternality (Heb. 9:14), and he performs acts commonly ascribed to God, such as creation (Gen. 1:2) and resurrection (Rom. 8:11). Finally, the Holy Spirit is set alongside the Father and the Son in a way that assumes their equality (Matt. 28:19; 2 Cor. 13:14; 1 Cor. 12:4-6; 1 Pet. 1:2). He is fully God, one of the three Persons of the divine Trinity.[6]

Only this understanding of who the Holy Spirit is enables us to appreciate what he does.

II. What Does the Holy Spirit Do?
The Holy Spirit Glorifies the Lord Jesus Christ

On the night before his death as he prepared his disciples for his imminent departure, Jesus said, "Because I have said these things, you are filled with grief. But I tell you the truth: It is for your good that I am going away. Unless I go away, the Counselor will not come to you; but if I go, I will send him to you" (John 16:6-7). Jesus must go so that the Spirit may come.

This is not to suggest that it was impossible for Jesus and the Holy Spirit to be with the disciples at the same time—as is the case, say, with Clark Kent and Superman. The progression has to do with God's plan of salvation. Jesus' going away inaugurates a new stage in God's saving work.

That same progression is mentioned in John's Gospel. Jesus said, "If anyone is thirsty, let him come to me and drink. Whoever believes in me, as the Scripture has said, streams of living water will flow from within him." John then adds, "By this [Jesus] meant the Spirit, whom those who believed in him were later to receive. Up to that time the Spirit had not been given, since Jesus had not yet been glorified" (7:37-39). Jesus' "glorification" in John's understanding was Jesus' death, resurrection, and ascension to the Father (cf. John 12:16,23; 13:31; 17:1). That death, that glorification, that "going away," introduces a new era in salvation history. Jesus' atoning sacrifice on the cross in taking away our sins and his victorious resurrection from the dead make possible the coming of

---

5 Cf. also 1 Cor. 3:16-17 and 6:19-20 in which to be inhabited by the Holy Spirit is to be a temple of God.

6 On the relationship between the three Persons of the Trinity, see Article 1, n. 28.

the Holy Spirit in a new way in the lives of God's people.

Jesus promised his disciples that the coming Counselor, the Holy Spirit, would be with them forever: "You know him for he lives with you and will be in you" (John 14:17). He then speaks of that time after his departure when "you will realize that I am in my Father, and you are in me, and I am in you" (14:20). How will we be "in him" and he "in us"? By the Spirit. This is how these words were understood by John, for he writes in his first epistle, "We know that we live in him and he in us, because he has given us of his Spirit" (1 John 4:13). Paul reflects this understanding also when he writes, "I pray that out of his glorious riches [the Father] may strengthen you with power through his Spirit in your inner being, so that Christ may dwell in your hearts through faith" (Eph. 3:16-17). Christ dwells in us through the Spirit. The Spirit makes Christ personally present in our lives.[7]

We must be careful when we speak this way, for the Spirit is not just Jesus in another form. We maintain a real distinction between the Persons of the Son and the Holy Spirit, for to deny that would be to fall into the ancient heresy of modalism. The Father, the Son and the Holy Spirit are not simply different modes of God's being, like an actor playing different roles or putting on different masks. The triune God is really three distinct Persons in one God. The Spirit is *another* Counselor. But in a mysterious way, the Bible teaches that the Holy Spirit is a Person who somehow joins us to Christ, allowing us to "know Christ" (Phil. 3:8) and all his benefits. The Spirit bridges the gulf created by time and space and unites us here today to the living Savior who lived in Palestine so long ago.

For this reason, Jesus says, "It is for your good that I am going away" (John 16:7). During Jesus' earthly ministry, his presence was limited to those who came into physical contact with him, and he impacted them from the outside. But because he went to the Father and sent the Spirit to us, Jesus' presence can extend beyond that small circle of followers in Palestine and expand across the whole world, and it can penetrate into the depths of our souls.

The Spirit's role, then, is not to magnify himself, but to bring glory to Jesus Christ. "When the Counselor comes, whom I will send to you from the Father, the Spirit of truth who goes out from the Father, he will

---

7 On this, see especially Rom. 8:9-11 in which Paul uses "the Spirit of God," the "Spirit of Christ," "Christ" and "the Spirit of him who raised Jesus from the dead" interchangeably.

testify about me," Jesus said (John 15:26). "He will bring glory to me by taking from what is mine and making it known to you" (John 16:14).

Supremely, the Holy Spirit will bring glory to Jesus Christ by making his saving work effective in the lives of sinful people. God's gospel—his gracious purpose to redeem a people for himself—*originates* in the eternal plan of the Father, which addresses our deepest human need. This gospel is *accomplished* by the earthly work of the Son, and this gospel is *applied* by the power of the ministry of the Holy Spirit. The Spirit glorifies Christ, first, in *evangelism* by convicting sinners of the truth; second, in *conversion* by bringing about a spiritual birth in which we are joined to Christ and are adopted into God's family; and third, in *discipleship* by empowering believers to be transformed into Christ's likeness so that he might be the firstborn among many brothers.

A. The Holy Spirit Glorifies Christ in Evangelism

Jesus came to his people preaching, teaching and performing miracles, but he was ultimately rejected and delivered to the Romans to be crucified. After his resurrection, he called his followers to continue his mission to the world. But one might well ask, What chance of success could they possibly have? If their Messiah had been rejected, why should people believe them when they declared that he had actually died not as a sinner, but as a sacrifice for sin which God validated by raising him from the dead? If people didn't believe in Jesus when he walked among them in the flesh, why should they believe in him now, when he was nowhere to be seen?

But people did believe. In fact, in the first public preaching of the gospel, Peter spoke to the same crowd in Jerusalem who had once cried, "Crucify him!" and he proclaimed the very last thing they wanted to hear: "Therefore let all Israel be assured of this: God has made this Jesus, whom you crucified, both Lord and Christ" (Acts 2:36). One might have expected a mob to lynch Peter there on the spot, but Luke tells us, "When the people heard this, they were cut to the heart" (v. 37), and about 3,000 people responded that day (v. 41).

What could explain this reaction? Jesus had assured his disciples that they would receive power when the Holy Spirit came upon them to be his witnesses (Acts 1:8), and on the Day of Pentecost that Holy Spirit had come. The Spirit gave power to Peter's preaching, and hardened hearts became receptive to the message of the gospel.

The Holy Spirit Convicts the World of Its Guilt

We believe that, in glorifying the Lord Jesus Christ, the Holy Spirit convicts the world of its guilt. Peter's preaching as recorded in Acts and the subsequent history of the church testify to this work of the Spirit, but our conviction rests ultimately on the promise of Jesus himself. In preparing his disciples for his departure, he declared plainly: "I tell you the truth: It is for your good that I am going away. Unless I go away, the Counselor will not come to you; but if I go, I will send him to you. When he comes, he will convict the world of guilt with regard to sin and righteousness and judgment" (John 16:7-8).

The Greek word for "Counselor"—*paraklētos*—had legal associations in its secular usage. A *paraklētos* was someone who would come alongside you in a court of law. But here he appears not as a counselor for the defense but as a prosecutor seeking a guilty verdict. The "conviction" suggested by the word used here, however, refers to more than just the judge's decision. It also refers to the guilty defendant's perception of that verdict. The defendant is to *see* that he is guilty by having his sin exposed and in that exposure to *feel* ashamed. Jesus is promising that the Spirit will work in that way when we act as his witnesses in the world. "When he comes, he will convict the world of guilt in regard to sin and righteousness and judgment."

In the compact phrases that follow this promise (John 16:9-11), Jesus proclaims that the Spirit will impress a realization upon human hearts that to reject him through unbelief is an offence against God. The Spirit will shine as a light exposing a false righteousness and revealing the righteousness of the One who has now gone to the Father. And he will disclose the truth that the death of Jesus was actually a condemnation of the prince of this world,[8] as Jesus' resurrection declared. The Spirit will convict the world of its spiritual blindness as he confirms the truth about Jesus.

Sin, righteousness and judgment are unfashionable moral categories in our world today. Our world would rather speak of psychological disorders, cultural differences, or genetic determinations. It glories in self-expressive behavior, self-fulfillment, tolerance and diversity of all sorts, with disdain for moral authority and accountability. Talk of sin, righteousness and judgment is considered impolite and uncivil. But the Bible declares that we are sinful, unrighteous and under God's judgment,

---

8 For this connection with Jesus' death, see John 12:31-33.

and until we are convicted of that fact we will never turn to the One who alone can free us from the bondage which that guilt entails. But Jesus promises the power of the Holy Spirit to be at work as we declare the gospel, convicting the world of the truth. In this way, Christ is glorified, for he is revealed as our gracious Savior.

B. The Holy Spirit Glorifies Christ in Conversion

The Evangelical Free Church was born of a revival movement within the state churches of Scandinavia in the eighteenth and nineteenth centuries. During that period, though most people professed Christian faith, they often showed little evidence of spiritual life. The revival movements there, and later in America, gave our forebears a strong conviction that the message of the gospel must change the hearts of sinners by the regenerating work of the Holy Spirit. They put great stress on the words of Jesus to Nicodemus in John 3: "You must be born again." That truth is just as relevant today.

1. The Holy Spirit Regenerates Sinners

Christianity is often seen as a means of self-help, giving us God's instructions for our self-improvement and self-fulfillment. But Jesus' words to Nicodemus reject that view. In entering God's kingdom, self-help is useless, for in our fallen state we are helpless and even lifeless.[9] We need more than even God's *help*. We need God's life-giving power at work within us, something which can only be described as a "new birth."[10]

Nicodemus, as "the teacher of the Jews," ought to have known this (John 3:10). The prophets, particularly Jeremiah and Ezekiel, had declared that the people of God had been given God's law and had been the recipients of God's love, but it was to no avail. It did them no good because they did not have a heart for God. They followed "the stubbornness of their evil hearts," Jeremiah says repeatedly (cf., e.g., Jer. 3:17; 9:14 13:10). "The heart is deceitful above all things and beyond cure. Who can understand it?" (Jer. 17:9; cf. Jer. 18:11-12). They needed more than moral instruction; they needed spiritual power.

And that spiritual power is what the prophets promised.

---

9 Cf. Eph. 2:1,5. For further discussion, see Article 3, sec. III.A.

10 "Regeneration" is simply the Latin form of this expression.

> "The time is coming," declares the Lord,
> "when I will make a new covenant
> with the house of Israel
> and with the house of Judah. . . .
> I will put my law in their minds
> and write it on their hearts.
> I will be their God, and they will be my people."
>
> (Jer. 31:31-34)

The God of the old covenant, who came to rule *over* his people through his Old Testament law, would come in his Son Jesus to live *alongside* them, and then he would come by his Spirit to dwell *in their hearts*. "I will give them a heart to know me, that I am the LORD. They will be my people, and I will be their God, for they will return to me with all their heart" (Jer. 24:7).

Or as the prophet Ezekiel put it:

> I will sprinkle clean water on you, and you will be
> clean; I will cleanse you from all your impurities and
> from all your idols. I will give you a new heart and put
> a new spirit in you; I will remove from you your heart
> of stone and give you a heart of flesh. And I will put
> my Spirit in you and move you to follow my decrees
> and be careful to keep my laws.
>
> (Ezek. 36:25-27)

This is the promise of the new covenant—a covenant with the power to bring life. This work of the Holy Spirit in regenerating sinners, causing us to be born again spiritually, is what we mean by the word "conversion." Spiritual rebels are turned around and become worshippers of the living God (1 Thess. 1:9). This is essential for a right understanding of the gospel and its work in our lives.

Regeneration is always accompanied by faith, but the logical order of these two is the subject of some dispute. Some contend that we believe and then are born again, giving priority to human freedom and responsibility. They point to passages such as Acts 2:38 in which Peter urges his hearers to repent and be baptized with the result that they would receive the Holy Spirit. Others reverse faith and regeneration, emphasizing the preeminence of God's free grace in the process of salvation. They base this primarily on the way the Bible speaks of our human condition—we are blind to God's truth (Isa. 35:5; John 9:39; Rev. 3:17), deaf to his Word (Isa. 42:19; 43:8) and spiritually dead in our trespasses and sins (Eph. 2:1,5). They contend that the Spirit himself must first give us new life or we will never believe. This debate continues among us, and our Free Church Statement of Faith allows for either order.[11]

The Holy Spirit brings spiritual life by applying the work of Christ to us. He does that by uniting us to Christ.

2. In the Holy Spirit Sinners Are Baptized Into Union With Christ

How do the benefits of Jesus Christ flow into our lives? How can the spiritual achievement of the One affect the many? The Bible speaks of a spiritual union of Christian believers and Jesus Christ such that what is true of him becomes true of us.

Our union with Christ is captured in that simple prepositional phrase "in Christ," used by Paul in one form or another 164 times. Only as we are "in Christ" are we chosen, called, regenerated, justified, sanctified, redeemed, assured of the resurrection and given every spiritual blessing (Eph. 1:4,7; Rom. 6:5; 8:1; 2 Cor. 5:17; Eph. 1:3). This union with Christ spans space and time—so that Paul can say that the Christian *has died* with Christ (Rom. 6:1-11; Gal. 2:20); the Christian *has been resurrected* with Christ (Eph. 2:5-6; Col. 3:1-2), the Christian *has ascended* with Christ to share *now* in his reign in the heavenly places (Rom. 5:17; Eph. 2:6) and the Christian is destined to share Christ's coming glory with him (Phil. 3:20-21; 1 John 3:2).

No wonder some call our union with Christ one of the central messages of the New Testament. Theologian John Murray called it "the central truth of the whole doctrine of salvation."[12] A. W. Pink said, "The

---

11 The framers of our 1950 EFCA Statement of Faith wanted to create a statement that was consistent with both Arminian/Wesleyan and Calvinist views but which required or endorsed neither. That is the intention of this revised Statement also. Here in Article 6 we are only discussing the Spirit's work. Articles 7 and 10 refer to the attendant human response. Both regeneration (the Spirit's work) and faith (our response) are essential for salvation, and this Statement affirms both without giving logical priority to either. Interestingly, the (Swedish) Evangelical Free Church Ministerial Association (1947) spoke of the Holy Spirit's work to "regenerate the *unbelieving* sinner" (as recorded in A. T. Olson, *This We Believe* [Minneapolis: Free Church Publications, 1961], p.135), while the 1950 Statement of Faith of the EFCA spoke of the Spirit's work to "regenerate the *believing* sinner" (italics added). Here we speak simply of the Spirit regenerating *sinners*.

12 *Redemption: Accomplished and Applied* (Grand Rapids: Eerdmans, 1955), 161.

subject of spiritual union is the most important, the most profound, and yet the most blessed of any that is set forth in sacred Scripture."[13] Cambridge scholar B.F. Westcott wrote: "If once we realize what these words 'we are in Christ' mean, we shall know that beneath the surface of life lie depths which we cannot fathom, full alike of mystery and hope."[14]

The Bible provides a variety of images that help us gain some insight into this "profound mystery" (cf. Eph. 5:32). Jesus used a horticultural metaphor: "I am the vine, and you are the branches. If a man remains in me and I in him, he will bear much fruit; apart from me you can do nothing" (John 15:5). In this vital union with Christ we draw our nourishment, our strength, our spiritual life.

Another way that we can understand our relationship with Christ comes through the Hebrew conception of the solidarity between a king and his subjects. When David was anointed as king, we read that all the tribes of Israel came to him to pledge their loyalty, and they said, "We are your own flesh and blood" (2 Sam. 5:1). He became their leader, their representative before God. When King David sinned, as he did when he made a census of the people (2 Sam. 24:1-15), the whole nation suffered. But when he was victorious in battle, the whole nation prospered.

This notion of royal representation was then transferred to the solidarity of the Messiah with his people. When we turn in faith to Jesus as the Messiah, and submit ourselves to him as our King, we are joined to him—he represents us, and we become like his own body, his "flesh and blood."[15]

The Apostle Paul speaks of our relationship to Christ like that of our body's relationship to its head—"He is the head of the body, the church" (Col. 1:18; cf. 1 Cor. 12:12,27; Eph. 4:16). This reflected Paul's own experience on the Damascus road. As a zealous Pharisee, Paul was intending to arrest leaders of this heretical sect of Christians when suddenly, in a brilliant flash of light, he encountered the glorious risen Jesus, who asked, "Paul, why are you persecuting me?" (Acts 9:4). In that instant Paul was confronted with the truth that to persecute the church

---

13 Cited in Philip Ryken, "Justification and Union with Christ", http://www. thegospelcoalition.org/articles.php?a=75.

14 *St. Paul's Epistle to the Ephesians* (New York, 1906; repr. Grand Rapids: Eerdmans, 1952) 186; cited in Lewis B. Smedes, *Union with Christ: A Biblical View of the New Life in Jesus Christ* (Grand Rapids: Eerdmans, 1970), 58-59.

15 Cf. also Lam. 4:20— "The Lord's anointed, our very life breath...."

was to persecute Jesus. Through the presence of the Spirit within them, Christians are one with Christ, united as a body is united with its head.

Paul not only uses a biological image to picture our union with Christ, he also uses an image from the world of architecture—the picture of a building, more specifically, a holy temple. We are united with Christ like stones in a building built on the cornerstone of Jesus Christ. In him we become a holy temple to God—a place where God dwells (Eph. 2:18-22; cf. also 1 Pet. 2:4-5).

From bodies and buildings, Paul moves to the much more intimate and personal metaphor of marriage to picture our relationship with Christ. This is especially helpful, for marriage had been used already in the Old Testament to describe the covenant relationship between the Lord and his people Israel. More than that, the biblical description of marriage stresses the new union that is created by the marriage bond: "the two will become one flesh" (Gen. 2:24). The physical union of husband and wife becomes an expression of an inward union of love, and the new social unit that marriage creates pictures well our union with Christ (Eph. 5:32).

In a marriage the couple assumes a new identity, no longer as individuals but as a couple. Their happiness and their sorrows are joined to one another inextricably. Marriage also has legal aspects, and so it is in our relationship with Christ. When we are joined to him, he assumes the debt of our sin, taking it upon himself and bearing it away, and we share his righteousness. God sees us not as isolated individuals, but through the lens of our marriage relationship with Christ. In union with Christ we are presented as a beautiful bride in the sight of God.

Paul speaks of a body (with Christ as its head), a building (with Christ as its foundation), a marriage (with Christ as the groom), and in Romans 5 and 1 Corinthians 15 Paul develops one other picture of solidarity that sheds light on our relationship with Christ, cosmic in its scope and embracing all humanity—the picture of our union with Adam: "For just as through the disobedience of the one man (Adam), the many were made sinners, so also through the obedience of the one man (Jesus Christ), the many will be made righteous" (Rom. 5:19).

By nature all humanity has been united with Adam, such that his sin has impacted us all. We are all now subject to the curse of death that was placed upon him. Every one of us now shares something of his self-centered, sinful nature.[16] But Jesus Christ has come to undo what Adam has done. By his obedience, Christ creates a new humanity, a people redeemed by his death, who now follow him in their lives. And whereas we are joined to Adam by nature, through our physical birth, we must be joined to Christ by faith, through a second, spiritual birth. Humanity in Adam and the new humanity in Christ—this is the contrast, and the choice, Paul sets before us.

The mystical union of believers with Jesus Christ can be pictured in rather ordinary images—a vine and its branches, a king and his subject, a building, a body, and a marriage. Our relationship with Adam opens up a new dimension which embraces all humanity. But one final image takes us to the very nature of God himself. Jesus tells us that our relationship with himself is in some sense a reflection of his own relationship with his Father in heaven. We are united to Christ in a way that reflects the mysterious union of the divine Persons of the Trinity—the Father, the Son and the Holy Spirit.

In his great prayer in John 17, Jesus addressed the Father on behalf of his disciples. He prayed "that all of them may be one, Father, just as you are in me and I am in you. May they also be in us so that the world may believe that you have sent me. I have given them the glory that you gave me, that they may be one as we are one: I in them and you in me" (John 17:21-23). This is indeed a profound mystery!

It must be emphasized that our union with Christ does not mean that we somehow become God—that we are joined to the divine being in the sense that we are divinized by absorption into the Godhead such that Creator and the created are indistinguishable. It is a spiritual union that is the work of the Holy Spirit— "we were all baptized by [or "in"] one Spirit into one body" (1 Cor. 12:13).[17] In this "Spirit-baptism"[18] the Holy Spirit bridges the chasm of space and time. He takes what happened then—the life, death and resurrection of Jesus—and brings its saving power into our lives now, by uniting us in a spiritual way with Christ.

---

16 On this, see Article 3, sec. III.

17 We concede that the translation of this key text is uncertain—Is it "by" one Spirit (agent) or "in" one Spirit (location or substance) that we are baptized? But regardless of the exegesis of that one verse, this, in fact, is what the Spirit does in theological terms—he unites us to Christ in a "Spirit-baptism" that occurs at our conversion. We deny the classic Pentecostal teaching which insists upon a post-conversion baptism in the Spirit which is evidenced by speaking in tongues.

18 We discuss water baptism, which expresses this spiritual reality in a visible way, in Article 7.

By the Spirit, Christ lives in us, and we in him. By the Spirit, we are now joined to Christ as a vine and its branches, as a king and his subjects, as a body and its head, as a building and its foundation, as a husband with his bride, and as the new humanity in Christ Jesus. The Spirit himself unites us with Christ and so applies all his saving work to our lives. He draws us into the new creation Christ inaugurates (2 Cor. 5:17). "We know that we live in him and he in us, because he has given us of his Spirit" (1 John 4:13).[19] "To sum up," as John Calvin expounds this theme, "the Holy Spirit is the bond by which Christ effectively unites us to himself."[20]

3. In the Holy Spirit Sinners Are Adopted as Heirs in the Family of God

One of the central benefits of our union with Christ which we highlight in our Statement is our adoption as heirs in the family of God.[21] In our union with the Son of God we share in a new filial relationship with God as our Father.

Contrary to common conception, the Bible does not speak of God as the Father of all humanity.[22] In the Old Testament Israel is described as God's son, his firstborn (cf. Exod. 4:22-23; Jer. 31:9,20; Hos. 11:1), as is the representative of Israel, the king (cf. Pss. 2:6-7; 72:1; 2 Sam. 7:14).[23] In the New Testament, Jesus, the Son of God, becomes the means by which sinful human beings are brought into a new relationship with God as Father (cf. John 14:6; Matt. 11:27,29). Though Jesus' teaching is rich with the message of God's fatherly love and care, it is only to his disciples that Jesus speaks in this way.[24]

---

19 Cf. 1 Cor. 6:17,19; Rom. 8:9-11; 1 John 3:24.

20 *Institutes* 3.1.1.

21 Cf. J. I. Packer's assessment that adoption "is the *highest privilege that the gospel offers*: higher even than justification. . . . [justification] is the *primary* and *fundamental* blessing of the gospel . . . But this is not to say that justification is the *highest* blessing of the gospel. Adoption is higher, because of the richer relationship with God that it involves....Justification is a *forensic* idea, conceived in terms of *law*, and viewing God as *judge*....Adoption is a *family* idea, conceived in terms of *love*, and viewing God as *father*" (*Knowing God* [Downers Grove: InterVarsity, 1973], 186-187).

22 Acts 17:29 comes close to speaking this way ("we are God's offspring"), but the emphasis there is on our creation in God's image and not on his relationship with us as "Father."

23 The Israelites themselves are also described as God's children (cf. Deut. 14:1; 32:5,19-20; Isa. 1:2,4; 43:6; 45:11).

24 The distinctive prayer Jesus taught his disciples begins with this address: "Our Father" (Matt. 6:9).

Living as a child of God is not our natural condition; it is a supernatural gift. It is not a result of our birth, but of our new birth—the regenerating work of the Spirit. John describes it this way, speaking of Jesus: "Yet to all who received him, to those who believed in his name, he gave the right to become children of God—children born not of natural descent, nor of human decision or a husband's will, but born of God" (John 1:12-13). We are sons and daughters of God not by nature, but by grace, as we come into a relationship with Christ the Son by faith. Paul writes to the Galatian believers: "You are all sons of God through faith in Christ Jesus, for all of you who were baptized into Christ have clothed yourselves with Christ" (Gal. 3:26-27).

The Apostle speaks of this relationship as an adoption: "In love [God] predestined us to be adopted as his sons through Jesus Christ" (Eph. 1:5; cf. Gal. 4:6-7; Rom. 8:15). As such we enter into a new status, for as adopted children we have "the full rights of sons" (Gal. 4:5) and become heirs of all the promises of God: "Now if we are children, then we are heirs—heirs of God and co-heirs with Christ" (Rom. 8:17; cf. Gal. 3:29-4:7; Eph. 3:6; Titus 3:7). The Holy Spirit himself becomes the down payment of our inheritance, "a deposit, guaranteeing what is to come" (2 Cor. 1:22; 5:5; Eph. 1:14). He is the "first fruits" of that future harvest when we enter into the full possession of all we possess in Christ (Rom. 8:23).

But it is not just a new status that we receive in this spiritual adoption. We also enter into a new experience of God. By the Spirit's work within us, we can know the love of the Father personally. Paul writes: "For you did not receive a spirit that makes you a slave again to fear, but you received the Spirit of sonship. And by him we cry, 'Abba, Father.' The Spirit himself testifies with our spirit that we are God's children" (Rom. 8:15-16). The very expression Jesus used in his own prayer to the Father, "Abba, Father" (cf. Mark 14:36), is now ours. The Spirit helps us realize with greater clarity what it means to be God's son or daughter in Christ and leads us into a deeper response to God in that relationship. "How great is the love the Father has lavished on us, that we should be called children of God! And that is what we are!" (1 John 3:1).

C. The Holy Spirit Glorifies Christ in Discipleship

The Holy Spirit works powerfully to bring glory to Jesus Christ. He works powerfully in evangelism to convict the world of its guilt. He works powerfully in conversion to effect spiritual birth, uniting sinners to Christ so that they are adopted into God's family. And the Spirit works powerfully in the lives of believers in the process of discipleship, so that they might be conformed to the image of Christ.

1. The Holy Spirit Indwells Believers

Our Statement presents a variety of ways the Spirit works in the lives of believers in a list that is by no means exhaustive. We begin by affirming simply that the Holy Spirit indwells all believers, for Paul asserts that if a person does not have the indwelling Spirit, "he does not belong to Christ" (Rom. 8:9; cf. 1 Cor. 3:16; 6:19; 12:13; 2 Cor. 1:22; Gal. 4:6).[25] By the Spirit, Christ lives in us (cf. Rom. 8:9-10). This, as we've noted, is a mystery, but it is, as Paul states, full of "glorious riches," for "Christ in you" is our "hope of glory" (Col. 1:27). The Spirit is the power of the coming age (Heb. 6:4-5), a source of divine life, the animating force in Jesus' own resurrection glory. "And if the Spirit of him who raised Jesus from the dead is living in you, he who raised Christ from the dead will also give life to your mortal bodies through his Spirit, who lives in you" (Rom. 8:11). By the indwelling Spirit the believer enters into a new life, one that will come to fulfillment when Christ returns. In this sense, through the Holy Spirit, God has "set his seal of ownership on us, and put his Spirit in our hearts as a deposit, guaranteeing what is to come" (2 Cor. 1:22; cf. Eph. 1:13; 4:30).

This indwelling of the Spirit can be distinguished from the "filling" of the Spirit, for Paul can speak of the former as a fact true of all Christians and call for the latter in an ongoing command: "be filled with the Spirit" (Eph. 5:18). This suggests that this filling can occur repeatedly in a believer's life. Though the filling of the Spirit can occur as God sovereignly equips believers for particular circumstances (Luke 1:5-8,41,67; Acts 4:8; 7:55; cf. Matt. 10:19-20) or to fulfill certain tasks (Luke 1:15-17; Acts 9:17; cf. 22:12-15; 26:16-23), here Paul is referring to the filling of the Spirit that ought to be the norm for healthy Christians (Acts 6:3,5; Act 11:24; 13:52; cf. also Luke 4:1). The context of Paul's command (Eph. 5:18-21) suggests that the filling of the Spirit entails a growing submission to God resulting in a heart desiring to worship the Lord in thanksgiving and to love others in humble service. Paul describes the qualities of

---

25 Our Statement affirms that Spirit-baptism is a single, transformative work of God at conversion, while the indwelling of the Spirit is the ongoing presence of the Spirit in the believer's life.

character brought forth by the Spirit's work in the believer's life—love, joy, peace, patience, kindness, goodness, faithfulness, gentleness and self-control—as "the fruit of the Spirit" (Gal. 5:22-23).

2. The Holy Spirit Illuminates Believers

The indwelling Spirit is at work restoring the corrupted image of God in every believer. That work involves a transformation of our minds as we are enabled by the Spirit to understand and apply God's truth to our lives. The same Spirit who inspired the Scriptures[26] now illuminates us as we hear, read and study them. This is the primary means by which the Holy Spirit teaches the believer.

The illuminating work of the Holy Spirit has a crucial cognitive dimension. That is, it enables us to overcome the blinding effects of sin so that we might see the truth of God's Word to us. "The man without the Spirit does not accept the things that come from the Spirit of God, for they are foolishness to him, and he cannot understand them, because they are spiritually discerned" (1 Cor. 2:14). The Spirit takes away the veil covering our hearts, Paul says (2 Cor. 3:15-16). As believers we have received the Spirit "that we may understand what God has freely given us" (1 Cor. 2:12). By the Spirit, God himself testifies to the truth of what he has revealed, so that our knowledge has a divine warrant (1 John 2:20).[27]

But the Spirit not only impacts our minds, enabling us to understand the truth of God's word. He also moves our hearts so that we may see that truth as a glorious thing, full of grace, goodness and beauty, something to rejoice in and to embrace as a source of life and love. By the Spirit, God shines his light in our hearts "to give us the light of the knowledge of the glory of God in the face of Christ" (2 Cor. 4:6). For that reason, the Apostle prays for the Spirit's work in the lives of believers so that "the eyes of your heart may be enlightened in order that you may know the hope to which he has called you, the riches of his glorious inheritance in the saints" (Eph. 1:18) and that "you, being rooted and established in love, may have power, together with all the saints, to grasp how wide and long and high and deep is the love of Christ" (Eph. 3:17-18). By the

---

26 Cf. Paul's words in Acts 28:25: "The Holy Spirit spoke the truth to your forefathers when he said through Isaiah the prophet...." (also, Acts 1:16; 4:25; Heb. 3:7; 10:15; 2 Pet. 1:21).

27 Through this inward testimony of the Spirit the Christian need not rely on evidence or argument as the basis for his or her knowledge of the things of God. This truth is, according to John Calvin, in effect "self-authenticating" (*Institutes*, 1.7.5).

Spirit's illumination, God's glorious truth is experienced and applied personally—we taste the Lord's goodness and love. That truth becomes knowledge sealed upon our hearts as well as revealed to our minds.

For this reason, our study of Scripture can never be a mere academic exercise. It must be accompanied by meditation and prayer with a humble and submissive heart eager to receive what God reveals.[28] The Spirit's illumination turns what seems to us mere words of men into a living word from God.[29]

3. The Holy Spirit Guides Believers

As our Counselor, the Holy Spirit also guides the believer. First, the Bible speaks of the Spirit guiding us *morally*, as "being led by the Spirit" is contrasted with "living according to the sinful nature" (Rom. 8:12-14; Gal. 5:16-18). "Live by the Spirit," Paul says, "and you will not gratify the desires of the sinful nature" (Gal. 5:16). Instead, you will bring forth the "fruit of the Spirit" (Gal. 5:22-23). The Spirit guides us into the purity and holiness of Christ.

The Bible also describes the Spirit guiding believers *practically*. Jesus himself was "led by the Spirit into the desert to be tempted by the devil" (Matt. 4:1; Luke 4:1). The Spirit told Philip, "Go to that chariot and stay near it" (Acts 8:29). While the disciples were worshiping the Lord and fasting in Antioch, the Holy Spirit said, "Set apart for me Barnabas and Saul for the work to which I have called them" (Acts 13:2; cf. Acts 15:28). And Paul declared that he was "compelled by the Spirit" to go to Jerusalem, knowing the danger that awaited him there (Acts 20:22-23; cf. 11:12; 13:4). The Spirit can guide us in practical ways by a mysterious inward prompting, which is spiritually discerned, or, more commonly, by simply leading us into godly wisdom through an understanding of the Word of God (cf. Eph. 1:17; 6:17).

4. The Holy Spirit Equips Believers

The critical work of the Spirit in uniting believers in the new community of the church will be discussed in the following chapter, but here we briefly mention the Spirit's role in equipping believers for

---

28 We also affirm the Spirit's work in the lives of other believers so that we understand Scripture with the help of the corporate body of the church.

29 To be clear, as Article 2 affirms, we believe the Bible to be the Word of God whether it is perceived to be such or not.

their service in that community. He does that through the distribution of spiritual gifts.

Paul begins 1 Corinthians 12 with the words, "Now about spiritual gifts," with the assumption that his readers knew what he was talking about. Unfortunately, the Apostle never defines the term, and we are left to understand it by its use. In five different lists (1 Cor. 12:8-11; 1 Cor. 12:28; Rom. 12:6-8; Eph. 4:11; 1 Peter 4:11) some twenty distinctive gifts are referred to in the New Testament (some refer to capacities, others to offices or people). No single gift occurs in all five lists, and thirteen occur in only one of the five lists, so it is likely that these are not exhaustive in scope.

The purpose of these gifts is the edification of the church (cf. 1 Cor. 12:7; 14:26; Eph. 4:12; 1 Pet. 4:10). The Spirit equips every believer (1 Cor. 12:11; 1 Pet. 4:10; Eph. 4:7) so that in some way he or she may serve in the body of Christ. The gifts are diverse—several relate to speaking (prophecy, teaching, exhorting), others refer to practical help (service, mercy, administration). They are distributed to each as God chooses (Heb. 2:4; Rom. 12:6), yet each gift is important and useful, just as the various parts of a body work together as a whole (1 Cor. 12:12-27). It is important to distinguish spiritual "gifts" from spiritual "graces" (or virtues)—that is, the marks of godly character. As the experience of the Corinthian church illustrates all too well, these two do not necessarily coincide. Without love, all gifts are of no ultimate value (1 Cor. 13:1-3).

A recent resurgence of interest in so-called "miraculous gifts" (e.g., the gift of tongues, the gift of healing, and the gift of prophecy) has led to much debate and considerable dissension in Evangelical circles. Our Statement of Faith does not take a position on whether such gifts are still operative in the church today, but we affirm that no spiritual gift serves as a sign either of the fullness of the Spirit or of the spiritual maturity of the believer.[30] Further, as our Article 2 affirms, the Scriptures remain our authority on all matters of faith and practice—any exercise of gifts must be done under the direction of the Word of God[31] and all our experience must be understood in the light of the teaching of that Word.

---

30 Again, we deny the classic Pentecostal teaching which insists upon a post-conversion baptism in the Spirit which is evidenced by speaking in tongues.

31 Cf., e.g., Paul's instructions regarding the gift of tongues in the context of the gathered assembly of the church in 1 Cor. 14:26-29.

5. The Holy Spirit Empowers Believers for Christ-Like Living and Service

Both the gift of the Holy Spirit and his gifts are presented in the New Testament as signs of Christ's victory, the fruits of the triumph of his life, death and resurrection (John 7:39; Acts 2:32-33; Eph. 4:8-10). By the Spirit, that victory is made effective as Jesus himself is made known in the world and people turn to him in repentance and faith. The Spirit convicts the world of its sin, regenerates sinners and unites them to Christ, and empowers believers to become conformed to the image of Christ.

The work of the Holy Spirit in the heart of the believer is perhaps the most distinctively new feature of the New Covenant. Instead of simply addressing his people from the outside through his law, God now works powerfully by the Spirit to change the heart: "I will give you a new heart and put a new spirit in you; I will remove from you your heart of stone and give you a heart of flesh. And I will put my Spirit in you and move you to follow my decrees and be careful to keep my laws" (Ezek. 36:26-27). In exalting the ministry of this new covenant that has now come in Christ, Paul declares that we "are being transformed into his likeness with ever-increasing glory, which comes from the Lord, who is the Spirit" (2 Cor. 3:18). In Christ, Paul declares, God has "condemned sin in sinful man in order that the righteous requirements of the law might be fully met in us, who do not live according to the sinful nature but according to the Spirit" (Rom. 8:4).

"He will bring glory to me"—that is how Jesus characterizes the work of this coming Counselor, the Holy Spirit (John 16:14). J. I. Packer describes it as the Spirit's "floodlight ministry." Like the floodlights that illuminate the Washington Monument at night, displaying its beauty in the best possible way, so the Spirit throws his light on Jesus, allowing us to see his glory, to hear his word, to go to him and receive life, and to taste his gift of joy and peace.[32] He applies the redeeming work of Christ to our lives by uniting us to our Savior, and, by dwelling within us as the down payment of our future inheritance, he begins our transformation into conformity with the image of Christ.

---

32 J. I. Packer, *Keep in Step with the Spirit: Finding Fullness in Our Walk with God,* 2nd ed. (Grand Rapids: Baker Books, 2005), 57.

Evangelical Convictions

A Theological Exposition of the Statement of Faith
of the Evangelical Free Church of America

Article 7

THE CHURCH

7. We believe that the true church comprises all who have been justified by God's grace through faith alone in Christ alone. They are united by the Holy Spirit in the body of Christ, of which He is the Head. The true church is manifest in local churches, whose membership should be composed only of believers. The Lord Jesus mandated two ordinances, baptism and the Lord's Supper, which visibly and tangibly express the gospel. Though they are not the means of salvation, when celebrated by the church in genuine faith, these ordinances confirm and nourish the believer.

God's gospel is now embodied in the new community called the church.

Sociologists have observed an interesting trend in America in recent years—the growing number of "unchurched believers." It used to be considered natural that if you claimed to be a Christian, you would be a part of a church. In fact, for most of Christian history it was believed that membership in a church was an essential part of Christian life. Already in the mid third century, the church father Cyprian declared "There is no salvation outside the church."[1] The "unchurched" were assumed to be "unbelievers."

But no more. More and more people who express some allegiance to Jesus view the church as simply an optional extra, a mere helpful tool, or perhaps even a detriment to spiritual life. In one poll, when asked, "Do you think that a person can be a good Christian if he or she doesn't attend church?", 88% of those who *don't* attend church said yes, but so did 70% of those who *do*.

A number of reasons may account for this shift in opinion. Americans are independent by nature; increasingly they separate spirituality from real life in the world; and, because of well-publicized scandals, many have grown cynical about "organized religion." But this "believing without belonging," this "faith without fellowship," bears little resemblance to what we see displayed in the pages of the New Testament. More than that, it reflects a fundamental misunderstanding of the gospel message itself.

From the beginning, when God declared that it was not good for man to be alone (Gen. 2:18), the divine design for human life included social relationships—a community that in some way reflected the community of love found within the Trinity.[2] Sin ruptured the relationship not only of man with God, but also between human beings. The image of God in the world was defaced.

But God in his grace has purposed to restore his fallen creation and to redeem a people for himself. In Jesus Christ God has acted to rescue sinful human beings from his wrath and to reconcile them to himself. This work of Christ in his cross and resurrection is now applied to us

---

1 Though in context Cyprian was specifically addressing the issue not of the unchurched but of heretical schismatics, the basic point still stands.

2 See Article 1, sec. I.F.

by the Holy Spirit, who unites us with Christ so that what is true of him becomes true of us. And in uniting us with Christ, the Spirit also creates a new community we call the church. The church, as those saved by God's grace and united with Christ by God's Spirit, becomes the embodiment of the gospel in the world.

God's gospel creates the church. We can say this, first, on the basis of what happened *historically*. When Jesus began his public ministry, he chose twelve disciples to accompany him as the nucleus of a new community (cf. Matt. 4:18-22).[3] When Peter first declared that Jesus was the Christ, the Son of the living God, Jesus commended him and then announced the consequence of this confession: "you are Peter, and on this rock I will build my church" (Matt. 16:18).[4] Jesus easily moved from Peter's Spirit-inspired recognition of who he was to the promise of the building of a new community. The two go together.

On the Day of Pentecost, Peter preached to the crowds in Jerusalem and 3,000 people responded in repentance and faith and were baptized that day. They did not go home to become followers of Jesus privately and independently, but "They devoted themselves to the apostles' teaching and to the fellowship, to the breaking of bread and to prayer. . . . And the Lord added to their number daily those who were being saved" (Acts 2:42,47). Saving faith entails a new community.

The account of the ministry of Paul in Acts (and the witness of his letters) reinforces this connection. During his first missionary journey, Paul and Barnabas went back to each of the cities in which they had preached, "strengthening the disciples and encouraging them to remain true to the faith" (Acts 14:22), and they "appointed elders for them in each church" (Acts 14:23). In his ministry of the gospel, Paul did not just make converts, he integrated those converts into new communities he called churches.[5] From the beginning, God's gospel created a new social solidarity (cf. Gal. 3:28).

---

3 The number twelve suggests a parallel to the community of Israel with its twelve tribes.

4 The referent of the "rock" metaphor has been the subject of much discussion with at least four views presented: 1) Peter is the rock; 2) Peter's confession is the rock; 3) all the disciples constitute the rock; 4) Christ himself is the rock. None of these provide a basis for the later Roman Catholic doctrine of the papacy based on Peter's supremacy.

5 This church planting strategy was important in the early days of the Free Church in Scandinavia. For example, Fredrik Franson (1852-1908), an influential Free Church revivalist preacher akin to D. L. Moody and founder of The Evangelical Alliance Mission, believed that evangelism led to conversions which led to new churches. Under the Headship of Jesus Christ, he also affirmed the autonomy of the local church.

The new community created by the gospel is evident historically, but it is also grounded theologically, and as such, contributes to a discussion of the nature of the church.

I. The Nature of the Church

The Greek term *ekklēsia* translated as "church" simply means "an assembly,"[6] but in the New Testament it is used with a particular theological meaning in two senses. It is important to distinguish between the two, but, as we shall see, they must not be separated.

A. The True Church

First, the Bible speaks of the church as the totality of all those united with Christ by faith, resulting in a new standing before God and a new relationship with one another.[7] In this sense, Paul can say that "Christ loved the church and gave himself up for her" (Eph. 5:25) and that Christ is the Savior of "the church" (Eph. 5:23; cf. also 1:22-23). We refer to this as the "true" church, for it is a community ultimately known only to God, for only God can know the depths of the human heart. Only he can perceive with absolute certainty whether the faith that is professed is truly believed.[8] We may consider the composition of the true church from two perspectives.

1. The True Church Comprises All Who Have Been Justified by God's Grace Through Faith Alone in Christ Alone

The doctrine of justification by faith alone is central to our understanding of the gospel. Martin Luther, who did so much to revive the church's understanding in this area, regarded it as "the article on

---

6 The English word "church" derives from the Greek word *kuriakon*, which means "pertaining to or belonging to the Lord." This word was used of church buildings and developed into the English term which also referred to the community of people which met in those buildings.

7 The relationship between the church and Israel is a subject of some disagreement within the Free Church, and this Statement of Faith does not define the nature of that relationship. All sides agree that as we move from the Old Testament to the New there are elements of continuity and of discontinuity between them. The main difference between the various positions lies in the degree of each. All also agree that ultimately there is only one people of God, symbolized by Paul as one olive tree (Rom. 11:17-24).

8 Cf. 2 Tim. 2:19— "The Lord knows those who are his."

which the church stands or falls,"[9] and John Calvin said it was "the main hinge on which religion turns."[10] At the core of the gospel is the good news that God has acted in Jesus Christ to rescue lost sinners from a condition of divine condemnation and wrath into a new relationship of favor with himself. Where once there was enmity and alienation, now there is peace. Justification is the act of God by which he brings about this new state of affairs. As Paul writes, "Therefore, since we have been justified through faith, we have peace with God through our Lord Jesus Christ" (Rom. 5:1).

Justification is a term that comes from the law court. It is a judicial acquittal of the innocent, contrasted with a conviction of the guilty (cf. Deut. 25:1; Prov. 17:15). Justification does not *make* a person righteous; it simply declares a person to be so. So when a judge renders a verdict of "not guilty," the defendant is "justified." But how then can God justify the wicked, as Paul says that he does (cf. Rom. 4:5)? Wouldn't that make God himself an unjust judge?

This is precisely the issue the Apostle deals with in the first four chapters of his letter to the Romans. From 1:18-3:20 Paul argues that sin is universal. Everyone knows about God, whether it be through the external evidence of creation, through the internal evidence of one's own conscience, or from God's revelation through his law. Yet each of us, in our own way, has turned away from him, refusing to allow him to be God in our lives. Consequently, we are all without excuse before him—we are all, Jew and Gentile alike, guilty of moral failure. Every mouth will be silenced before the judgment of God (Rom. 3:19).

Then in Romans 3:21-25 Paul sets forth a wonderful truth in what Luther called, "The chief point, and the very central place of the Epistle, and of the whole Bible":

> But now, a righteousness from God apart from the
> law, has been made known, to which the Law and
> Prophets testify. This righteousness from God comes

---

9 This phrase reflects Luther's thought even if the phrase itself was not used until the seventeenth century (cf. Alistair E. McGrath, *Justitia Dei: A History of the Christian Doctrine of Justification. Vol. 2: From 1500 to the Present Day* [Cambridge: University Press, 1986], 193, n. 3). In Luther's lecture on Psalm 130:4 (1532/33), in speaking about the doctrine of justification, he did say, "this verse is the sum of Christian doctrine . . . ; for when this article stands, also the church stands; when this article falls, the church falls so" (cited in Bernhard Lohse, *Martin Luther's Theology: Its Historical and Systematic Development*, trans. Roy A. Harrisville (Minneapolis: Fortress Press, 1999), 258, n. 1).

10 *Institutes* III.11.1.

through faith in Jesus Christ to all who believe. There
is no difference, for all have sinned and fall short
of the glory of God, and are justified freely by his
grace through the redemption that came by Christ
Jesus. God presented him as a sacrifice of atonement,
through faith in his blood. He did this to demonstrate
his justice, because in his forbearance he had left the
sins committed beforehand unpunished—he did it to
demonstrate his justice at the present time, so as to be
just and the one who justifies those who have faith in
Jesus.

(Romans 3:21-25)

Paul is insistent that God is righteous in justifying sinners, both Jewish
and Gentile. His case rests on three factors, reflecting the hallmarks of
the rediscovery of the gospel at the time of the Reformation.

First, the *source* of our justification is found in God and his grace.
This justification comes to sinners "freely by his grace" (Rom. 3:24). In
ourselves, on the basis of our own merits, no one could be in the right
with God, for all have sinned (Rom. 3:23), and the wages of sin is death
(Rom. 6:23).[11] If we are to be justified at all, it must be by God's grace
alone.

Second, Paul insists that we are justified freely by his grace "through
the redemption that came by Christ Jesus" (Rom. 3:24). That is, the
ground of our justification is not in ourselves, but in Jesus Christ. "God
presented him as a sacrifice of atonement" (Rom. 3:25), a propitiatory
sacrifice.

God is just; he is the righteous judge who maintains the moral order
of his creation. Yet in his grace he is also the justifier. In his love he acts
righteously to save unrighteous sinners. He forgives them by acquitting
them of their moral offenses, and God's justice and his justifying grace
are held together (Rom. 3:25) by the atoning sacrifice of God's own Son,
Jesus Christ. Jesus, as the God-man, acts as our righteous substitute,
bearing our sin and the death that it deserves. In Christ, God the Judge,
who is himself the offended party, bears his own judgment, propitiating

---

11 On the depth of our sin and our utter inability to save ourselves, see our discussion of
the human condition in Article 3, sec. III.

his own wrath.[12] We are justified solely by God's grace because that saving work of God comes through Christ alone and not on the basis of our own deeds.

But how can *Christ's* death on a cross result in *our* justification? How does Christ's sacrifice apply to us personally? If the source of our justification is God's grace alone and its ground is Christ alone, then the *instrument* of justification must be faith alone. Three times in this passage Paul affirms it— "This righteousness from God comes through faith in Jesus Christ to all who believe"[13] (Rom. 3:22; also vv. 25,26). Faith is not our contribution to the saving work of God, it is simply the means of receiving it. Faith is not a meritorious work; it is the beggar's empty hand. And our faith itself is only possible through the grace of God, leaving us with no grounds to boast before God (John 6:65; cf. also Eph. 2:8-9). For that reason, faith and grace are complementary (cf. Rom. 4:16), for our faith rests on the righteousness of another.

Faith receives God's salvation, for faith, on our part, is what joins us to Christ.[14] That union is not a reward of our faith, but simply a consequence of it. Jonathan Edwards uses the illustration of marriage to make this point:

> As when a man offers himself to a woman in marriage, he does not give himself to her as a reward of her receiving him in marriage. Her receiving him is not considered as a worthy deed in her for which he rewards her by giving himself to her; but it is by her receiving him that the union is made, by which she hath him for her husband. It is on her part the union itself.[15]

---

12 For more on this atoning work of Christ, see our discussion of Article 5.

13 The English words "faith," "trust" and "belief" (or "believe") all translate a single Greek word in its noun or verb form, *pistis* or *pisteuō*. On the nature of faith, see further in Article 10, sec. I.C.

14 Some theologians have helpfully said, "Faith justifies not because of itself, insofar as it is a quality in man, but on account of Christ, of whom faith lays hold."

15 Jonathan Edwards [1734], "Justification by Faith Alone" in *Sermons and Discourses, 1734-1738,* ed. M. X. Lesser, *The Works of Jonathan Edwards,* vol. 19, (New Haven: Yale University Press, 2001), 201.

So by faith, and faith alone,[16] we are joined to Christ such that he bears our sin and we receive his righteousness (cf. 2 Cor. 5:21; Phil. 3:9).[17] This is no legal fiction, for by virtue of this union with Christ, God actually constitutes a new legal status. God can justify the ungodly, for though they are ungodly in themselves, they are now righteous by virtue of their union with Christ (cf. Rom. 5:19). His righteousness is imputed, it is credited or reckoned, to us.[18] In justifying us, God declares to be what he, in his grace, has established. When Jesus died on a Roman cross, the judgment of the Last Day was brought back into the midst of history, and in our union with Christ by faith the final verdict is anticipated. In Christ our sins were condemned, our punishment was borne, we receive his righteousness, and by God's grace we are now justified in his sight.

Justification is a judicial act recognizing that we have been put in the right with God. But this legal expression has an important communal component. Our justification by God means that we are members in good standing of the company of God's covenant people. In that sense justification is integral to our understanding of the church, and we affirm that all who are justified by God's grace through faith alone in Christ alone are members of the true church.

2. The True Church Comprises Those United by the Spirit into the Body of Christ of Which He Is the Head

In our consideration of the work of the Holy Spirit in Article 6 (sec. II.B.2), we have already seen how in the Spirit we are baptized into union with Christ. There our focus was on the new relationship with Christ which this union creates. But our "vertical" union with Christ also has important "horizontal" implications. We each come alone to God, but in coming to God we do not remain alone—we are simultaneously constituted into the corporate body of believers. Thus, if in union with Christ, God becomes our Father, then all other believers similarly united to Christ become our brothers and sisters. And if, by virtue of our union

---

16 James 2:24 appears to deny that one is saved by "faith alone," but the type of faith referred to there appears to be mere intellectual assent without real spiritual life. It is a "dead faith" that bears no fruit (cf. 2:14-26). On the evidence of faith in its fruits, see Article 8.

17 For further discussion of the nature of saving faith, see Article 10, sec. I.C.

18 An Old Testament image of this notion of imputation is that of being clothed with God's righteousness. Cf. Isa. 61:10— "I delight greatly in the LORD; my soul rejoices in my God. For he has clothed me with garments of salvation and arrayed me in a robe of righteousness, as a bridegroom adorns his head like a priest, and as a bride adorns herself with her jewels."

with Christ, we are a part of his body, then we are fellow members of that body with every other person who is also in communion with Christ (cf. 1 Cor. 10:16-17; 12:27). Therefore, we affirm that the true church comprises all those united by the Spirit into the body of Christ.

This distinctively Pauline metaphor of the body is used by the Apostle to emphasize both the unity and diversity that exists among Christians (Rom. 12:5; 1 Cor. 12:12). Through our Spirit-created union into one body, social distinctions (and even the distinction between Jew and Gentile) no longer divide us (1 Cor. 12:13). But that same Spirit also distributes various gifts, creating a diverse community with a wide variety of roles (1 Cor. 12:4-31). Each is to serve the other in a community of love. The church is united under the authority of Christ as its Head (Eph. 1:22-23; 4:14-15; 5:23; Col. 1:18, 24), from whom "the whole body, joined and held together by every supporting ligament, grows and builds itself up in love, as each part does its work" (Eph. 4:14-15).

This is a wonderful body, a body full of variety, with people of all sorts, differing in their interests and skills and gifts, but each playing a vital part in the well-being of the whole. Just as with our physical bodies, each member is important and should be valued by all, and each should be guided by the Head, who is Christ himself.

But already we have begun to move from a discussion of the true church, universal in scope and encompassing all true believers of all time, to the real-life community of people interacting in relationships found in what we call the local church. So we now consider the second sense in which we understand the word "church."

B. The Local Church

1. A Visible Community Manifesting the True Church in the World

One can speak of the church as a body known only to God, for in an ultimate sense only God knows those who are truly his. But generally in the New Testament, the church refers to a community visible in the world. And though the term can refer to the community of Christians within a large geographical area,[19] it more commonly denotes a local gathering of

---

19 One instance of such use can be found in Acts 9:31— "the church throughout Judea, Galilee and Samaria." For the more common use, cf. 1 Cor. 16:19— "The churches in the province of Asia" (also 1 Cor. 16:1).

believers in one place.[20] Here in this local network of relationships the gospel is embodied in the world and worked out in our lives.

This community of Christians in the local church is a microcosm of the universal church. In that sense, the local body is not simply a part of the whole, but a manifestation of the whole, encapsulating in itself its essential qualities as a community of believers redeemed by the blood of Christ. Paul can speak both of all Christians constituting the body of Christ (Eph. 1:22-23) and of a local community as that same body (1 Cor. 12:27).[21] In each local church Christ is present (Matt. 18:20), and in the love displayed in its midst (cf. John 13:35; 17:20-22) and in the quality of the lives of its members living in the world (cf. Matt. 5:16; 1 Pet. 2:9-12), each local church is to demonstrate to the world something of the truth and beauty of the gospel of Christ.

2. Local Church Membership Should be Composed Only of Believers

Because the local church is to manifest the true church in the world, the essential requirement for membership in each should be the same—a saving faith in the Lord Jesus Christ.[22] Therefore, we affirm that membership in the local church should be composed only of believers, regenerated by the Holy Spirit.

---

20 So, for example, "Aquila and Priscilla greet you warmly in the Lord, and so does the church that meets at their house" (1 Cor. 16:19), or "when you come together as a church" (1 Cor. 11:18).

21 This understanding of the nature of the church, among other things, is used to support the notion of local church autonomy and congregational church government. The Articles of Incorporation of the Evangelical Free Church of America mandate that the EFCA "shall be an association and fellowship of autonomous but interdependent congregations of like faith and congregational government" (II.A). Our polity, however, is not a part of our Statement of Faith (note the distinction in the Articles of Incorporation made between "like faith and congregational government"). We recognize that true, Bible-believing Christians through the centuries have differed on the way the church should be governed. Congregationalism is not considered an essential feature of our faith but simply the way we think best accounts for the teaching of the Bible. By excluding our polity from our Statement of Faith we allow those who agree to live under our congregational polity to join with us as full members even though they may come to us from churches with other forms of government and may believe that the Bible supports those forms as well. For further discussion of congregational church government in the EFCA, see Appendix 2.

22 Because the local church is a community of believers who covenant together, agreeing to live as a community in certain ways (often expressed in church constitutions and bylaws), a class for prospective members discussing the particular organization and expectations of a local church is also a reasonable requirement for membership. On the relationship of church membership to baptism, see n. 52 below.

This element of our Statement reflects a strong feature of our Free Church heritage. Coming out of state churches in Scandinavia that incorporated into their membership all who had been baptized, irrespective of their personal commitment to Christ, the early Free Church believers formed congregations of those who explicitly gave testimony to and showed evidence of personal conversion.

In saying that local church membership "should" (rather than "must") be composed only of believers, we are simply recognizing that we do not have infallible knowledge of who is actually a member of the true church. We can only make a judgment on the basis of a credible profession of faith. Membership in the local church is a corporate affirmation of a person's profession, but we must not give the false impression, leading to a false assurance, that such an affirmation is unerring. Jesus has warned us that some who appear to be sheep are really wolves in disguise (Acts 20:29-30), that the profession of some will prove false (Matt. 7:21-23) and that some will be surprised by the verdict on the Last Day (Matt. 25:31-46).

In making a judgment about whether a person is a member of the true church, we cannot demand what is impossible to accomplish. However, we strongly affirm here that the local church is to be a fellowship of believers. The local church ought to be composed of those who have personally embraced the gospel of Jesus Christ in faith and have been brought into his body by the regenerating work of the Holy Spirit, and local church membership ought to reflect that.

II. The Ordinances of the Church

The gospel creates the church. In their efforts to reshape the church that emerged from the Middle Ages, the Evangelical Reformers[23] of the sixteenth century affirmed this principle by insisting that an essential mark of a church must be a true proclamation of the gospel. But the church is to be a visible community, and so they also declared that a further identifying mark of the church was the proper administration

---

23 The Reformers preferred for themselves the term "Evangelical" over the term "Protestant," for their emphasis was first on reclaiming the gospel (the *evangel*) more than on simply protesting the practices of the Roman Catholic Church. The work of these Reformers is critical to our Evangelical history and identity.

of the ordinances (or sacraments[24]).[25] These ordinances, baptism and the Lord's Supper,[26] help to define who are part of the church as they visibly and tangibly express the gospel. We will discuss the nature of the ordinances, considering their source and purpose, before describing each more specifically.

A. The Nature of the Ordinances

1. Their Source: The Ordinances Are Mandated by the Lord Jesus

The description of the practices of baptism and the Lord's Supper as "ordinances" reflects their source—they come to us by way of an authoritative order, a mandate, from the Lord Jesus himself. Jesus' Great Commission found in Matthew's Gospel mandates that in making disciples we are to baptize in the name of the Father, the Son and the Holy Spirit (Matt. 28:19). The Book of Acts records how baptism was a practice of the church from the Day of Pentecost (Acts 2:38-41).[27]

The church's practice of the Lord's Supper began with the disciples' last meal with Jesus on the night before his death. When he shared the Passover meal with them, he gave them bread and wine and said, "Do this in remembrance of me" (Luke 22:19). The early Christians took this to be a command with abiding significance, extending beyond that night to include all believers in the ongoing life of the church. When Paul instructs the church in Corinth regarding their conduct when they gathered to share the Lord's Supper, he says, "I received *from the Lord*

---

24 These two terms can be interchangeable, but because of certain theological associations commonly attached to them, we prefer the former.

25 Cf. the Lutheran Augsburg Confession: "The Church is the congregation of saints in which the Gospel is rightly taught and the Sacraments are rightly administered" (Art. VII), or the statement of John Calvin: "Wherever we see the Word of God purely preached and heard, and the sacraments administered according to Christ's institution, there, it is not to be doubted, a church of God exists" (*Institutes* 4.1.9). Later Reformed tradition included a third mark: the proper exercise of church discipline, though this could be seen as simply an extension of the second. The administration of the ordinances generally separates a church from a parachurch organization.

26 This ordinance is also often referred to as "Communion" or, occasionally, as "the Breaking of Bread." The term "Eucharist" (from the Greek for "thanksgiving") is not common among us because of some of its traditional associations with a Roman Catholic understanding of the Lord's Supper (cf. 183-187).

27 Baptism was practiced before this time during the ministry of Jesus, but too little is said of it to know exactly how it was practiced and why (cf. John 3:22; 4:1-2).

what I also passed on to you" (1 Cor. 11:23).

These two practices, baptism and the Lord's Supper, come to us as outward signs given by Jesus himself, and they have been practiced by the church in some form throughout church history. We accept only these two as ordinances with this divine warrant.[28] Their distinctiveness among the commands given by Christ to the church is reflected in their unique purpose.

2. Their Purpose: The Ordinances Visibly and Tangibly Express the Gospel

Why have these ordinances been given to the church? What purpose do they serve? Most significantly, baptism and the Lord's Supper visibly and tangibly express the gospel. Certainly, the mere application of water or the eating of bread and the drinking of the cup[29] do not have inherent meaning. For that reason, these acts must always be set within a context that includes the proclamation of the Word of God. When the gospel is preached in conjunction with these ordinances, they become, in the words of Augustine, "visible words." These observable acts speak to us of the wonderful truths of the gospel—Christ's sacrificial death, our union with him, the new life that is ours and his glorious coming by which God's saving purpose will be brought to completion.

Yet the ordinances are not only seen, they are also experienced physically—we "eat and drink" and we are "washed," hence, the term "tangibly" in our Statement. In our participation in baptism and the Lord's Supper, the preached gospel is personalized, and we are individually engaged in a tangible response. These are God-given means by which we respond to the gospel personally as it is set before us in these visible and tangible ways.

a. The Ordinances Are Not the Means of Salvation

The biblical story amply illustrates the common human fallacy of confusing the sign with the reality it signifies. Israel was prone to

---

28 Through developments during the Middle Ages, the Roman Catholic Church considers five other rites as sacraments also: confirmation, penance, marriage, ordination and extreme unction. Following the Reformers of the sixteenth century, we do not believe that these have biblical sanction as ordinances of the church.

29 In the celebration of the Lord's Supper in Free Churches, most use grape juice, some use wine.

confuse the physical temple in Jerusalem with the God who was to be worshipped there, assuming that the presence of the former assured them of the saving presence of the latter. Jeremiah warned them that that was not the case (Jer. 7:1-29). Or they trusted in the outward act of animal sacrifice and ignored the inward commitment to the Lord and his ways that such an act was meant to express (cf., e.g., Isa. 1:2-20). Such confusion has also often plagued the church.

Our Scandinavian Free Church forebears lived in a Christian culture in which participation in the ordinances was too often devoid of spiritual commitment.[30] It was commonly believed that a person experienced forgiveness of sin and was brought into a right relationship with God merely through the act of baptism or through participating in the Lord's Supper. Our Statement is explicit in rejecting that misunderstanding. These ordinances are signs, pointing us to the reality of Jesus' saving work in his death and resurrection. We are saved by God's grace through faith alone in Christ alone.

b. When Celebrated by the Church in Genuine Faith
The Ordinances Confirm and Nourish the Believer

The ordinances are not the means of our salvation, but this does not mean that they are devoid of any spiritual benefit. Far from it. They are given to the church[31] by our Lord for our good as a God-ordained means of spiritual growth and edification. In that sense, though not "the means of salvation," they can nonetheless be considered "means of grace." Like the preaching of the Word, corporate worship, prayer and our fellowship with other Christians, these ordinances are means God uses to strengthen us in our faith.

Because of their spiritual benefit coming through their connection to the gospel, the ordinances are to be "celebrated" by the church. We are to practice them with a spirit of thanksgiving and praise for the wonderful gospel they express. As we come in faith to be baptized or to share in the Lord's Supper, God the Holy Spirit works in our hearts to attest to the gospel of which they speak—the one confirms the new believer in

---

30 In the context of a state church, baptism was often considered merely a civic duty and a means of citizenship.

31 These are ordinances "of the church." By this we affirm that these are not private acts but are most appropriately done under the auspices and authority of a local church. They are celebrated corporately and have individual benefit—both are important.

the inaugural act of faith[32] and the other nourishes[33] the believer in the ongoing Christian life.[34] Both serve to separate the believer from the world and to give a visible designation of those who belong to the body of Christ.

Again, we stress that the ordinances are not efficacious in and of themselves.[35] They do not edify apart from the subjective spiritual response which they both presuppose and foster—what we call here "genuine faith."[36] These are signs which point us to the reality of the gospel. We must not confuse the two.[37] It is through faith in Christ alone, not our participation in these ordinances, that we are saved.

B. A Description of the Ordinances

1. Baptism

We first describe the ordinance of baptism, and we discuss it as it was most clearly practiced in the New Testament—as an act involving believers. We present a theology of baptism that all Evangelical churches could affirm when baptizing professing believers.[38] The practice of baptizing infants of believing parents,[39] also allowed under our Statement

---

32 Or, in the case of infant baptism, it affirms the gracious promise of the gospel to the children of Christian parents (who must subsequently come to a personal faith).

33 We use this term metaphorically to mean "to strengthen," "to edify" or "to enhance spiritual health."

34 For this reason, historically it has been the near universal practice in churches of all denominations to require baptism (in some form) before participation in the Lord's Supper. In the EFCA this is a matter that is left to the local church.

35 To use the common theological term, they do not operate *ex opere operato* (Latin for "on account of the work which is done"). We reject the Roman Catholic notion that simply participating in the ordinances confers saving grace. This is sometimes referred to as "sacramentalism."

36 Admittedly, the term "faith" ought not to need a qualifier, but one is used here for emphasis—similar to the Apostle Paul's expression "sincere faith" in 1 Tim. 1:5; 2 Tim. 1:5. On the subject of faith, see Article 10, sec. I.C.

37 We say this recognizing that biblical writers can so associate the sign with the thing signified that they can sometimes speak of the two interchangeably. So, the act of baptism can stand for the whole process of conversion (cf. Rom. 6:3-4; Acts 2:38; 1 Pet. 3:21).

38 This is referred to as "believer's baptism" or "credobaptism" (from the Latin *credo*, meaning "I believe").

39 Also referred to as paedobaptism (from the Greek *paidion*, meaning "child").

(see further below),[40] has to be understood in a different way.[41]

The practice of baptism emerges in the New Testament without preparation or explanation in the ministry of John the Baptist who came to Israel preaching a baptism of repentance. Jesus himself responded to John's call and submitted to his baptism, identifying himself with a sinful Israel,[42] though he himself was without sin. Then in his Great Commission, Jesus commanded his disciples to make disciples of all nations through baptism and teaching (Matt. 28:19).

On the day of Pentecost after the dramatic outpouring of the Holy Spirit and after Peter had finished preaching his powerful sermon in Jerusalem, the people cried out and asked, "Brothers, what shall we do?" To which Peter responded, "Repent and be baptized, every one of you, in the name of Jesus Christ for the forgiveness of sins" (Acts 2:37-38). And we read, "Those who accepted his message were baptized, and about three thousand were added to their number that day" (Acts 2:41).

This pattern continued—the apostles preached, and people responded in faith and were baptized (cf. Acts 8:12-13, 36-38; 9:18; 10:47-48; 16:14-15, 31-34; 18:8). In the Book of Acts there seems to have been no conception of an unbaptized believer.[43] Baptism was a universal practice in the church.

But what does baptism mean? One could expound its significance by considering the three actors who play a part in every act of baptism.

---

40 We recognize that the interpretations of Scripture on the relevant points regarding the two positions on baptism differ with one another and are in some ways incompatible. We allow different interpretations, not because we think Scripture is intrinsically ambiguous on the matter, nor because we think Scripture provides so little information that it is unwise to hold any opinion, but because some of us think the credobaptist position is in line with Scripture and that the paedobaptist position is mistaken, and some think the paedobaptist position is in line with Scripture and that the exclusively credobaptist position is mistaken. In other words, both sides hold that Scripture speaks to the matter, but each side holds a view that excludes the other. However, we do not believe that our differing views on this matter (among others) should prevent our unity in the gospel in full local church fellowship. It is in this sense, and only in this sense, that the Statement of Faith "allows" both views.

41 Many Free churches practice infant dedication, which simply recognizes a child as a gift from God for which we give thanks, seeks God's blessing on that child's life, and calls the parents, and the church family, to fulfill their responsibilities in bringing that child up in the love and instruction of the Lord. This is not to be confused with infant baptism.

42 Jesus' role as Israel's promised Messiah is discussed further in Art. 4, sec. I.D. In identifying himself with Israel, Jesus is also identifying himself with all sinful humanity.

43 Note also that Paul's argument in Rom. 6:1-14 assumes that all believers in Christ have been baptized.

a. Baptism as a Believer's Profession

First, from the perspective of the person who comes to be baptized, baptism is something we do. Ananias said to Paul, after he had received his vision of the risen Lord, "Now what are you waiting for? Get up, be baptized and wash your sins away, calling on his name" (Acts 22:16). Baptism is an act by which a person publicly calls upon the name of Jesus as Lord and Savior. From the perspective of the person being baptized, baptism is the subjective response to the objective truth of the gospel. It is the biblically prescribed public[44] action that corresponds to a personal response of faith to the gospel.[45]

b. Baptism as the Church's Affirmation

But it is important to remember that a new believer can only *ask* to be baptized, or better, respond to the command to be baptized[46]—no one baptizes him- or herself. Baptism requires a second actor: the local church. In baptism, the first actor comes as one professing faith in Christ. The second actor, the church, *hears* that profession and *affirms* that profession and then publicly recognizes the one baptized as a Christian brother or sister.

Baptism has, from the beginning, been seen as the point of entry into the visible body of Christ.[47] In Galatians 3:26-29 Paul describes those who have been baptized into Christ as sons of God and part of a new community—a community of Jew and Greek, slave and free, male and female.[48] Baptism in the name of the Father, Son and Holy Spirit is baptism into the body of Christ, and so into the church. Baptism was the point at which a person was publicly recognized as a Christian.[49]

---

44 On the importance of a public profession of faith, cf. Matt. 10:32; Rom. 10:9.

45 If baptism is to be a profession of faith, it must be both free and informed. This has important implications for the way baptism is to be practiced.

46 Cf. Ananias's words to Paul (Acts. 22:16).

47 Cf. Acts 2:41— "those who accepted his message were baptized, and about three thousand were added to their number that day."

48 Baptism here refers to the whole conversion experience, though we recognize that some think that Paul is referring to "Spirit-baptism" rather than baptism in water at this point.

49 Cf. the story of Lydia in Acts 16:14— "The Lord opened her heart to respond to Paul's message," and she was baptized. She then says, *"If you consider me a believer in the Lord* [with the presumption that he did], come and stay at my house" (Acts 16:15). Baptism says: "We, as a church, consider you a believer in the Lord and now regard you as a brother or sister in Christ."

Becoming a Christian is very personal, but it is never private, for being adopted as a child of God[50] means being a part of a family—a very visible and tangible family embodied in a local church.[51] Baptism is the initial means by which we are recognized by that family and are welcomed into that family to enjoy its privileges and to bear its responsibilities.[52] The responsibility of the church, then, toward those who come to be baptized is to affirm those who offer a credible profession of faith.

c. Baptism as God's Promise

Baptism is something *we* do, and baptism is something *the church* does, but, most importantly, baptism is also something that *God* does. Consider the illustration of a wedding. A baptismal profession is like our matrimonial "I do." At our baptism, we pledge our faith to God and promise to follow Christ all the days of our lives. But in a wedding there are *two* who promise. And in baptism, our promise is but a response to the prior promise of God. In baptism that promise of God is reaffirmed, made visible and, in fact, acted out, in the very act of baptism itself. When we are plunged under the water,[53] we are buried with Christ into his death (Rom. 6:2-4). We go with him to the cross; we enter his tomb— and in union with Christ our old sinful life dies. Baptism, first of all, proclaims God's promise that Christ's death has become our own and that he has borne our judgment.[54]

But in baptism we don't stay under the water! We are raised up with Christ to new life: "We were therefore buried with him through baptism into death in order that, just as Christ was raised from the dead through the glory of the Father, we too may live a new life" (Rom. 6:4). In baptism,

---

50 On our adoption, see Article 6, sec. II.B.3.

51 On the community of faith, the disciples of Jesus, the church, as a new family, cf. Matt. 12:46-49; 19:29; Gal. 6:10; 1 Tim. 3:15; 5:1-2, and the constant use of family language— "brothers and sisters"—to describe fellow believers.

52 In both baptism and church membership the church affirms a person's profession of faith. In the former, a person is recognized as a part of the global church (that is, the visible church around the world [In that sense there is "one baptism" (Eph. 4:5)]). In church membership, one is formally linked to a local church. Both baptism and church membership are important for every believer, and in normal circumstances baptism as the biblically prescribed act of Christian initiation (in whatever form regarding time or mode) ought to precede church membership.

53 Here we are assuming baptism by immersion. Our Statement does not require that mode.

54 Peter compares the water of baptism to the overwhelming flood of judgment in the days of Noah (1 Pet. 3:20-21).

Peter says, we are like Noah in his ark, saved out of the judgment that threatens us through God's gracious provision (1 Pet. 3:20-21).

And in that passage, Peter reminds us that the water is not only a symbol of judgment, it also symbolizes *cleansing*. That water washes us clean from the dirt of our sin. Paul recounts the words of Ananias to him, "Get up, be baptized and *wash your sins away*, calling on his name" (Acts 22:16). In Hebrews 10:22 we read, "let us draw near to God with a sincere heart in full assurance of faith, having our hearts sprinkled to cleanse us from a guilty conscience and *having our bodies washed* with pure water."[55] Baptism pictures God's gracious promise of moral cleansing.

In some parts of the early church, those who were baptized actually took off their old clothes—the symbol of their old life of sin, and when they came out of the water they were given new clothes to symbolize their putting on the righteousness of Christ. This was meant to capture the affirmation of Paul: "You are all sons of God through faith in Christ Jesus, for all of you who were baptized into Christ have clothed yourselves with Christ" (Gal. 3:26-27).

Baptism is the picture of a promise, the visible sign of an invisible grace. In baptism, God's promise in the gospel is made personal to the one who is baptized as it is displayed before our eyes. This symbolic act displays God uniting us to Christ in his death and resurrection, washing our sins away and clothing us with new garments of righteousness. For this reason, Paul is probably referring to the time of their baptism (which represents the whole process of conversion[56]), when he says to the Corinthians, who once were as immoral as any pagans could be (cf. 1 Cor. 6:9-11), "But you were washed, you were sanctified, you were justified in the name of the Lord Jesus Christ and by the Spirit of our God" (1 Cor. 6:11).

d. Baptism and the Holy Spirit

This naturally raises the question: What is the relationship between baptism and the saving work of the Holy Spirit? Isn't it the Spirit who washes us and who unites us with Christ in his death and resurrection and who joins us to the body of Christ, the church (cf. 1 Cor. 12:13)? How

---

55 Cf. also Eph. 5:26— "Christ loved the church and gave himself up for her, to make her holy, *cleansing her by the washing with water through the word.*"

56 Paul's way of speaking here can cause confusion among those who fail to distinguish between the sign and what is signified in baptism (cf. n. 37).

are baptism in water and baptism in the Spirit related?

Interestingly, in the Book of Acts the temporal connection between water baptism and the reception of the Spirit is varied, as sometimes the former occurs before, sometimes simultaneous with, and sometimes after the latter.[57] This suggests that God is sovereign and can act however he likes and that the work of his Spirit is not tied to any outward act. On the other hand, enough of a connection is established that conceptually the two should be linked, leading one to believe that baptism in water is the outward act that pictures the inward regenerating work of the Holy Spirit. It is the sign of the new covenant promise of the prophets:

> I will sprinkle clean water on you,
>   and you will be clean;
> I will cleanse you from all your impurities
>   and from all your idols.
> I will give you a new heart and put a new spirit in you;
> I will remove from you your heart of stone
>   and give you a heart of flesh.
>
> (Ezek. 36:25-26)

Baptism in the name of the triune God depicts our union with Christ, and through our union with Christ, we are brought into the new age of the Spirit. In that sense, Christian baptism is not a baptism of *preparation*, like that of John the Baptist, looking forward to what was to come; it is a baptism of *participation*—picturing our present participation in Christ, and so our participation in the new age of and by the Spirit.

Because of this conceptual connection between baptism and the giving of the Spirit, we can say that not only is baptism a sign of God's promise to us in the gospel, it also serves as a visible seal of that promise.[58] In other words, by the Spirit, God acts in baptism to confirm the truth of the gospel in our hearts. When we come in faith and are baptized into the triune name, God visibly declares a reality that has already been effected by the Spirit—he puts his seal upon us; he claims us as his own; we belong to him; we are his.[59] Baptism functions like a wedding ring, providing a

---

57 Baptism first: Acts 8:14-17; 19:5-6; Simultaneous (presumably): Acts 2:38; Reception of the Spirit first: Acts 10:47-48.

58 On the Holy Spirit as a "seal" of God's promise in the life of the believer, cf. 2 Cor. 1:22; Eph. 1:13.

59 In this sense, this reflects the voice of the Father from heaven at Jesus' own baptism:

physical representation of a promise given and a promise received.

Baptism is a visible form of the gospel, but not just the gospel proclaimed. Baptism also displays the gospel being believed and received. In one symbolic act, baptism unites God's grace displayed, human faith exercised, and the church celebrating them both by publicly welcoming a new believer into the global body of Christ, the family of God.

e. What About Infant Baptism?

This discussion of baptism has assumed that the person coming to be baptized is a professing believer, as this is the most explicit form of baptism practiced in the Book of Acts. However, many through church history have argued, based primarily on the baptism of "households" (cf. Acts 16:15,33; 1 Cor. 1:16) and a biblical parallel between baptism and the Old Testament practice of circumcision,[60] that the infant children of believers are also to be baptized.[61] In fact, infant baptism was practiced early in the post-apostolic period and has been practiced by most churches throughout history. Though most churches in the Evangelical Free Church of America practice only believer's baptism, our Statement allows for infant baptism also. Again, our Statement affirms that baptism does not save a person. We deny that baptism in water is the instrumental cause of regeneration and that the grace of God is effectually conveyed through the administration of the ordinance itself.[62] We affirm that one must come to personal faith in Christ to benefit from his saving work. Those in the Free Church who practice infant baptism do so within this framework.

Our Free Church forebears determined that neither the "time" of baptism (whether during infancy for the children of believers or at a point of personal profession) nor its "mode" (whether practiced through immersion or the sprinkling or pouring of water) would be considered an essential point of doctrine over which they would separate from other Christians. Therefore, our Statement of Faith is silent on this issue, and in Free churches either form of baptism (in both "time" or "mode") is

---

"You are my Son, whom I love; with you I am well pleased" (Luke 3:22).

60 The passage most frequently cited to make this connection is Col. 2:11-12.

61 Peter's words in Acts 2:39 are also used to support the notion that, as in the Old Covenant, the New Covenant promises extend to the children of believers (cf. also Gen. 17:7; 1 Cor. 7:14).

62 This position is known as "baptismal regeneration."

acceptable.[63] We continue to debate this issue, but we do not allow it to divide us.

This position is held in the Free Church while maintaining both that local church membership should be composed of believers only and that baptism is not the means of salvation. An acceptance of infant baptism, given the theological understanding of baptism outlined above, may be justified if one compares the presentation of the gospel in baptism to an act of preaching. The validity of preaching is not nullified by a failure of the hearers to repent and believe. But when they do, that preaching achieves its appointed end. On this ground, the baptism of someone who was baptized as an infant and who has come to faith in Christ can be accepted as a valid baptism, though only their subsequent Spirit-prompted response of faith has completed that baptism and made it effective as a true picture of the saving work of God in that person's life.[64] In whatever form, baptism is an integral aspect of the Christian life as an ordinance given by our Lord.[65]

2. The Lord's Supper

When Jesus gathered with his disciples in that upper room on the night he was betrayed, they celebrated the traditional Jewish Passover meal together. Through this meal the Jews renewed the memory of that single, defining moment in the history of the people of Israel when the angel of death "passed over" the houses of Israel without harm but brought death to every firstborn in the houses of the Egyptians. The families of Israel were spared because by faith in God's gracious provision, they had sacrificed a lamb and had dabbed the blood of the sacrificial lamb on

63 This distinguishes Free churches from Baptist churches. However, since many are convinced that baptism properly ordered according to God's design is to picture both the objective promise of God in the gospel and the divinely-inspired subjective response of faith by the person being baptized, many Free churches will baptize as believers those who had been baptized as infants, if this is requested. This remains a matter left to personal conscience.

64 Certainly, in infant baptism, the role of the church in affirming the faith of the one baptized must be shifted to a later point of public profession (either at some form of "confirmation" or at the reception into church membership). Our Statement does deny that infant baptism in itself makes one a full member of the body of Christ.

65 In Free churches practicing credobaptism, children of believing parents need not be seen as mere outsiders, but as "baptismal candidates in training." This is similar to the category of "catechumen" used in the early church for those not yet full members of the church, but no longer considered as pagans. The children of believing parents do, however, need to believe the gospel by turning to Him in repentance and personally receiving the Lord Jesus Christ.

their doorposts. On the next day the Israelites were set free from their many long years of bondage and began their exodus from Egypt and their movement toward the land of God's promise. Moses declared: "This is a day you are to commemorate; for the generations to come you shall celebrate it as a festival to the LORD—a lasting ordinance" (Exod. 12:14). And so every year in every Jewish home those events would be re-lived; they would come alive in their minds; and the Jews of each new generation would understand themselves as the ones whom God had rescued.

a. The Lord's Supper Is a Remembrance of Christ's Death

Jesus took that Passover meal and gave it a new significance, pointing it to himself. As he broke the bread, he gave it to his disciples and said, "This is my body, which is for you; do this in remembrance of me" (Luke 22:19). Offering them the cup he said, "Drink from it, all of you. This is my blood of the covenant, which is poured out for many for the forgiveness of sins" (Matt. 26:27-28). Jesus was giving up himself for his people, like that Passover lamb whose death substituted for the death of the firstborn of Israel.[66] This Christian meal is meant, in Paul's words, to "proclaim the Lord's death" (1 Cor. 11:26). In the Lord's Supper, Jesus was providing a symbolic picture to help us keep in mind forever what he was doing for us.

How many men in previous generations, when going off to war, gave their wives or fiancées pictures of themselves as a remembrance until they returned. Referring to a picture prominently displayed by her bedside, a woman might have said, "This is Richard, my husband." The picture helped to keep him present in her mind and heart. So Jesus Christ has left such a memento of himself for his bride—the bread and the cup, which set before our eyes his broken body and shed blood. The Lord's Supper is a remembrance of Christ's death—it vividly reminds us of the cross, and in celebrating this meal, Christians of each new generation understand themselves as those for whom Christ died.

b. The Lord's Supper Is a Communion with Christ's Life

The Lord's Supper is an act of remembrance, but the eating and drinking in the context of a fellowship meal suggests that it may entail more than that. After all, what bride ever ate the photograph of her absent

---

66 Cf. Paul's words in 1 Cor. 5:7: "Christ, our Passover lamb, has been sacrificed."

husband? In addition, why did the early Christians choose Sunday and not Friday on which to celebrate this meal, for it was on a Friday that he died?

The bread and the cup point us to Christ's atoning death, but our eating and drinking what Jesus describes as his body and blood symbolize that we also share in Christ's resurrection life. The words of Jesus himself point to this connection, expressing it in such a graphic way that many found it offensive— "I tell you the truth, unless you eat the flesh of the Son of Man and drink his blood, you have no life in you" (John 6:53).[67] Elsewhere Jesus used organic imagery to describe our vital relationship with him— "I am the vine, you are the branches" (John 15:5). His very life flows through us, and the Lord's Supper displays this vital union with Christ. We call this meal the *Lord's* Supper, and in it we "commune" with Christ (cf. 1 Cor. 10:16).

The precise nature of this communion with Christ has been understood in various ways through church history. Roman Catholics have so identified the sign (the bread and the wine) with what is signified (the body and blood of Christ) that the sign, when consecrated by the priest, essentially ceases to exist and only appears to be bread and wine.[68] The Protestant Reformers of the sixteenth century—including Martin Luther, John Calvin and Huldrych Zwingli—rejected this view, along with other attendant aspects of Roman Catholic sacramental theology,[69] and so do we. We insist that the sign and what is signified must be distinguished and that failing to do that distorts the gospel.

However, the Evangelical Reformers were not in agreement among themselves about how the sign and what is signified were related and about how we commune with Christ at the Lord's Supper.[70] The Lutherans contended that Christ is truly present "in, with, and under" the physical

---

67 We do not assume that Jesus was referring directly to the Lord's Supper in John 6. For Christian readers, however, these words would certainly bring this to mind.

68 This is called transubstantiation—the "substance" of the bread and the wine literally become the body and blood of Christ while maintaining their outward appearance. This idea is based on an Aristotelian distinction between substance and accident (i.e., appearance).

69 This would include the doctrine of the sacrifice of the mass, in which the priest makes an offering of Christ (in effect, sacrificing him again) on behalf of the people, somehow earning merit, and the notion that the sacraments confer grace *ex opere operato* (that is, apart from faith in the one who receives them [see note 35 above]).

70 At the famous Marburg Colloquy of 1529 Luther and Zwingli debated this very issue but could come to no common understanding, though they were in full agreement on the essentials of the gospel.

elements of the bread and the wine (though "in a supernatural and heavenly manner"[71]), followers of Zwingli understood the language regarding Christ's body and blood metaphorically and the Lord's Supper primarily as a meal of remembrance,[72] while the Calvinists sought a real, though spiritual, presence of Christ in the communion elements.[73] Most in the Free Church would be closest to Zwingli in their understanding.[74] Nonetheless, these Evangelical leaders agreed, and this Statement

---

71 See the *Formula of Concord*, VII.6. Following Martin Luther, Lutherans take the statement of Jesus— "This is my body"—in a straightforward, literal way. In addition, they take the declaration that Jesus is now seated at the right hand of the Father in a metaphorical sense to describe his authoritative rule of the cosmos (cf. Matt. 28:18). Lutherans believe in the ubiquity of Christ—that is, they believe that Christ's humanity shares in his divine omnipresence (*communicatio idiomatum*). Hence Christ can be fully present at the Supper.

The Lutheran view of the presence of Christ in the Lord's Supper is often referred to as "consubstantiation," though Lutheran theologians generally reject this term. They contend that it was coined by their opponents in the mid-sixteenth century to associate their view with Roman Catholic conceptions of the Lord's Supper, which they vehemently deny. Evangelical Lutherans insist that we are saved by grace alone, through faith alone in Christ alone, and that the Lord's Supper has benefit only for those who receive it in faith. Moreover, the presence of Christ is not located in the elements statically, such that they should be the object of adoration (as Roman Catholics believe), but dynamically, that is, only during the actual practice of the Lord's Supper itself. The Lutheran view of the Lord's Supper was often rejected by Free Church leaders of the past because of the popular perception that, as in the Roman Catholic view, the Lord's Supper confers God's grace apart from personal faith in Christ. This perception persists, even among many Lutherans, and in articulating our position we must guard against any misunderstanding— we are saved by grace alone through faith alone in Christ alone.

72 This is often referred to as the "memorialist" view. However, Zwingli did believe that in the Lord's Supper, by faith in the promises of God, we do feed on Christ in our hearts and commune with him spiritually. In his words: "So then, when you come to the Lord's Supper to feed spiritually upon Christ, and when you thank the Lord for his great favour, for the redemption whereby you are delivered from despair, and for the pledge whereby you are assured of eternal salvation, when you join with your brethren in partaking of the bread and wine which are the tokens of the body of Christ, then in the true sense of the work you eat him sacramentally. You do inwardly that which you represent outwardly, your soul being strengthened by the faith which you attest in the tokens" (*An Exposition of the Faith* [1531; 1536]).

73 In the words of Calvin: "The truth of God, therefore, in which I can safely rest, I here embrace without controversy. He declares that his flesh is the meat, his blood the drink, of my soul (John 6:53f); I give my soul to him to be fed with such food. In his sacred Supper he bids me take, eat, and drink his body and blood under the symbols of bread and wine. I have no doubt that he will truly give and I receive" (*Institutes* IV.17.32). He makes clear, however, "that the Scripture, when it speaks of our participation with Christ, refers its whole efficacy to the Spirit" (Ibid., IV.17.12).

74 We must beware of the danger voiced by Millard Erickson: "Out of a zeal to avoid the conception that Jesus is present in some sort of magical way, some have sometimes gone to such extremes as to give the impression that the one place where Jesus most assuredly is not to be found is the Lord's Supper. This is what one Baptist leader termed 'the doctrine of the real absence' of Jesus Christ" (*Christian Theology*, 2nd ed. [Grand Rapids: Baker Academic, 1998], 1130).

affirms, that the Lord's Supper is not a means of communicating God's grace apart from the "genuine faith" of those who share in this meal. We give latitude in how our communion with Christ in the Lord's Supper is understood[75] and in what sense those who celebrate this ordinance in genuine faith are "nourished." We must be clear, however, that in our celebration of the Lord's Supper, our communion with Christ in whatever manner is by God's grace and spiritual benefit can only come as we subjectively appropriate the meaning of this meal (that is, the gospel) through faith.

c. The Lord's Supper Is a Fellowship in Christ's Body

The Lord's Supper is not something that we do alone. It is a practice of the church. As a fellowship meal, at least in symbolic form, it speaks not only of our communion with Christ but also of our communion with one another as believers. Paul writes to the Corinthian Christians, "Because there is one loaf, we, who are many, are one body, for we all partake of the one loaf" (1 Cor. 10:17). Our unity as a church is to be evident in our sharing in the Lord's Supper, for it is precisely there that we focus on what Christ has done for us all.[76]

The Lord's Supper is "a participation in the body of Christ" (1 Cor. 10:16), visibly displaying our unity with other Christians (v. 17). For that reason this meal is for Christian believers, signifying our unity in Christ as those who come in faith before God, confessing their need of forgiveness, and professing Jesus as their Lord and Savior. In other words, it is the same requirement for those who present themselves to be baptized. And whereas baptism is to be the once-and-for-all, formal point of visible admission into Christ's body, the Lord's Supper is to be the ongoing affirmation of it. So most churches through history have affirmed that this meal is to be shared by baptized believers who come in faith,[77] and church discipline often entailed the exclusion of an

---

75 In that sense, as with the "time" and "mode" of baptism, this is something about which our Statement is silent. We may disagree on some points related to the Lord's Supper, but we choose not to divide over those disagreements. On this, see also n. 40 above, which applies to debates on the Lord's Supper as well as to baptism.

76 For this reason, many believe that Paul's exhortation in 1 Cor. 11:27 not to share in this meal "in an unworthy manner" refers especially in its context (cf. 11:17-33) to examining ourselves with regard to how we are treating other members of the body of Christ (cf. v. 29), that is, the church.

77 There is no Free Church policy regarding who may participate in the Lord's Supper in the local church, but Free churches commonly practice "open communion," meaning that participants should be believers, but need not be members in that local church.

unrepentant member from participation.

d. The Lord's Supper Is a Foretaste of Christ's Coming

In our celebration of the Lord's Supper, not only do we look back in remembrance of what Christ has done, experience his presence with us now, and affirm our present connection to his body, the church, as we come to this table we also look forward to what is yet to come. Jesus told his disciples at that Last Supper that he would not drink from the fruit of the vine until that day when he would drink anew with them in his Father's kingdom (Matt. 26:29). Paul says that in the Lord's Supper "we proclaim the Lord's death *until he comes*" (1 Cor. 11:26).

One of the biblical pictures of that glorious future is that of a great banquet—a messianic wedding feast, at which the church as the bride of Christ is received by her husband (cf. Isa. 25:6; Matt. 8:11; 22:4; 2 Cor. 11:2; Rev. 19:7; 21:2,9). A small morsel of bread and a sip of wine or grape juice is no feast, but it is to be a token of one—a taste, a glimpse, a pointer to our great hope. Even today when Jews celebrate Passover, they end the meal by looking forward, saying, "Next year in Jerusalem," signifying their hope in the coming of the Messiah. When Christians celebrate the Lord's Supper we look *back* to Jerusalem, and Jesus' death and resurrection there, and we look forward to what is yet to come, saying, "Next year in the glorious kingdom of God."[78] For when we eat and drink, our souls are nourished in faith as we anticipate that glorious future when our faith will become sight.

C. A Summary of the Ordinances

To summarize our understanding of the ordinances, our Statement affirms:

1. Christ has given his church two ordinances, baptism and the Lord's Supper, and the practice of these ordinances is an essential distinguishing mark of a church;

2. these ordinances are signs, that is, visible and tangible expressions, of the gospel, and as such they serve to strengthen our faith— "confirming and nourishing the believer";

---

78 The kingdom of God is a dynamic and multivalent biblical concept, its relationship to the church is complicated, not least because both 'church' and 'kingdom' are used in more than one way. It is probably best to speak of the kingdom as a power and the church as a people which is created by the kingdom and witnesses to it. In the age to come these two will become one.

3. the signs (water in baptism, the bread and grape juice or wine in the Lord's Supper) must be distinguished from what they signify (God's saving work in the gospel and Christ's presence with us);[79]

4. the practice of these ordinances does not save us, and we receive spiritual benefit from them only when they are celebrated in "genuine faith" in Christ.

5. the ordinances serve to separate the believer from the world and to give a visible designation of those who belong to the body of Christ.

Our Statement denies that:

1. either baptism in water or participating in the Lord's Supper is the instrumental cause of regeneration;

2. the grace of God is automatically and effectually conveyed through the administration of the ordinances themselves.

In addition, our Statement does not prescribe the "time" or "mode" of baptism (allowing for both credo- and paedobaptist practices) nor does it define the precise manner in which Christ is present in the Lord's Supper (allowing for a variety of historic Evangelical views).

III. Conclusion: The Church and the Gospel

God's gospel is now embodied in the new community called the church. This means not only that the gospel creates the church, but also that the church proclaims the gospel. And the church proclaims the gospel not simply in what the church is called to do,[80] but in what the church is.

The church is the centerpiece of God's purposes for humanity. For the promise of the gospel is that God will redeem a people composed of those from every nation, tribe, people and language who will find their unity solely in their common relationship with Jesus Christ as they are united to him by the Spirit (cf. Rev. 5:9; 7:9). And it is in the church that this people-to-come is now being made visible to the world.

In a sense, in the church the gospel message finds its initial realization. Paul in Ephesians 2:11-3:13 describes the creation of the one new humanity united in Christ as the purpose of God in all ages now revealed: "[God's] intent was that now, through the church, the manifold

---

79 Thus we deny baptismal regeneration and the doctrine of transubstantiation.

80 On this, see our exposition of Article 8.

wisdom of God should be made known to the rulers and authorities in the heavenly realms, according to his eternal purpose which he accomplished in Christ Jesus our Lord" (Eph. 3:10-11).[81]

In this way, the church is the "first fruits" of what is to come. As one writer put it, "The church does communicate to the world what God plans to do, because it shows that God is beginning to do it."[82] In Christ a new age has dawned, and the church is to be an anticipatory presence of that new age and an initial signpost of its coming.

The church is not just the bearer of the message of reconciliation, the church is a part of the message itself. The church's existence as a community reconciled to God and to one another is what gives the message its credibility, for such a community is itself the manifestation of the gospel it proclaims. Jesus said as much. In speaking to the Father of his disciples in John 17, Jesus prayed, "I have given them the glory that you gave me, that they may be one as we are one: I in them and you in me. May they be brought to complete unity *to let the world know* that you sent me and have loved them even as you have loved me" (17:22-23). One way the gospel is to be declared to the world is through the loving unity of Christians.

The church is to be a provisional expression of that new humanity united in Christ which God has graciously purposed to create for his own glory. So the church is missional in its very nature—who we *are* is an important part of our proclamation of the gospel to the world. For God's gospel is embodied in this new community called the church.

If this is so, then shouldn't every Christian be a committed member of a church? If you believe, then you must belong. Many still persist in church-hopping, always searching for something that might satisfy their desires. Evidently this is not a new problem, for a colleague of Martin Luther in the sixteenth century, Philip Melanchthon, made this remark: "Let us not praise those tramps who wander around and unite with no church, because they nowhere find their ideals realized [because] something is always lacking."[83] We must not be church dabblers. We must dig in and discover the riches that can be had as we live out God's purpose in real fellowship in the life of a local church. For without a commitment to the local church, we haven't rightly understood God's gospel.

---

81 On this initial realization of the gospel in the church, cf. also Heb. 12:18-24.

82 John Howard Yoder, *The Royal Priesthood: Essays Ecclesiastical and Ecumenical*, ed. Michael G. Cartwright (Scottdale, Pennsylvania: Herald Press, 1998), 126.

83 *Loci*, 3rd ed., Jacobs, *SCF*, 415, cited in Thomas Oden, *Life in the Spirit. Systematic Theology: Volume Three* (New York: Harper, 1992), 302.

Evangelical Convictions

A Theological Exposition of the Statement of Faith of the Evangelical Free Church of America

Article 8

CHRISTIAN LIVING

8. We believe that God's justifying grace must not be separated from His sanctifying power and purpose. God commands us to love Him supremely and others sacrificially, and to live out our faith with care for one another, compassion toward the poor and justice for the oppressed. With God's Word, the Spirit's power and fervent prayer in Christ's name, we are to combat the spiritual forces of evil. In obedience to Christ's commission, we are to make disciples among all people, always bearing witness to the gospel in word and deed.

God's gospel compels us to Christ-like living and witness to the world.[1]

The Christian message has been commonly misunderstood in two equally dangerous directions. On the one hand, the *legalists* believe that being a Christian is a matter of obeying the law. We are made right with God by what we do, whether that is conceived in terms of observing the torah of Moses received on Mt. Sinai or conforming to the standards of Jesus' Sermon on the Mount. But the gospel message assumes that we have all broken the law and can now do nothing to save ourselves. "By observing the law no one will be justified," Paul writes (Gal. 2:16), for "all have sinned" (Rom. 3:23). Our salvation does not depend on how we have lived (cf. Titus 3:4), but on Christ's life given for us. Paul's hope is not in his own righteousness that comes from the law, but that which is through faith in Christ (Phil. 3:9). In union with Christ, our sins are forgiven, our guilty consciences are washed clean and the righteousness of Christ is now ours—all apart from our good works (cf. Eph. 2:8-9).

On the other hand, some, seeing that our salvation is not a matter of how we live, conclude that how we live doesn't matter. From the ditch of legalism these people lurch to the opposite ditch of *license*. In the book of Jude we read of certain "godless men" who, having infiltrated the church, "change the grace of our God into a license for immorality" (Jude 4), and people have been following in their miry footsteps ever since.

In his letter to the Romans, the Apostle Paul addresses this very issue. After setting forth the depth and breadth of human sin and the even greater power of God's grace in the first five chapters, contending that where sin increased, grace increased all the more (5:20), Paul raises the question that ought to be in the minds of his readers: "What shall we say, then? Shall we go on sinning so that grace may increase?" (6:1).[2]

---

1 Though this Article has no parallel in the 1950 EFCA Statement of Faith, it does expand what is stated at the conclusion of Article 4 of that Statement which refers to the Holy Spirit's work to "empower the believer for godly living and service." This new article also reflects our Free Church heritage as evidenced by the concluding Article 12 of the 1912 Norwegian-Danish Evangelical Free Church Association Statement of Faith: "We believe that the sole duty of the Christian Church is to proclaim the Gospel to the whole world, and to assist charitable institutions, to work for righteousness and temperance, for unity and cooperation with all believers, and for peace among all people and nations on the whole earth."

2 Martin Lloyd-Jones makes the astute observation that true preaching of the gospel of God's grace will always lead to the possibility of this charge being brought against it (*Romans. An Exposition of Chapter 6: The New Man* [Grand Rapids: Zondervan, 1972], 8).

In other words, can we be indifferent to the moral character of our lives? Paul's answer is an emphatic No!

> By no means! How can we who died to sin go on living in it? Do you not know that all of us who have been baptized into Christ Jesus were baptized into his death? Therefore we have been buried with him by baptism into death, so that, just as Christ was raised from the dead by the glory of the Father, so we too might walk in newness of life.
>
> (Rom. 6:2-4)

Paul is pointing us to the secure path that avoids the pitfalls on both sides. For the Christian, grace and godliness coexist, for both are found in our union with Christ. Using the outward sign of baptism as a symbol of that Spirit-forged union, Paul declares that believers now have a new identity. We have died with Christ, who has atoned for our sin, and we have been raised with him to live a new life. Therefore, in our Statement we affirm that God's justifying grace must not be separated from his sanctifying power and purpose.[3]

I. Grace and Godliness: God's Justifying Grace and His Sanctifying Power and Purpose

We have declared already that we are justified by God's grace alone through faith alone.[4] As a once-for-all act of God, our justification means that "There is therefore now no condemnation for those who are in Christ Jesus" (Rom. 8:1). But God's saving work is not limited to the forgiveness of sins and our rescue from God's wrath. The God who justifies us also works in us to conform us to the image of Christ, so that we might share in his glory (cf. Rom. 8:29-30) in an on-going process we call sanctification.[5] As Paul writes in 2 Timothy 1:9, God "has saved us

---

3 Paul speaks of the danger of having a form of godliness but denying its power—its power to change us through the regenerating work of the Spirit (cf. 2 Tim. 3:5; Tit. 1:16). Linking grace and sanctification has been a part of our Free Church heritage as we have sought to join Christian freedom with responsibility and accountability.

4 See Article 7, sec. I.A.1.

5 This term can have different senses in the New Testament, referring either to a position or status of holiness in God's sight (e.g. 1 Cor. 1:2; 1 Pet. 1:1-2) or to the process of becoming holy in our lives (e.g., 1 Thess. 4:3-4; 5:23). Here we use the term in the second sense. Moreover, the

and called us to a holy life—not because of anything we have done but because of his own purpose and grace."

Justification and sanctification must never be confused, but neither can they be separated.[6] Both are aspects of God's gracious work in our lives, and both are consequences of our union with Christ by the Spirit. We are first *declared* righteous as, in union with Christ, we are clothed with his righteousness. Then we progressively *become* righteous in ourselves as we live out our new life in Christ by God's power.[7] God's grace in the gospel compels us to seek godliness. As Paul instructs Titus[8]:

> For the grace of God that brings salvation . . . teaches
> us to say 'No' to ungodliness and worldly passions,
> and to live self-controlled, upright and godly lives in
> this present age, ... [Jesus Christ] gave himself for
> us to redeem us from all wickedness and to purify for
> himself a people that are his very own, eager to do
> what is good.
>
> (Titus 2:11-12,14)

A proper understanding of the gospel leaves no room for nominal Christianity—being a Christian in name only. Without some evidence of God's sanctifying work in a person's life, without a concern for godliness, we have no reason to believe that a person who makes a Christian profession has, in fact, been truly justified by God's grace. Again, our good works earn us nothing (cf. Eph. 2:8-9), but there is such a thing as a dead faith—in James' words, a faith without works, the faith of demons (James 2:14,19,26; cf. Titus 1:16). We are saved by God's grace alone through faith alone, but that saving faith never stands alone. It is always accompanied by the regenerating work of the Spirit, which introduces us into a new sphere of life (cf. 2 Cor. 5:17). Therefore, the faith that saves is a faith that works,

---

process is often worked out where the word "sanctification" is not used (e.g., Phil 3:12-14).

6 In this sense, orthopraxy (how we behave) becomes a part of orthodoxy (what we believe).

7 This is the distinction between Christ's *imputed* righteousness and his *imparted* or *infused* righteousness. In Roman Catholic theology, this "imparted" righteousness is the ground of justification. This we deny.

8 On this connection between God's grace and the call to godliness, cf. also Titus 3:3-8; Acts 20:32; Eph. 2:8-10; 2 Pet. 1:10. "This allows for the positions of the perseverance of the saints (some refer to this as "eternal security") and for apostasy (some refer to this as "losing salvation"). This article neither demands nor precludes either position."

bearing the fruit of the indwelling Spirit in the life of the believer.[9]

Grace and godliness are ultimately inseparable. Consider the words of the nineteenth-century Anglican bishop J. C. Ryle:

> He who supposes that Jesus Christ only lived and died and rose again in order to provide justification and forgiveness of sins for His people, has yet much to learn. Whether he knows it or not, he is dishonouring our blessed Lord, and making Him only a half Saviour. The Lord Jesus has undertaken everything that His people's souls require; not only to deliver them from the *guilt* of their sins by His atoning death, but from the *dominion* of their sin, by placing in their hearts the Holy Spirit; not only to justify them, but also to sanctify them.[10]

The Christian life entails growth, for we are to "continue to work out [our] salvation" (Phil. 2:12). But we live in the assurance that "it is God who works in [us] to will and to act according to his good purpose" (Phil. 2:13), confident "that he who began a good work in [us] will carry it on to completion until the day of Christ Jesus" (Phil. 1:6).

One of the most beautiful sights in the picturesque city of Cambridge, England, is King's College Chapel, a magnificent Gothic building completed during the reign of Henry VIII. One of the great attractions of the chapel is a painting by one of the Old Masters, Peter Paul Reubens, entitled, "The Adoration of the Magi." But in 1974 in an act of political protest, a vandal entered the chapel and defaced this magnificent painting by scratching the letters "IRA" deeply into the canvas. It was thought then that this irreplaceable work of art was ruined forever, but soon there appeared a notice alongside it that announced, "It is believed that this masterpiece can be restored to its original condition." And it was—in all its glory.

That is the message of the gospel: this masterpiece of the human person, created to glorify God as his image but defaced by the ravages of

---

9 The nature of saving faith is discussed more fully in Article 10, sec. I.C.

10 *Holiness: Its Nature, Hindrances, Difficulties, and Roots*, 2nd ed. (Grand Rapids: Baker, 1979 [reprinted from the 1883 edition]), 24. To put it another way, we have been saved from the penalty of sin, we are being saved from the power of sin and we will be saved from the presence of sin.

sin, can be restored to a glory even beyond its original condition. This is God's sanctifying purpose, and by his gracious power we are to grow in godliness and so display the glory of God. As Paul writes: "For it is by grace you have been saved, through faith—and this not from yourselves, it is the gift of God—not by works, so that no one can boast. For we are God's workmanship, created in Christ Jesus to do good works, which God prepared in advance for us to do" (Eph. 2:8-10).

What are these "good works" that God, the Master Craftsman, has in mind when restoring his creation? The statements that follow in this Article describe three ways in which we are to live out our faith to the glory of God: obeying the Great Commandment, engaging in the Spiritual Battle and carrying out the Great Commission.

II. The Great Commandment

> "Of all the commandments, which is the most
> important?" Jesus was asked. "The most important
> one," answered Jesus, "is this: 'Hear, O Israel, the Lord
> our God, the Lord is one. Love the Lord your God
> with all your heart and with all your soul and with
> all your mind and with all your strength.' The second
> is this: 'Love your neighbor as yourself.' There is no
> commandment greater than these."
>
> (Mark 12:28-31)

What does God want from us? To live lives of love. He has saved us from our sin for this very purpose.

A. We Are to Love God Supremely

First, God commands us to love him supremely—with all our heart, soul, mind and strength. This is the first and greatest commandment because God himself is love (1 John 4:8,16). He has existed eternally as a loving union of three equally divine Persons—the Father, the Son and the Holy Spirit. Love is central to who he is. Creation is an outpouring of that eternal love. And in creation, God has made one special creature to be like him—a personal creature who could love as he loves. As human beings, we were created to govern the good world God had made, living under his loving authority.

And who could be more worthy of our love than God himself—he who is of unfathomable glory and goodness and who is the source of all beauty and joy? To love God with all our heart, soul, mind and strength is simply what it means to function properly as a human being. That function has been corrupted by sin. But in our union with Christ that proper function begins to be restored as we come to share in the Son's relationship with the Father and enter into the triune life of love.[11] Loving God is not only our supreme duty but our highest privilege and the source of our deepest joy, as we respond to the God who has first loved us (1 John 4:10).

What does it look like to love God with our heart, soul, mind and strength? Loving God means, first, that he is the supreme object of our worship. In loving him, we declare his worth above all else. Worship is not only an expression of our love for God; it is also a means of loving him more. When we worship we call to mind just how worthy God is of our love—we hear of his greatness in his work of creation and of his goodness in his work of redemption. Our worship is an act of love.

We love God when we express to him our thanksgiving and our praise. We love him when we long to hear his voice through the reading and exposition of his Word. We love him when we acknowledge our dependence upon him as we come to him in prayer. We love him when we guard our affections, lest we be drawn away after other objects of our devotion, for anything that usurps God's place in our hearts becomes an idol. We love God when we humbly submit our wills in obedience to him. "If you love me," Jesus said, "you will obey what I command" (John 14:15; also vv. 21,23-24; 15:9-10). And, as we shall see, we love God when we love our neighbor.

God's sanctifying purpose is that his image in us be restored—that image that was displayed in all its glory in his Son Jesus. And that image is properly displayed when all our loves, all our desires, are rightly ordered, and our love for him is above all else. "Love the Lord your God with all your heart and with all your soul and with all your mind," Jesus said. "This is the first and greatest commandment" (Matt. 22:37-38).

B. We Are to Love Others Sacrificially

"And the second is like it," Jesus said, "'Love your neighbor as

---

11 Cf. John 17:20-23. To experience this divine love is part of what it means to "participate in the divine nature" (2 Pet. 1:4), for the highest quality Peter lists as evidence of our knowledge of Christ is love (2 Pet. 1:7).

yourself" (Matt. 12:39). There is an obvious reason why this should be so important: If we love God, we must love other human beings, because they are created in his image—they are his representatives on earth.

If the President of the United States sent an ambassador to a foreign leader who disrespected and abused that ambassador, the President himself would be insulted. So it is with God. He is represented in the world through every human being created in his image. How we treat his representatives is how we treat the One whom they represent.[12]

James points out the absurdity of not honoring this connection— "With the tongue we praise our Lord and Father, and with it we curse men, who have been made in God's likeness. . . . My brothers, this should not be" (James 3:9). John puts it even more bluntly: "If anyone says, 'I love God,' yet hates his brother, he is a liar. For anyone who does not love his brother, whom he has seen, cannot love God, whom he has not seen" (1 John 4:20). To love the one is to love the other; to hate the one is to hate the other.

Jesus says, "Love your neighbor as yourself." Contrary to what is commonly taught in some Christian pop-psychology, there is no hidden command to love ourselves here. Self-love is all too natural to us all— in the sense of doing what we perceive to be for our own good. We feed ourselves, we clothe ourselves, we indulge ourselves in all sorts of ways. Self-love in this form is simply assumed; the command is to curb that self-love, and to turn it outward toward other people—to that neighbor, whoever he or she may be, that God is setting before you.[13]

"A new command I give you: Love one another," Jesus said. "As I have loved you, so you must love one another" (John 13:34). And how did Jesus love us? John tells us: "This is how we know what love is: Jesus Christ laid down his life for us. And we ought to lay down our lives for our brothers" (1 John 3:16). So we say, we are to love others *sacrificially*— not conveniently, not just when it suits us, when it fits easily into our schedule, when it doesn't put us out, or when it doesn't cost us anything. The world loves that way, loving only those who love them (cf. Matt. 5:46-47). But we have come to know the love of God, and we have seen the love of Christ. We are to love others sacrificially (cf. 1 John 4:8-10;

---

12 Cf. Prov. 14:31; 19:17; Heb. 6:10.

13 Cf. Jesus' parable which answers the question, "Who is my neighbor?" in Luke 10:29-37. In this age of globalization and media coverage, determining whom we should care for is difficult, but the Bible tells us that our responsibility for our neighbor begins with our own families (1 Tim. 5:8), moves to the family of believers (Gal. 6:10) and extends to the world.

also Eph. 5:25). And when we do, both individually and corporately, the world will take notice.

Our Statement picks out three ways that our sacrificial love is to be expressed. This is certainly not an exhaustive list, but these three do reflect important biblical mandates.

1. Caring for One Another

We are to live out our faith in the way we care for one another. Here we are speaking about the special love that we are to have for our brothers and sisters in the family of believers, the church of Jesus Christ. This is what Jesus was referring to when he said, "By this all men will know that you are my disciples, if you love one another" (John 13:35). Followers of Jesus must display love toward one another, or the world has a right to ask if they really are his disciples.

The New Testament is laced with calls to this kind of love, with a myriad of "one another" passages. We are to—

- "be devoted to one another" (Rom. 12:10)
- "honor one another above ourselves" (Rom. 12:10)
- "live in harmony with one another" (Rom. 12:16; 1 Pet. 3:8)
- "stop passing judgment on one another" (Rom. 14:13)
- "accept one another, just as Christ accepted you" (Rom. 15:7)
- "instruct one another" (Rom. 15:14)
- "greet one another with a holy kiss" (2 Cor. 13:12)
- "serve one another in love" (Gal. 5:13)
- "be kind and compassionate to one another" (Eph. 4:32)
- "speak to one another with psalms, hymns and spiritual songs" (Eph. 5:19)
- "submit to one another out of reverence for Christ" (Eph. 5:21)
- "bear with each other and forgive whatever grievances you may have against one another" (Col. 3:13; Eph. 4:2)
- "teach and admonish one another with all wisdom" (Col. 3:16)
- "encourage one another and build each other up" (1 Thess. 5:11)
- "spur one another on toward love and good deeds" (Heb. 10:24)
- "love one another deeply, from the heart" (1 Pet. 1:22)

- "offer hospitality to one another without grumbling" (1 Pet. 4:9)
- "clothe ourselves with humility toward one another" (1 Pet. 5:5)

Part of the power of the early church's witness to the world was the way in which they put this "one another" love into practice. In the Book of Acts we read:

> All the believers were one in heart and mind. No one claimed that any of his possessions was his own, but they shared everything they had. There were no needy persons among them. For from time to time those who owned lands or houses sold them, brought the money from the sales and put it at the apostles' feet, and it was distributed to anyone as he had need.
>
> (Acts 4:32,34-35)

"Therefore, as we have opportunity," Paul wrote, "let us do good to all people, especially to those who belong to the family of believers" (Gal. 6:10). Paul says "especially," but certainly he did not mean "exclusively." Our love is not to be restricted to our fellow Christians, for when Jesus was asked, "Who is my neighbor?", he told a story pointing to the example of that good Samaritan, that religious outsider, who showed love to a man he happened to meet along the road while traveling down to Jericho. His neighbor was the person God had placed in his path. We are called by God to love our neighbor, whoever that may be. And Jesus calls us to love even our enemies, for that is the way God loves (Matt. 5:43-47; Rom. 5:8-10).

2. Acting with Compassion Toward the Poor

Another category of people that we are especially called to love in the Bible is those who are poor, which we take to include any who are needy, powerless and vulnerable, such as widows and orphans, the elderly, the disabled, the unborn, the immigrant, the minority or the mistreated (cf. Zech. 7:10; Luke 14:13). The Bible is quite explicit and realistic about this responsibility: "There will always be poor people in the land. Therefore I command you to be openhanded toward your brothers and toward the poor and needy in your land" (Deut. 15:11).

This biblical instruction is clear:

Prov. 14:21— "He who despises his neighbor sins,
                        but blessed is he who is kind to the needy."
Prov. 22:9— "A generous man will himself be blessed,
                        for he shares his food with the poor."
Prov. 28:27— "He who gives to the poor will lack nothing,
                        but he who closes his eyes to them receives
                        many curses."

Jesus condemned that rich man who lived in luxury every day and ignored the beggar Lazarus who lay at his gate (Luke 16:19-31). James tells us that "Religion that God our Father accepts as pure and faultless is this: to look after orphans and widows in their distress and to keep oneself from being polluted by the world" (James 1:27).

We are called to have compassion[14] for the poor because this reflects God's concern. God identifies himself with those who have no value in the eyes of the world:

Prov. 14:31— "He who oppresses the poor
                        shows contempt for their Maker,
                        but whoever is kind to the needy honors God."
Prov. 19:17— "He who is kind to the poor lends to the LORD,
                        and he will reward him for what he has done."

Though perhaps referring particularly to believers, Jesus nonetheless identifies with those who are poor and needy when he says that inasmuch as you have met the needs of the least of these my brothers you have done it to me (Matt. 25:31-46).

Showing kindness to the poor and giving with compassion to meet their needs is an act of love toward God. It demonstrates a sincere and selfless love, since it promises no return in this world. Jesus commended this kind of love when he said:

When you give a . . . dinner, do not invite your friends,
your brothers or relatives, or your rich neighbors; if
you do, they may invite you back and so you will be

---

14 Compassion is a divine attribute that is most clearly evidenced in the person and ministry of Jesus (cf. Matt. 9:36; 14:14; Mark 8:2; Luke 10:33; 15:20). When we show compassion to others (cf. Heb. 10:34) we are exhibiting the character of Christ.

> repaid. But when you give a banquet, invite the poor,
> the crippled, the lame, the blind, and you will be
> blessed. Although they cannot repay you, you will be
> repaid at the resurrection of the righteous.
>
> (Luke 14:12-14)

Those who are poor in this world have no resources of their own to depend on; they have no one to turn to. Therefore God, in his compassion becomes their defender. "Has not God chosen those who are poor in the eyes of the world to be rich in faith and to inherit the kingdom he promised those who love him?" (James 2:5; cf. also 1 Cor. 1:26-29).

A life of generosity toward the poor flows out of our experience of the gospel (Matt. 10:8). Paul encourages the Corinthians to contribute to his offering for the poor in Jerusalem[15] by reminding them of God's gift in Christ: "For you know the grace of our Lord Jesus Christ, that though he was rich, yet for your sakes he became poor, so that you through his poverty might become rich" (2 Cor. 8:9). Jesus became poor for us; he entered into our poverty, for before God we are all "wretched, pitiful, poor, blind and naked" (Rev. 3:17). Hearts touched by the gospel, those who have experienced God's compassion toward them in their own poverty (Matt. 5:3), cannot help but extend that compassion toward others.[16] But the Bible also warns that those indifferent toward the poor may find God indifferent toward them: "If a man shuts his ears to the cry of the poor, he too will cry out and not be answered" (Prov. 21:13).

The church, at her best, has always lived out the gospel in this way. In the early church, it was evident in the way God's people cared for those with physical needs, especially among those whom society marginalized.[17] This compassion was also seen in how the church cared

---

15 Paul's eagerness to meet this need is evidenced in Gal. 2:10.

16 Paul sees our willingness to be generous as a test— "But just as you excel in everything . . . see that you also excel in this grace of giving. . . . I want to test the sincerity of your love" (2 Cor. 8:7-8).

17 Whether giving or receiving, all was done under the sovereign hand of God, leading to gratitude and humility in both giver and receiver. Gerhard Uhlhorn, a German Lutheran theologian and historian, referring to the early church's ministry of compassion, writes, "The rich gave what he gave to God, and the poor received what he received from God. Thus the temptation of the rich to exalt themselves above the poor, and the humiliation of the poor at being obliged to receive assistance from others, were removed, while at the same time discontent and murmuring, as well as insolent demands and presumptuous requests, were done away with" (*Christian Charity in the Ancient Church* [New York: Charles Scribner's Sons, 1883], 146).

for those who were converted from a profligate life, thus losing their means of livelihood. Such were received into the church family and provided for. In another example, inspired by the Spirit-prompted Great Awakening that infused life into the church and a recommitment to the gospel, William Wilberforce started or supported over 60 humanitarian works. This "compassion for the poor" was rooted in his understanding of the gospel.

Acting with compassion toward the poor—showing mercy toward those in need—is one of the ways we love our neighbor.

3. Seeking Justice for the Oppressed

Contrary to the one-sided views often heard from those on the political left or on the political right, the Bible speaks of various ways that people find themselves in poverty and need. Sometimes such a state is the result of circumstances beyond their control—disaster, famine, illness, injury, or the death of a provider, like a husband or a father. Consider Jacob and his family fleeing to Egypt during a famine in Israel or the frequent mention of the plight of the widow and the orphan.[18]

Sometimes people are poor because of their own deficiencies—they lack self-discipline or enduring effort: "All hard work brings a profit, but mere talk leads only to poverty" (Prov. 14:23; also 6:9-11; 24:30-34). Our own failures or irresponsibility, of course, did not stop God from showing compassion to us.

But another cause of poverty mentioned often in the Bible is injustice and oppression: "A poor man's field may produce abundant food, but injustice sweeps it away" (Prov. 13:23). We live in a fallen world, and the structures of this fallen world often lead to unjust conditions and ill-treatment. People in authority take advantage of others, and the rich and powerful make the laws which generally protect their own interests. Because of these structural forms of evil in society, our love for our neighbor ought also to include not just compassion for the needy but also a desire for justice for the oppressed.

We must take to heart the biblical teaching on this important theme. The commands of Scripture are explicit and unambiguous:
- "Defend the cause of the weak and fatherless;
  maintain the rights of the poor and oppressed.
  Rescue the weak and needy;

---

18 Consider particularly the example of Ruth.

deliver them from the hand of the wicked" (Ps. 82:3-4).
- "The righteous care about justice for the poor,
but the wicked have no such concern" (Prov. 29:7).
- "Speak up for those who cannot speak for themselves,
for the rights of all who are destitute.
Speak up and judge fairly;
defend the rights of the poor and needy" (Prov. 31:8-9).
- "'He defended the cause of the poor and needy, and so all
went well. Is that not what it means to know me?' declares
the LORD" (Jer. 22:16).
- "Stop doing wrong, learn to do right!
Seek justice, encourage the oppressed.
Defend the cause of the fatherless,
plead the case of the widow" (Isa. 1:16-17).

In the Bible the Lord is on the side of the poor because no one
else is. And he is on the side of the poor because he is on the side of
justice:
- "Do not exploit the poor because they are poor
and do not crush the needy in court,
for the LORD will take up their case
and will plunder those who plunder them"
(Prov. 22:22-23; 23:10-11).
- "I know that the LORD secures justice for the poor
and upholds the cause of the needy" (Ps. 140:12).
- "A father to the fatherless, a defender of widows, is God in
his holy dwelling" (Ps. 68:5).
- "Do not take advantage of a hired man who is poor and
needy, whether he is a brother Israelite or an alien living
in one of your towns. Pay him his wages each day before
sunset, because he is poor and is counting on it. Otherwise
he may cry to the LORD against you, and you will be guilty
of sin" (Deut. 24:14-15).[19]

This concern for justice[20] is dear to God's heart. Therefore, we read,

19 Cf. also Lev. 19:13; Mal. 3:5; 31:13-15; Pss. 10:14; 12:5; 14:6; 146:7; Prov. 3:27-28; James 5:1-6.

20 There are, of course, various ways of defining justice. The biblical teaching gives emphasis to procedural or structural inequities that tend to oppress people without power or

"To do what is right and just is more acceptable to the LORD than sacrifice" (Prov. 21:3). And the Lord through the prophets Isaiah[21] and Amos[22] refused to accept Israel's worship when their hands were guilty of injustice to the poor and needy.

It is important to recognize that the church in the New Testament is not in the same situation as Israel under the old covenant. Israel was a nation-state with the coercive power of a judicial system and taxation at its disposal. The church is a spiritual family comprised of people from all nations. Ours is a spiritual power that comes through the gospel. How we seek justice must bear these differences in mind, as well as the difference between the corporate action of the church and the work of individual Christians. But whether it be, for example, through the proclamation of God's truth about the dignity of every human being deserving of respect and honor, or through the efforts of Christians involved in the actual affairs of the political process, we are called to seek justice for the oppressed as an aspect of our love for our neighbor in the world.

The early church was committed to biblical righteousness in caring for the "least of these." In the *Didache*,[23] an early post-apostolic writing, abortion was spoken against strongly as it was considered murder: "you shall not murder a child by abortion nor kill that which is born." Later in church history, a similar commitment to biblical righteousness bore fruit in the abolition of slavery in Britain.[24]

Regarding ministries of compassion and justice, the church has often vacillated between two extremes, either focusing on the physical needs of people while assuming or neglecting the spiritual or seeing people only as "souls to be saved" and disregarding their tangible suffering in this world. The example of the early church in Acts 6 provides a helpful

wealth (cf., e.g., Isa 10:1-2). However, because poverty can be the result of a variety of factors (see above), not all societal inequalities are the result of injustice. The notions of justice and righteousness are closely tied in the Bible (of the more than 30 such references, cf., e.g., 1 Kings 10:9; 29:14; Ps. 9:8; Isa. 5:16) such that these together point to a rightly ordered society under God's rule.

21 Cf. Isa. 1:1-17.

22 Cf. Amos 5:7-15.

23 Cf. *Didache: The Lord's Teaching Through the Twelve Apostles to the Nations*, Chapter 2. The Second Commandment: Grave Sin Forbidden.

24 After William Wilberforce's conversion (1785), his commitment to the gospel of Christ led him to labor for most of his parliamentary career to abolish the slave trade and ultimately slavery. Largely due to his efforts, the Slave Trade Act was passed in 1807 and the Slavery Abolition Act in 1833, three days before Wilberforce's death.

model. In response to the inequitable distribution of food among widows, the apostles saw to it that some were assigned to address that situation. But they did so while maintaining the priority of their ministry of the Word and prayer (Acts 6:2-4). The church today must do the same. Ministries of compassion have been a strong part of our Free Church history, both in America and around the world, through the establishment of orphanages, homes for the elderly and hospitals.[25] We now have a ministry known as TouchGlobal dedicated to this purpose.[26] Certainly, our highest priority must be the proclamation of the gospel, for the gospel alone can address our deepest need, and the church alone can bring this gospel to the world.[27] But while maintaining this priority, we ought not to neglect the very pressing material needs of those around us. Love requires no less.

The poet Robert Browning once wrote, "Take away love and our earth is a tomb."[28] That is true, for if you take away love, you take away the presence of the very life of God. Jesus said that loving God and loving our neighbor was the fulfillment of the law of God, for it is the perfect expression of the character of God. And love is the essence of that new life to which we are called. John says, "We love, because [God] first loved us" (1 John 4:19), and he has demonstrated that love supremely in the gospel of Jesus Christ. It is this love that leads to our next theme: our call to engage in a battle.

III. The Spiritual Battle

The gospel gives us solid grounds for great joy in this life, but the Apostle Paul, who himself urges us to "rejoice in the Lord always" (Phil. 4:4), often wrote of the hardships he endured (see esp. 2 Cor. 11:23-29). In describing one experience he lamented, "We were under great pressure, far beyond our ability to endure, so that we despaired even of life" (2 Cor. 1:8). We can never forget that we are called to follow in the footsteps of a *crucified* Messiah.

---

25 For further information on these activities, see Jim Forstrom, *A Living Legacy: Evangelical Free Church of America, A Pictorial History* (St. Louis, MO: G. Bradley Publishing, 2002), 57-61.

26 TouchGlobal was begun in 1993 as an arm of the EFCA International Mission (now known as ReachGlobal).

27 Our Article 10 affirms the eternal consequence of dying apart from Christ. We believe we ought to seek to alleviate all human suffering, but especially that which is eternal.

28 *Fra Lippo Lippi,* line 54.

As Paul's experience illustrates, the Christian life involves struggle and conflict. Jesus promised no less. He told his disciples, "In this world you will have trouble" (John 16:33). Paul urges his young protégé Timothy to "fight the good fight" (1 Tim. 1:18) and to "Endure hardship with us like a good soldier of Christ Jesus" (2 Tim. 2:3; cf. also Phil. 1:29-30). Being a follower of Jesus means that we will be engaged in a struggle, a fight, a battle.

We must be clear—ours is not a political or military battle. We cannot establish a "Christian nation" on this earth, for God's kingdom cannot be contained by any political party, nor can it be imposed by military force. Jesus was a King, but he commanded no earthly armies, and to Pilate the Roman governor he declared, "My kingdom is not of this world. If it were, my servants would fight to prevent my arrest by the Jews. But now my kingdom is from another place" (John 18:36). His is a spiritual kingdom, not a political one, and the battle we are called to is a spiritual battle, not a military one. "For our struggle," Paul writes, "is not against flesh and blood, but against the rulers, against the authorities, against the powers of this dark world and against the spiritual forces of evil in the heavenly realms" (Eph. 6:12). God's kingdom advances not through force of arms, but through the spread of the gospel. God's rule is manifest where spiritual rebels turn to Jesus Christ in repentance and faith, and God's glory is exhibited as the gospel flows out in acts of love.

A. Our Duty: To Combat the Spiritual Forces of Evil

Our responsibility is clear: we are to combat the spiritual forces of evil in the world. The reality of this spiritual opposition, centered in a personal devil,[29] is assumed throughout the Scriptures. Peter urges us, "Be self-controlled and alert. Your enemy the devil prowls around like a roaring lion looking for someone to devour. Resist him, standing firm in the faith" (1 Pet. 5:8-9). Jesus spoke of the devil as "a strong man" who must be bound if men and women were to be set free (Matt. 12:25-29). He is a powerful creature who, in his encounter with Jesus in the desert, spoke of all the world's glory and splendor having been given to him, and Jesus doesn't contest that claim (Luke 4:5-8). John writes in his first letter, "the whole world is under the control of the evil one" (1 John 5:19). Though Satan's power is great, as followers of Jesus we must oppose him and all that he stands for.

In his call to arms, Paul includes "the rulers, the authorities, the

---

29 On the devil, see Article 3, sec. II.A.

powers of this dark world" as well as the "spiritual forces of evil in the heavenly realms" (Eph. 6:12). There is some debate about the specific meaning of these terms, but the contrast with "flesh and blood" in this verse supports the notion that Paul is referring to demonic, spiritual powers working within the human institutions, cultural enterprises, bureaucracies and power structures of our world. These spiritual powers shape the "spirit of our age"[30]—and the spirit of our age, or any age, will inevitably conflict with the new age (Matt. 12:32; Eph. 1:21; Heb. 6:5) Jesus has come to bring. The battle has been joined, and every day we will be challenged in some way by the devil's work.

B. Our Means

To fight this battle we must be properly armed. "Put on the full armor of God," Paul writes, "so that you can take your stand against the devil's schemes" (Eph. 6:11). Since this is a spiritual battle, we must use spiritual means— "The weapons we fight with are not the weapons of this world" (2 Cor. 10:3). Our Statement lists three of the most powerful resources the Lord has put at our disposal.

1. God's Word

The devil's primary tactic is deception. Jesus said that "there is no truth in him. When he lies, he speaks his native language, for he is a liar and the father of lies" (John 8:44). From the beginning in the garden, the devil sowed doubt about the truth of what God had said (Gen. 3:1,4). He denies and distorts the truth, so that his lies might appear attractive to us. So to combat the devil's lies, we need God's truth given to us in his Word.

Paul's description of our divine armor using the model of the Roman soldier in Ephesians 6 emphasizes this point. His list begins with "the belt of truth" and the following pieces of equipment all relate to God's truth in some way. Finally, the notion of truth again becomes explicit, as Paul speaks of "the sword of the Spirit which is the word of God" (Eph. 6:17). This one offensive weapon repels the spiritual forces of evil like no other, as seen so clearly in Jesus' own confrontation with the devil in the desert (Matt. 4:1-11). The devil is defenseless against the truth of God's Word.

---

30 In 2 Cor. 4:4 Satan is described as "the god of this age."

2. The Spirit's Power

Our second resource, closely related to the first, is the Spirit's power. As we have seen already,[31] the Holy Spirit gave power to the apostolic preaching to convict the world of its guilt so that hardened hearts might be receptive to the message of the gospel (cf. Acts 2:14-41). Against the enemy and his work of blinding the minds of unbelievers (2 Cor. 4:4), the Spirit opens blind eyes (cf. Acts 9:17-18) and hard hearts (Acts 16:14) to the truth, exposing the devil's lies. He who inspired God's written Word brings that Word to life so that the God who spoke in the past speaks now with power in our hearts (cf. Rom. 10:17; James 1:18; 1 Pet. 1:23). Those so enlightened and softened by the Spirit to see and receive the truth in Christ are transferred from the domain of darkness into the kingdom of the beloved Son (Col. 2:13).

To those thus transferred, the Spirit also works to encourage and equip us for this battle. It is important to remember that we do not engage in this battle in the flesh. The weapons of our warfare have divine, Spirit-wrought power to destroy strongholds and to take every thought captive to Christ (2 Cor. 10:3-5). Since the works of the devil have been destroyed (1 John 3:8), we, through the Spirit, have the authority to render his power powerless (cf. Luke 10:17-19; Heb. 2:14). Indeed, greater is the one who lives within us than the one who is in the world (1 John 4:4; 5:18). When we do not know how or what to pray as we engage in the battle, the Spirit intercedes on our behalf (Rom. 8:26). Likewise, in our stand against the schemes of the devil, we intercede on behalf of others (Eph. 6:18). He enables us to resist the adversary, standing firm in our faith (James 5:7-8; 1 Pet. 5:8-9). Ultimately it is only through the Spirit that we have the power to overcome (cf. Rev. 12:10-11).

3. Fervent Prayer in Christ's Name

As we combat the spiritual forces of evil, we are to depend upon the truth of God's Word, we are to draw on the power of the Holy Spirit, and, to round out this Trinitarian arsenal, we engage in fervent prayer in Christ's name.

This, in fact, is where Paul is led in his discussion of spiritual armor: "And pray in the Spirit on all occasions with all kinds of prayers and requests" (Eph. 6:18). Prayer could be another part of the armor, but it

---

31 See a our discussion of Article 6, sec. II.A.

may be better to see prayer as the activity that stands behind the entire battle. To use the military analogy, prayer is the supply line as we engage the enemy on the front. In prayer the truth is made personal as we do not merely talk about God; we talk to him.

Our faith is activated as we pray, and God acts when we pray. But he acts not because of who we are, for we have no right in ourselves to come before him or to ask anything of him. God acts when we pray because we now come to the Father in the name of our Lord Jesus Christ. We come in his authority and under his provision. Six times in the Gospels Jesus urges us to pray in this way: "You may ask me for anything in my name, and I will do it" (John 14:14); "Until now you have not asked for anything in my name. Ask and you will receive, and your joy will be complete" (John. 16:24). Because of our union with Christ, we can expect God to act through us in this cosmic battle.

We Do Not Fight Alone

It is important to notice the "we" in our Statement— "*we* are to combat the spiritual forces of evil." We need each other in this spiritual battle (cf. Heb. 3:13; 10:25), for who wants to be alone behind enemy lines? And in prayer we can supply protective cover for others who may be in the line of fire themselves. Paul concludes his words on spiritual warfare this way: "With this in mind, be alert and always keep on praying for all the saints" (Eph. 6:18). Even Paul requested prayer for courage to go forth in battle (Eph. 6:19-20). "I urge you, brothers, by our Lord Jesus Christ and by the love of the Spirit, to join me in my struggle by praying to God for me" (Rom. 15:30). He encourages the Colossians by informing them that Epaphras "is always wrestling in prayer for you, that you may stand firm in all the will of God, mature and fully assured" (Col. 4:12). We must not fight alone, and we must strengthen others through our prayer, confident that Jesus himself is our Intercessor before the Father (Heb. 7:25; Rom. 8:34) and that the Spirit intercedes for us even when we don't know how to pray (Rom. 8:26-27).

C. Our Confidence: In Jesus Christ Our Victory Is Assured

Although the spiritual battle in which we are engaged is demanding, we should never become discouraged. The gospel declares that our victory is assured, for Jesus has won the decisive battle through his sacrificial death and his glorious resurrection. Satan, the accuser, can accuse us no longer, for "there is now no condemnation for those who are in Christ Jesus" (Rom. 8:1). God has "disarmed the powers and authorities" and has "made a public spectacle of them, triumphing over them by the cross" (Col. 2:15). Though not totally destroyed, the devil is a defeated enemy, for Jesus Christ is risen from the dead. "In this world you will have trouble," Jesus said. "But take heart! I have overcome the world" (John 16:33). As Revelation reminds us, though Satan accuses believers day and night, we overcome by holding fast to the saving blood of the Lamb (Rev. 12:10-11). We have this assurance: greater is he who is in us, than he who is in the world (1 John 4:4).

IV. The Great Commission: We Are to Make Disciples

As we fight *against* the spiritual forces of evil, we are also contending *for* the cause of Christ and the kingdom of God. As followers of Christ we have been commissioned to engage the world with the gospel and to make disciples of Jesus Christ among all people.

Our marching orders as believers have come from the Lord Jesus himself. His final words to his disciples as recorded in Matthew's Gospel make this clear: "All authority in heaven and on earth has been given to me. Therefore go and make disciples of all nations, baptizing them in the name of the Father and of the Son and of the Holy Spirit, and teaching them to obey everything I have commanded you. And surely I am with you always, to the very end of the age" (Matt. 28:18-20). Luke and John record their own versions of this Great Commission.[32] We have been given an assignment of eternal significance, and we stand under a divine command—we are to go and make disciples.

What Is a Disciple?

Our English word "disciple" commonly translates the Greek word *mathētēs*,[33] which comes from a verb which means "to learn, or to be instructed." A disciple, then, is a pupil or student. Jesus uses the word in this sense when he says, "A student [*mathētēs*] is not above his teacher" (Matt. 10:24). A disciple of Jesus is one who learns from him.

---

32 Cf. Luke 24:45-48; Acts 1:8; John 20:21. The longer ending of Mark (which is probably a later addition) also includes this commission (Mark 16:15).

33 Interestingly, this term occurs in the New Testament only in the Gospels and Acts. The noun occurs 246 times and the verb form occurs four times (Matt. 13:52; 27:57; 28:19; Acts 14:21).

This student/teacher model, however, can be deceptive if we think of it simply in our modern Western sense, for it involves more than simply the passing on of information. In the Jewish world in which Jesus taught, a person became a disciple by attaching himself to a teacher in a relationship of loyalty and submission, and what was learned was more than mere facts or skills, but a way of life. Again, Jesus refers to this when, after saying that "A student [that is, disciple] is not above his teacher," he continues, "It is enough for the student [disciple] to be like his teacher" (Matt. 10:25).

We might use the word "apprentice" to capture this idea. An apprentice attaches himself to a master craftsman. He carefully observes the craftsman as he demonstrates his skill, and he listens to his instruction and does what he says under the craftsman's watchful eye so that, over time, the apprentice can become like him. So a disciple of Jesus is a follower of Jesus who humbly learns from Jesus so that he may become like Jesus in a process that takes a lifetime and will only be brought to completion when we are glorified with Christ.

A disciple is not a special kind of Christian. One does not become a Christian and then later become a disciple. "Disciple" is the term used in the Bible for anyone who is a Christian.[34] To become a Christian is to attach oneself to Jesus and to become a lifelong learner, an apprentice of Jesus Christ—with the goal of becoming more like him. All Christians are called to be disciples, and all are commissioned to make disciples.

A. We are to Make Disciples Among All People

In this Great Commission, Jesus commands his disciples to break out of their national and religious boundaries. We are not to restrict ourselves to those who share our Christian heritage or who embrace our moral values. Jesus said, "Go and make disciples of all nations" (Matt. 28:19).

The word "nations" here is the Greek term *ethnē*, from which we get our word "ethnic." It refers more to a cultural community, rather than a political nation-state. For that reason our Statement affirms that Jesus commissions us to make disciples "among all people." Every people-group of whatever sort is to be the object of our efforts. In whatever language, in whatever part of the world, with whatever educational or socio-economic status or cultural customs or religious tradition—we are to seek to bring this good news of God's love in Christ to them all.

For this reason, from the beginning there has been a need for those

---

34 Cf. Acts 6:1-2,7; 9:1,19; 11:26

specially called to take the gospel across the borders of language and culture to new parts of the world. These servants we commonly call "missionaries." In the pattern of the early church, they move from their own cultural home (Jerusalem) to those nearby but different (Judea and Samaria), and then to the ends of the earth (Acts 1:8).

The gospel is truly trans-national, embracing people from all backgrounds and uniting them in Christ into a new community (cf. Col. 3:11). John in the Book of Revelation gives us a picture of a future in which this has happened:

> After this I looked and there before me was a great
> multitude that no one could count, from every nation,
> tribe, people and language, standing before the throne
> and in front of the Lamb. They were wearing white
> robes and were holding palm branches in their hands.
> And they cried out in a loud voice: "Salvation belongs
> to our God, who sits on the throne, and to the Lamb."
>
> (Rev. 7:9-10)

In obedience to Christ's commission we are to seek to realize on earth what will be true in heaven as we endeavor to make disciples among all people.[35]

B. We are to Make Disciples by Bearing Witness to the Gospel in Word and Deed

How do we make disciples? If a disciple is a follower of Jesus, then obviously we must first introduce people to him. The process of making disciples begins with evangelism—the process of communicating the *evangel*, the good news that God has come in the flesh in Jesus Christ to rescue us from our sin and to redeem a people for himself. We must call people to respond to this message in repentance and faith.

The biblical expression often used to express evangelism is translated

---

35 In our Free Church history, making disciples among all nations was one of the primary reasons for partnering together as an association of local churches. Together they could do more and be more effective than individually. In 1885, one year after the formation of the Free Church Association in Boone, Iowa, Edward Thorell and Matilda Johnson were sent as the first missionaries to Utah to evangelize the Mormons. In 1887 H. J. Von Qualen was sent to China.

in English as "to testify" or "to bear witness."[36] A person testifies to what he or she has personally experienced, and the use of this term suggests that evangelism is a highly personal form of communication. In a sense, our own lives are a part of the message, in that the difference it has made in how we live communicates something to our hearers.

Words often attributed to Francis of Assisi are frequently quoted in this regard: "Preach the gospel all the time; if necessary use words." This is misstated, for our words are necessary, just as God's words are necessary for us to understand his message. But it is true, nonetheless, that how we live provides the context for the content of the message we proclaim. It provides the music that accompanies the lyrics of the gospel—the music which helps to display the beauty of those lyrics to the world. Thus, proclaiming the gospel in words and living the gospel through loving service to others ought to go hand in hand. Actions without words are insufficient, but words without actions lack credibility. We declare God's love to the world with more power when we also demonstrate that love in how we live.

For this reason we affirm that we are to bear witness to the gospel in both word and deed. Jesus taught that we are to let our light shine before men, that they may see our good deeds and praise our Father in heaven (Matt. 5:16). Peter insists that we are to live such good lives among the non-Christian neighbors that, though they accuse us of doing wrong, they may see our good deeds and glorify God on the day he visits us (1 Pet. 2:12). Making disciples begins with evangelism, offered in a demonstration of loving service, setting before others in word and deed the wonderful news of God's love in Jesus Christ and urging them to receive that love by putting their trust in him and becoming followers of Jesus.

In his Great Commission of Matthew 28:18-20, Jesus mentions two other aspects of the disciple-making process. First, it includes baptism, which, as we have seen,[37] is a picture of our union with Christ by the Spirit and our public reception into the visible body of Christ. Baptism reminds us that becoming a disciple of Jesus, though very personal, is never private, for it unites us with a new community of those who become fellow-travelers in our journey of faith.

---

36 Cf., e.g., Acts 1:8: "you will be my witnesses;" John 15:27; 21:24; Acts 4:33; 10:42; 22:5; 23:11; 2 Tim. 1:8; 1 John 1:2

37 On the meaning of baptism, see Article 7, sec. II.B.1.

Second, Jesus speaks of "teaching them to obey all that I have commanded you." A disciple is one who wants to learn how to become like Christ. In the context of grace-filled relationships within the community of the church, we teach one another, we encourage one another and we hold each other accountable to live out the new life that is ours in Christ, "considering how we may spur one another on toward love and good deeds" (Heb. 10:24).

We are called not simply to make converts, but disciples—apprentices of Jesus who are being conformed to his image. "We proclaim [Christ]," Paul says, "admonishing and teaching everyone with all wisdom, so that we may present everyone perfect in Christ" (Col. 1:28). Or, using a more graphic image, Paul writes, "I am in the pains of childbirth until Christ is formed in you" (Gal. 4:19). This is the goal of disciple-making—complete, mature followers of Christ.

Conclusion

"[God] has saved us and called us to a holy life—not because of anything we have done but because of his own purpose and grace" (2 Tim. 1:9). The same grace of God that takes away our sin also gives us new life—a life that reflects a new desire to love God and love our neighbor, to enter into the spiritual battle and to obey Christ's Great Commission. God's gospel, by its very nature, compels us to Christ-like living and witness to the world.

Evangelical Convictions

A THEOLOGICAL EXPOSITION OF THE STATEMENT OF FAITH
OF THE EVANGELICAL FREE CHURCH OF AMERICA

Article 9

CHRIST'S RETURN

9. We believe in the personal, bodily and premillennial return of our Lord Jesus Christ. The coming of Christ, at a time known only to God, demands constant expectancy and, as our blessed hope, motivates the believer to godly living, sacrificial service and energetic mission.

God's gospel will be brought to fulfillment by the Lord Himself at the end of this age.

Human beings ordinarily experience the world in three dimensions. With two eyes operating simultaneously and through the subtle effects of light and shadow and our knowledge of the relative sizes of objects, we can distinguish between near and far. Our sense of depth perception enriches our experience of life, much as a hologram enhances a two-dimensional photograph. Our lives are impoverished without this fullness of perception.

The three dimensions we experience in *space* remind us of the three dimensions we experience in *time*. We live, of course, only in the immediacy of the present, but we also remember the past and anticipate the future. The failure to learn from the past and the inability to prepare for the future are decided deficiencies that hinder healthy living. This temporal depth perception is an essential quality that must be developed if we are to live as God intended in this world, for a holistic understanding of the gospel requires an appreciation of its three temporal dimensions.

God's gospel has been accomplished in the *past*. In the life, death, and resurrection of Jesus Christ, God has acted to save us. Through that sacrificial death of Christ on the cross our sins have been taken away. We have been justified by God's grace, we *have been* saved, and we are no longer subject to the penalty of sin.

Now, in the *present,* that gospel is applied to our lives by the work of the Holy Spirit. Through the new birth, the Spirit unites us to Christ and to the new community called the church, and he empowers us to live in a new way. We are being sanctified by God's Spirit; we *are being* saved, as we are progressively set free from the power of sin.

But God's gospel also has a *future* dimension, for God's saving purpose is not yet complete. Jesus Christ has been raised from the dead, and his resurrection is but the first fruits of what is to come. Christ has been seated at the right hand of the Father, but his authority is not yet recognized by all. We still live in a fallen world, and sin and evil abound. We are still plagued by the weakness of our mortal bodies, and we have not yet been glorified with Christ in the new heaven and the new earth. But the gospel declares that in the future we *will be* saved by God's power when we are delivered from even the presence of sin.

The Bible promises us that God's gospel—his gracious purpose to redeem a people for himself in Jesus Christ—will be brought to fulfillment by the Lord himself at the end of the age when Jesus Christ returns to this earth in glory.

I. The Return of Jesus Christ

In Acts 1 Luke tells us that after his resurrection, Jesus showed himself to his disciples "and gave many convincing proofs that he was alive. He appeared to them over a period of forty days and spoke about the kingdom of God" (Acts 1:3). Then at the end of that period, the disciples were together on the Mount of Olives near Jerusalem, and Jesus "was taken up before their very eyes, and a cloud hid him from their sight" (v. 9).

In this reserved and unadorned account, free from the wild extravagance of legend or tradition, we cannot be sure exactly what the disciples saw, for though Jesus was lifted up before their eyes, a cloud hid him from their sight. The cloud throughout Scripture not only symbolizes the powerful presence of God[1] but also the movement of God, for "the Lord rides on a swift cloud" (Isa. 19:1), and the clouds are "his chariot" (Ps. 104:3). In Daniel 7 the Son of Man rode the clouds as he approached the throne of God (Dan. 7:13). Here the disciples receive a visible representation of a spiritual reality—this Jesus whom they had known and loved was taken up into the very presence of God to be seated at his right hand.

The immediate effect of this event on the disciples was confusion, as they were left wondering if they would ever see Jesus again. This response elicited a mild rebuke from the angelic figures beside them: "Men of Galilee, why do you stand here looking into the sky? This same Jesus, who has been taken from you into heaven, will come back in the same way you have seen him go" (Acts 1:11). Jesus would come back to them gloriously riding on the clouds.

The disciples ought to have known this, for Jesus himself had spoken of it. In his Olivet Discourse[2] Jesus taught that in the last days there would be a time of great distress. "At that time . . . [all the nations] will see the Son of Man coming on the clouds of the sky, with power and great glory. And he will send his angels with a loud trumpet call, and they will gather his elect from the four winds, from one end of the heavens to the other" (Matt. 24:30-31). Again in Matthew 25:31 Jesus had said, "When the Son of Man comes in his glory, and all the angels with him, he will sit

1 Cf. e.g., Exod. 16:10; 19:9; 24:16, and, in the New Testament, Matt. 17:5.

2 See Matt. 24-25; Mark 13; Luke 21.

on his throne in heavenly glory," judging the nations. Jesus Christ who rose from the dead and ascended to his Father to sit at his right hand would come again in glory.

This conviction became a critical element of apostolic instruction. Paul is most explicit. He assures the Thessalonians who were suffering for their faith that God is just and that justice would be done. "This will happen when the Lord Jesus is revealed from heaven in blazing fire with his powerful angels" (2 Thess. 1:7). And he assures them also that they need not worry about those believers who have already died, for they will not miss out on this glorious event.

> According to the Lord's own word, we tell you that we who are still alive, who are left till the coming of the Lord, will certainly not precede those who have fallen asleep. For the Lord himself will come down from heaven, with a loud command, with the voice of the archangel and with the trumpet call of God, and the dead in Christ will rise first. After that, we who are still alive and are left will be caught up together with them in the clouds to meet the Lord in the air. And so we will be with the Lord forever.
>
> (1 Thess. 4:15-17)

"[O]ur citizenship is in heaven," Paul writes. "And we eagerly await a Savior from there, the Lord Jesus Christ (Phil. 3:20). "We wait for this blessed hope: the glorious appearing of our great God and Savior, Jesus Christ" (Titus 2:13).[3]

Peter also speaks of that day when "Jesus Christ is revealed" (1 Pet. 1:7,13; 4:13) and when "the Chief Shepherd appears" (5:4), and on that day God's people will receive a crown of glory.[4] James urges patience "until the Lord's coming" (James 5:7-8). In his first epistle John instructs, "And now, dear children, continue in him, so that when he appears we may be confident and unashamed before him at his coming" (1 John 2:28), with the encouragement that "when he appears, we shall be like him, for we shall see him as he is" (3:2). The Revelation of John is centered on

---

3 In Paul, cf. also Rom. 8:22-24; 1 Cor. 1:7; 15:23; 16:22; Gal. 5:5; Eph. 4:30; Phil. 1:6, 20; 2:16; Col. 3:4; 1 Thess. 2:19; 3:13; 5:23-24; 2 Thess. 1:9-10; 2:1-12; 1 Tim. 6:14; 2 Tim. 4:1.

4 Cf. also Peter's words in Acts 3:20-21 and his reference to the "coming of the day of the Lord" in 2 Pet. 1:16; 3:12.

this glorious reality, as Jesus declares, "Behold, I am coming soon!" (Rev. 22:7,12).[5] And in Hebrews we read, "Christ was sacrificed once to take away the sins of many people; and he will appear a second time, not to bear sin, but to bring salvation to those who are waiting for him" (Heb. 9:28). The return of Jesus Christ was a central conviction of the apostles. Jesus Christ is coming again!

II. The Nature of Christ's Return

A. A Personal Return

How should we conceive of this coming of Christ? First, we affirm that it will be personal. Paul affirms that *"the Lord himself* will come down from heaven" (1 Thess. 4:16). This is not the coming of a spiritual force, or an idea, or a new form of government or a new way of life. The Bible affirms the coming of Jesus Christ himself— "this same Jesus... will come back" (Acts 1:11). Just as surely as he once came to us as a carpenter, so he himself will come again as a king.

B. A Bodily Return

Jesus will come again personally, and he will come again bodily. The angels told the disciples on the day of Jesus' ascension, "This same Jesus, who has been taken from you into heaven, will come back in the same way you have seen him go into heaven" (Acts. 1:11). As he ascended in his glorified resurrection body, so he will return in that same glorified body. We will see him, and we will become like him, in a bodily existence fit for the new heaven and the new earth (Phil. 3:20-21).

Some through history have conceived of Christ's return in only spiritual terms. The Jehovah's Witnesses, for example, maintain that Christ came to begin his reign over the earth on October 1, 1914. But this conception of the second coming of Christ has little in common with what the Bible describes. We believe that Jesus will come bodily for all to see, as visible as lightning that flashes across the sky (cf. Matt. 24:27).

C. A Premillennial Return

A third description of the return of Christ in our Statement—that it is premillennial—certainly relates to the *time* of that return (which

---

5 In John's Gospel, cf. John 21:22.

we will consider below), but more importantly it also reflects its nature. Rather than being a single great event which ushers in the new heaven and the new earth, our Statement affirms that Christ's return ushers in an "intermediate kingdom" between the present age and the eternal state, a kingdom in which Christ's identity as Lord and King will be publicly vindicated on earth. This period of great earthly blessedness under the rule of Christ is also known as the millennium, and we affirm that Christ will return *before* this kingdom is realized on earth. Hence, we describe his return as *pre*-millennial.

Premillennialism is distinguished from two other views regarding this messianic kingdom. Some contend that through the preaching of the gospel around the world and the powerful work of the Holy Spirit in conversion, a large proportion of the world's population will become believers in Christ. Moral conditions in the world will dramatically improve as the gospel transforms individuals, families, churches, communities and cultures.[6] This hope has gripped many during times of great revival, including the renowned Evangelical pastor-theologian Jonathan Edwards in the Great Awakening of the eighteenth century. Because Christ will return only *after* this time of earthly blessing, this view is called *post*-millennialism.

A third view of this earthly kingdom, and the most common through the history of the church, understands this rule of Christ as operative during the present age, for he is even now at the right hand of the Father and he has been given all authority in heaven and earth (cf. Matt. 28:19). When Christ returns he will immediately usher in the new heaven and the new earth. Because no intermediate millennial kingdom of Christ is posited, this view is commonly referred to as *a*-millennialism,[7] though some adherents prefer the term "inaugurated millennialism," for they believe that the millennial rule of Christ has already begun.[8]

Premillennialists insist upon a future millennial kingdom coming after Christ's return on the basis of the teaching of Revelation 20:1-

---

6 A theologically liberal version of this view asserts that this transformation will take place simply through political efforts promoting social justice (the so-called "social gospel"). Evangelical proponents of postmillennialism would not agree with this humanistic version and would ascribe this transformation to God's power and grace at work in the world.

7 The "a" represents the negative prefix in Greek.

8 This view necessarily entails a very different conception of what is meant by the "millennium."

10.[9] The Book of Revelation is apocalyptic literature, relating heavenly visions full of peculiar creatures and extraordinary events, with serpents coming up out of the sea and locust-like armies invading from the east, culminating in the arrival of a rider on a great white horse. John is taken up into heaven in order to see the world from a divine perspective. He is given a glimpse behind the scenes of history so that he can see what is really going on in the events of this world. John speaks in models and metaphors, not literal descriptions. But the book, nonetheless, uses this symbolic language to convey truth about what is real. The battle of good and evil is real, the final victory of God is real, the new heaven and the new earth is real, and, we believe, the intermediate millennial kingdom of Revelation 20:1-10 is also real.

Interpreters of the book differ greatly as to the nature of what is described there, reflecting differing interpretive frameworks for the book as a whole. Described as a "preterist" view,[10] some believe John is simply describing events of his own day, culminating, perhaps, in the fall of Jerusalem in A.D. 70. The "historicist" perspective views the book as a description of the events that will take place during the whole of church history from the time of the apostles to the end of this age. An "idealist" interpretation argues that the symbols do not relate to historical events at all but to timeless spiritual truths. Finally, the "futurist" interpretation holds that the book relates events yet to come, from John's perspective and ours. Each of these interpretive frameworks has value, as we must assume that the book had significance both for John's original readers and for the church throughout this age. An eclectic approach, incorporating the strengths of each view is probably best, but we must insist that some future dimension remains, for the future coming of Christ in glory is clearly taught elsewhere in the New Testament and the glorious future of chapters 21-22 has certainly not yet arrived.[11]

---

9 In the New Testament, 1 Cor. 15:20-28 is also cited as a passage that at least suggests an intermediate kingdom of Christ. Those operating within a Dispensationalist framework (see further below) see numerous passages in the Old Testament that point to the millennium. However, not all in the Free Church hold to this Dispensational understanding, and, therefore, there is no consensus among us whether certain Old Testament prophecies (e.g. Ps. 72:8-14; Isa. 11:6-9; Zech. 14:5-17) refer to the church age, to the millennium or to the new heaven and the new earth. Nor do we have a settled view on whether passages such as Ezek. 40-48 require a literal fulfillment in some future Jewish kingdom or were intended by their authors to be understood to refer to real future events but in a symbolic sense.

10 The word "preterist" refers to a past action or state.

11 We therefore deny a "hyper-preterist" position which holds that Christ "returned" in

But when does this millennial rule of Christ take place? Some interpret the Book of Revelation as a series of overlapping and recapitulating cycles, with the seals, trumpets and bowls all recounting basically the same reality from different perspectives, and all ending with the culmination of Christ's return at the end of the age. They consider the binding of Satan and Christ's millennial kingdom (Rev. 20:1-10) as yet another recapitulation describing the present age of the church. But even if the earlier cycles of chapters 6-18 cover the same ground, the events of chapters 19-22 are by their very nature temporally sequential. The glorious coming of Christ (chap. 19) must come before the final judgment (20:11-15) which, in turn, must precede the establishment of the new heaven and the new earth (chaps. 21-22). The millennium (20:1-10) fits into this sequential series of events and is best seen as coming after Christ's return and before the final judgment.

The description of this millennial kingdom develops in three parts. First, John describes the binding of Satan (Rev. 20:1-3). Although some equate this with the "binding" Jesus refers to in Mark 3:27 which takes place during his ministry, the very strong language of Revelation suggests otherwise. The dragon's activity is not simply curtailed; he is absolutely bound in the abyss (or prison) with a key and a "great chain." He is totally "sealed" in it (the same term used in the "sealing of the saints" in 7:1-8). Moreover, he can no longer "deceive the nations" (v. 3), the very thing God allows him to do in this age (cf. Rev. 12:9; 13:14; 18:23; 19:20). So this binding probably refers to a period following the present age.

In the second section of the passage, vv. 4-6, the saints reign. Those on "thrones" are described as the martyrs (v. 4), but this description should probably include all the saints (vv. 6,9). Those who died now "come to life," a verb that does not refer, as some argue, to spiritual life after conversion or during the intermediate state but, consistent with its use elsewhere, to physical resurrection (cf. Matt. 9:18; John 11:25; Rom. 14:9; Rev. 1:18, 2:8, 13:14). Further, the vindication of the martyrs during this period is in stark contrast to their situation in 6:9-11 in which they are told to wait for the time at which their blood would be avenged. Therefore, it appears that this millennium refers to a period after Christ's return.

Finally, vv. 7-10 tell of the final defeat of Satan. His release from captivity is in some sense a divine necessity (20:3). Certainly, the flocking of the nations after this deceiver proves their absolute depravity and

A.D. 70 and that there is no future coming in glory at the end of the age.

218

leads to the exigency of eternal punishment in 20:11-15. Satan "gathers them for battle" (v.8),[12] but they meet their final defeat (v. 9), paving the way for the judgment to follow and the coming of the eternal state.

This passage speaks of a period of "a thousand years" (Rev. 20:2-7), but we recognize that numbers are often used symbolically in this type of literature in general and in the Book of Revelation in particular.[13] Therefore, though many interpret this "thousand years" literally, we do not insist on a literal interpretation of this number here. The millennium will be a period of time under God's sovereign control in which he will perfectly work out his good purpose in overcoming evil in the redemption of his creation. Though the "thousand years" may not be literal, the event this number describes will certainly be a historical reality that extends for some period of time.

Revelation 20:1-10 depicts a transition between the present world order and the age to come. As a transition it is in some ways continuous with and different from both the present age and the eternal state. Conceptions of this millennial kingdom often differ on whether it is more like our present experience or more like that glorious (and unimaginable) future reality. In any event, it serves to tie together two central themes in the Book of Revelation and of the Bible as whole.

First, the events surrounding the millennial kingdom finalize the defeat of the dragon, "that ancient serpent, who is the devil, or Satan" (Rev. 20:2), a battle which began in the Garden of Eden. The theme of the ultimate futility of Satan before the sovereignty of God in the Book of Revelation is brought to a close. Evil will receive its just punishment in the "second death" which will deal with death itself (Rev. 20:14). The true nature of human depravity is revealed in those who enjoy the goodness of the rule of Christ himself for an extended period but who still join in rebellious allegiance to Satan when he is released for a final outburst of evil (20:7-10). Therefore, God's ways in judgment and eternal condemnation are justified.

Second, the glory of the Lamb upon the throne, fully revealed only

---

12 The wording here is exactly the same as in 16:14, and amillennialists take vv. 7-9 to be synonymous with the battle of Armageddon. However, the details are different, supporting a similar but distinguishable battle. If this is simply a recapitulation of earlier events, it offers a rather pale description of what is a climactic event in the book—the coming of Christ in glory (described vividly in 19:11-21).

13 See especially the use of the numbers 4, 7, 10 and 12 (and numbers derived from them) in the book. Each of these numbers commonly signifies wholeness or completeness throughout Scripture.

in heaven (Rev. 5), will be made known *on earth*. Jesus Christ, the King of kings and Lord of lords, will be vindicated in a public and visible way, as will his faithful saints who reign with him (cf. Rev. 2:26-27; 3:21; 6:11; 8:2-5). One can view the millennial kingdom as a restoration of God's good creation in Eden. Jesus, as the second Adam, fulfils the priestly and regal dimensions of the first Adam's God-given role in creation (found in Gen. 1:26-27; 2:16-17), and his people will share with him in this role as kings and priests (cf. Rev. 20:6). Thus, the millennial kingdom is the penultimate fulfillment of God's promise of blessing to his people in the context of this fallen world, while the new Jerusalem coming down from heaven (Rev. 21:2) is the ultimate realization of that promise in the context of the fully transformed cosmos when the distinction between heaven and earth will be no more and God will fully dwell with his people.

Some within the Free Church understand the millennial reign of Christ not so much in terms of a restoration of Eden but as a restoration of Israel. This view, associated particularly with a theological system known as Dispensationalism,[14] insists on a strict distinction between Israel in the Old Testament and the church in the New. Consequently, Dispensationalists believe that the promises to the nation of Israel are still in effect and will be fulfilled on earth in some visible and tangible way. The millennial kingdom, then, is the sphere in which national Israel is reconstituted and God's promises of blessing to Israel are realized.

This Dispensational view also entails that before the institution of this Jewish kingdom, the Lord will take his (largely) Gentile church out of this world before a period of great tribulation lasting seven years in which God's wrath will be poured out. This exodus will occur when Christ comes from heaven to "rapture"[15] his church into heaven (see 1 Thess. 4:13-18), before returning in glory with them at the end of this tribulational period to inaugurate his millennial kingdom. This view is referred to as "pre-tribulational premillennialism," and it has been very popular in Free Church history and continues to be widely embraced. The last few

---

14 This term was coined for this view based on the importance given by it to the various ways God has ordered his relationship to human beings, known as "dispensations." It tends to stress the discontinuity between the Old and New Testaments, emphasizing the continuing significance of the nation of Israel. A contrasting viewpoint highlighting the continuity of the two Testaments is often referred to as Covenantalism, which affirms the church as existing throughout redemptive history.

15 This term comes from the Latin translation of 1 Thess. 4:17, where Paul says that believers who are still alive will be "caught up" *(rapiemur)* in the clouds to meet the Lord in the air.

decades have seen the development of Progressive Dispensationalism, a variation of Dispensationalism, which has gained a number of adherents in the EFCA. It maintains a less strict separation of the church and Israel and a broader understanding of how the prophesies of the Old Testament may be fulfilled.

Another position, known as "historic premillennialism" (which has become increasingly common in the Free Church in recent years), holds that the promises to Israel may be fulfilled in Christ, in the church, in the millennium or in the new heaven and the new earth. The millennium will be focused on the church, not on Israel. Consequently, historic premillennialists see the coming of Christ not in two stages but as one great event. The "rapture" referred to in 1 Thessalonians 4:17 in which believers will "meet the Lord in the air" describes a royal welcome in which those visited by a king go out to meet him as a form of honorific greeting.[16] There will be a time of tribulation on earth, but Christ will not come until *after* this has been completed. Both the "post-" and "pre-tribulational" views of the coming of Christ are accepted within the Free Church.[17]

In summary, our affirmation of the premillennial return of Christ in this Statement entails the following:

1. The kingdom of God will not reach its culmination and fulfillment on earth before Jesus Christ comes in glory.

2. God's purposes include the public vindication of Christ. He will be seen to be the King of kings and Lord of lords by all, and he will establish his reign on this earth.

3. God's people will be vindicated with Christ in a public and visible way.

4. The coming of Christ will not simply usher in some spiritual heaven divorced from this created order. In an intermediate stage, Jesus must reign until he has put all enemies under his feet, before he hands over the kingdom to God the Father, ushering in the new heaven and the new earth in the eternal

---

16 The expression used in this verse (*eis apantēsin*) is also used of the virgins going out to meet the bridegroom in Matt. 25:6 and of the believers going out to meet Paul as he was about to arrive in Rome (Acts 28:15).

17 Other accepted views of the coming of Christ in relation to the tribulation referred to in Revelation are "mid-tribulationalism," which holds that Christ will return in the middle of the seven-year tribulation period, and "pre-wrath," which holds that Christ will return some time after the mid-point but before the end of the tribulation. Since these views also affirm a two-stage return of Christ, they are really variations of the Dispensational pre-tribulational view.

state.

5. Evil will not be overcome fully and completely when Christ returns in glory, but only after an intermediate kingdom which must precede that final victory of God. There will be one more uprising of the evil one at the end of the millennium, before the dawning of the new heaven and the new earth.

Further, we can also say what this Statement affirming premillennialism does not mean:

1. It does not require a specific position on when Christ will come in relation to a time of great tribulation.
2. It does not require a certain way of reading the Bible regarding the fulfillment of the prophecies of the Old Testament, whether that fulfillment is found in the nation of Israel, in Christ, in the church, in the millennium or in the new heaven and the new earth.
3. It does not entail a particular understanding of Israel and the church or of the current nation-state of Israel.
4. It does not necessarily mean that Christ's earthly reign must be a period of precisely one thousand years.

1. A Brief History of Millennial Theology[18]

We acknowledge that the premillennial position affirmed here has not been the consensus of the church through the ages. It is generally held that most of the best-known ante-Nicene church fathers (pre-A.D. 325), including Justin Martyr, Irenaeus and Tertullian, had roughly premillennial views, though these were often vaguely defined.[19] Certainly by the fourth century, when the Roman Empire became formally Christian, most of the preeminent church fathers had turned away from premillennialism.

This turn could be explained by a number of factors, including a

---

18 This section draws largely from a presentation by Doug Sweeney, Professor of Church History and the History of Christian Thought, Director, Jonathan Edwards Center entitled "Keeping Watch Until He Comes: A History of Christian Millennialism" presented at the EFCA Ministerial Association's Midwinter Conference in Bollingbrook, IL, on Jan. 27, 2000.

19 Some argue that a form of amillennialism may have been as widely held during this time as premillennialism. Cf., e.g., Charles E. Hill, *Regnum Caelorum: Patterns of Millennial Thought in Early Christianity*, 2nd edition (Grand Rapids: Eerdmans, 2001).

reaction against the radical prophetic practices of the Montanists;[20] the spread of the allegorical hermeneutics of the Alexandrian school with its aversion to any earthly, physical or sensuous depictions of the millennial age; and the more prominent social status of Christianity within the Empire. It became more difficult to associate Roman officials with the anti-Christ, and the millennial hopes of a persecuted minority became less fervent as the Christian believers became more at home in a Christianized Roman Empire.

The most significant influence in the decline of premillennialism, however, was the teaching of Augustine, expounded in his *City of God*.[21] After the time of Augustine, amillennialism became increasingly common among Catholics, and millennialism of any kind, such as that propounded by the twelfth-century Cistercian monk Joachim of Fiore, for example, was increasingly viewed with suspicion as dissension against the Catholic hierarchy.

The Magisterial Reformers of the Reformation era, such as Luther and Calvin, believed they were living in the last days and fervently believed in the imminent return of Christ, but they continued in the amillennialism they inherited. Millennial thought was beginning to stir at this period, however, particularly among the Anabaptists and in England.

The roots of modern Anglo-American eschatology are found in the millennial resurgence of the Puritans of the seventeenth century. Though, again, millennial positions were not clearly delineated, Puritan millenarianism could take both premillennial and, more commonly, postmillennial forms, and the latter, at this stage, were rarely liberal or optimistic about human progress. Indeed, for most of the English Puritans, including many amillennialists, the time preceding the final judgment would be one of unprecedented spiritual revival and one in which the Jewish people, especially, would come to faith. The Anglican Daniel Whitby (1638-1725) was the leading postmillennial voice, influencing many, including Jonathan Edwards. Another Anglican, Joseph Mede (1586-1638), was the best-known English premillennialist, popularizing the views of the German Calvinist, Johann Heinrich Alsted (1588-1638).

The nineteenth century saw a further resurgence of premillennial thought, though in a distinctively Dispensational form. Beginning

---

20 On the Montanists, see Article 2, n. 13.

21 This extremely influential work was written after the fall of Rome over a period of years (ca. 412-426).

in Great Britain, it was inspired chiefly by two men. The first, Edward Irving (1792-1834), was a famous Scottish charismatic, who broke with the Presbyterian Church to form his own denomination, the "Catholic Apostolic Church." This caused many to see premillennialism as both dangerous and sectarian.

The second popularizer of Dispensational premillennialism, John Nelson Darby (1800-82), was one of the early leaders of the Plymouth Brethren and is known as the founding father of Dispensationalism. The most distinguishing features of his eschatology were the doctrine of the secret (pre-tribulational) rapture and his commitment to divide the New Testament into national Jewish texts and church texts. Darby himself traveled widely, but his views were disseminated even more through the publication of the Scofield Bible in 1909 and Bible prophecy conferences such as those held at Niagara-on-the-Lake, Ontario, which were very popular in the late-nineteenth century. His views later formed the foundation of best-selling books such as Hal Lindsey's *The Late Great Planet Earth* in the 1970s (which, for a time, was the best-selling book in America apart from the Bible) and the *Left Behind* series of novels by Tim LaHaye and Jerry Jenkins in the 1990s. In addition, the Bible school movement of the late-nineteenth and early-twentieth centuries, which founded such schools as Moody Bible Institute, also promoted this Dispensational premillennialism, and this perspective was dominant in Free Church circles in its formative periods.

The rise of the Evangelical movement in the mid-twentieth century under the leadership of men like Carl F. H. Henry and Kenneth Kantzer led to some new theological developments, including a renewal of historic premillennialism. This view held to an intermediate millennial kingdom but without the Dispensational theological framework that had become so tied with it in North America. This form of premillennialism has become increasingly common in the EFCA.

2. The Place of Premillennialism in Our Statement of Faith

This brief historical survey underlines the fact that premillennialism is but one of several positions that has been held in the church, even within the Evangelical tradition. Furthermore, the millennial issue has not been defined in any major ecclesiastical creed or confessional statement. This reticence reflects the view of Justin Martyr, one of the early Christian apologists writing in the mid-second century. Justin himself espoused a belief in the millennial reign of Christ on earth, but he did not make this position a criterion for orthodoxy, conceding that "many who belong to the pure and pious faith, and are true Christians, think otherwise."[22]

We in the EFCA often speak of our desire to "major on the majors and minor on the minors" in delineating our core doctrinal convictions, and our Statement of Faith largely reflects that. We have set forth those doctrines which are very closely connected to the gospel itself and which have been widely held by Bible-believing Christians through all ages. We deliberately do not take a position on such significant issues as whether the regenerating work of the Spirit occurs before or after faith, or the time and mode of baptism—issues which have divided Christians through the centuries. And we recognize that Evangelical believers with strong convictions regarding the inerrant authority of the Scriptures have taken different positions on the millennium. In light of our distinctive ethos in the EFCA of uniting around the central doctrines of the faith, the inclusion of premillennialism in our Statement of Faith seems to many to be out of place.

In the period leading up to the revision of our Statement of Faith in 2008, we in the EFCA wrestled with whether to include premillennialism among our core theological convictions. In the end, the EFCA Board of Directors, after initially proposing three drafts without it,[23] decided to present to our Conference a revised Statement that did include premillennialism. The Board determined that though many among us recognized that it was not a doctrine central to the gospel, it remained

---

22 *Dialogue with Trypho*, LXXX. Justin's view has been echoed in our day by Free Church leader Kenneth Kantzer: "Some doctrines—the Trinity and the Incarnation, for example—are more integrally related to the person of Christ or to the gospel. Yet other doctrines, such as baptism or the nature of the elect, may be very important, but do not demand universal allegiance. One can possess an enduring and consistent Christian faith and differ with another believer over this kind of doctrine. Explanations about the second coming of Christ fit this description. It is an important slice of biblical theology, but it does not require a single interpretation among Christians" ("Our Future Hope: Eschatology and Its Role in the Church" [Christianity Today Institute], *Christianity Today* 31/2 [February, 1987], 1-I-14-I).

23 The original proposal for Article 9, which circulated publicly for some time, read: "We believe in the personal, bodily and glorious return of our Lord Jesus Christ with His holy angels when He will bring His kingdom to fulfillment and exercise His role as Judge of all. This coming of Christ, at a time known only to God, demands constant expectancy and, as our blessed hope, motivates the believer to godly living, sacrificial service and energetic mission." Interestingly, the Evangelical Free Church of Canada, which also adopted a new Statement of Faith in 2008, chose to use this version of Article 9. Their Statement is identical to that of the EFCA apart from this article and its introduction and headings which explicitly link each article to the gospel.

to many others a distinctive theological position of our movement that they would very strongly oppose changing. Consequently, the Board concluded that attempting to remove premillennialism at this time would create significant disunity and disruption. The General Conference agreed with that decision in voting to adopt the revised Statement of Faith. We expound it here with the understanding that we do not claim that it is an essential doctrine of Evangelical faith, but it remains a distinctive theological position of the EFCA.[24]

III. The Time of Christ's Return

Speculation about the time of the return of Christ has been a constant temptation in the life of the church. Thus far, no prediction has proved true.[25] The Bible warns us against such speculation in the clearest terms.

A. The Time of Christ's Return Is Known Only to God

Jesus spoke of signs of the end, including earthquakes, famine, political upheaval, false messiahs, persecution amid world-wide gospel preaching, and even the fall of Jerusalem (Matt. 24; Mark 13; Luke 21), but none of these can be used to pinpoint a particular moment in history when the end will come. "You do not know on what day your Lord will come," he told his disciples (Matt. 24:42). In fact, "No one knows about that day or hour, not even the angels in heaven, nor the Son, but only the Father" (Matt. 24:36; cf. 1 Tim. 6:14-15). Speculation is fruitless, and it can be dangerous. Jesus warned against false prophets who would come and deceive many concerning his coming (Matt. 24:4,11,24). He will come "like a thief in the night," Paul writes (1 Thess. 5:2; also 2 Pet. 3:10).

B. Christ's Return Demands Constant Expectancy

This uncertainty regarding its time demands that the proper attitude toward Christ's coming is one of constant expectancy. "Therefore, keep

---

24 For the minutes of the 2008 EFCA National Conference recording the debate on the Conference floor regarding the revision of the Statement of Faith, see http://www.efca.org/files/document/pastoral-care/ministerial-forum-12-08.pdf.

25 The story is told of an English preacher, William Partridge, who in 1695 distributed a religious tract prophesying that the world would end in 1697. In 1698 he distributed another tract, this one claiming that the world had indeed ended in 1697 but that no one cared to take notice!

watch, because you do not know on what day your Lord will come" (Matt. 24:42). Jesus will come like a thief in the night, so we are not to be caught sleeping, but should be alert and self-controlled (1 Thess. 5:6; Rom. 13:11-14; 2 Pet. 3:10-12; Rev. 3:3). Jesus urged his followers to be faithful servants, vigilant in their duty. "So you also must be ready, because the Son of Man will come at an hour when you do not expect him" (Matt. 24:44; Luke 12:40). The question remains: when he comes, will our Lord find us living in faith (Luke 18:8)?

The conviction that Jesus Christ could return at any time was compelling to many early Free Church leaders in this country. They believed the Lord's coming was imminent and that this return was the next great event to transpire in God's plan of salvation. Because the word "imminent" became associated with a particular theological position (the pre-tribulational coming of Christ) that is not required in the EFCA, we have chosen in this Statement to express their concern in other terms. Echoing the biblical language, we are to be constantly expectant.

But does this demand for constant expectancy imply that there can be no "signs" of Christ's coming? Some contend that if any signs must occur before Christ's return or if Christ's coming will take place only after a defined period of intense tribulation, the biblical call to vigilance is undermined. It appears to many, however, that the Bible is not clear on this point. Despite the call to constant vigilance, when Jesus' disciples asked him about the time of his coming, he spoke at some length of various things that must happen first, including the gospel being "preached in the whole world as a testimony to all nations" (cf. Matt. 24:14,33-34). The day of the Lord will come like a thief in the night, but Paul teaches the Thessalonians that "you, brothers, are not in the darkness so that this day should surprise you like a thief" (1 Thess. 5:4). In his second letter to them, he appears to go even farther: "Don't let anyone deceive you in any way, for that day will not come until the rebellion occurs and the man of lawlessness is revealed" (2 Thess. 2:3).

We should concede that it is possible that some signs must first take place before Christ returns (including a time of great tribulation), but we must also humbly acknowledge that we may not be able to discern those signs clearly enough to determine contemporaneously whether they have, in fact, already taken place.[26] Our best course is to assert what the Bible most clearly affirms: Only the Father knows the time of the Son's return, and until he comes we must maintain constant expectancy.

---

26 For example, how can we determine whether the gospel has indeed been preached to all nations (cf. Matt. 24:14)?

We are called to live as "sons of the light and sons of the day" (1 Thess. 5:5), with constant moral vigilance and enduring faith and hope.

IV. The Effect of Christ's Return

A. Our Blessed Hope

The first Christians were inspired by an eager expectation—the Lord Jesus Christ is coming back! "Our citizenship is in heaven," Paul writes, "And we eagerly await a Savior from there, the Lord Jesus Christ" (Phil. 3:20). To Titus he declares, "[W]e wait for the blessed hope—the glorious appearing of our great God and Savior, Jesus Christ" (Titus 2:13). John in his first epistle echoes that eager hope: "Dear children, this is the last hour; . . . we know that when he appears, we shall be like him for we shall see him as he is" (2:18; 3:2). In almost the last words of the New Testament, the risen Jesus declares, "I am coming soon!" And this declaration evokes the response, "So be it. Come Lord Jesus!" (Rev. 22:20).

These Christians were waiting for the coming of their Lord Jesus, and they expected him to return soon. Paul seems to expect it within his own lifetime when he tells the Thessalonians that "we who are still alive, who are left till the coming of the Lord, will certainly not precede those who have fallen asleep" (1 Thess. 4:15). "The hour has come for you to wake up from your slumber, because our salvation is nearer now than when we first believed. The night is nearly over; the day is almost here" (Rom. 13:11-12). James expresses this expectation: "Be patient and stand firm, because the Lord's coming is near" (James 5:8). Peter, too, states it clearly, "The end of all things is near" (1 Pet. 4:7).

Were they mistaken in their belief in the "nearness" of the coming of Christ? Even during the apostolic age, scoffers were asking, "Where is this 'coming' he promised?" (2 Pet. 3:4). After two thousand years can we still have the same expectation, the same hope?

We can and we must. Theirs was an eager expectation, but they were not misled, nor were they mistaken. As we have already seen, alongside the New Testament statements about the nearness of Jesus' coming are those which speak of or presuppose a delay or which declare the time of his coming as uncertain and even unknowable. The "nearness" of his coming speaks of the possibility of its taking place soon. In that sense, the Lord's coming was near then, and it is near now, for we do not know when it will be.

Further, our perception of time is limited. "And do not forget this one thing, dear friends:" Peter reminds us, "With the Lord a day is like a thousand years, and a thousand years is like a day" (2 Pet. 3:8). There is a purpose in the delay (if we may even call it a delay), for through it the Lord is testing our faithfulness and allowing the opportunity for salvation. "The Lord is not slow in keeping his promise, as some understand slowness. He is patient with you, not wanting anyone to perish, but everyone to come to repentance" (2 Pet. 3:9).

In the meantime, we are sustained by the Lord's great and precious promises (2 Pet. 1:4). More than that, Paul speaks of the down payment that has already been made, the seal of the Holy Spirit who now lives within our hearts, and who guarantees that we shall receive what God has promised to his people (Eph. 1:14). As we await the "not yet," we enjoy the "already."

The early Christians spoke of Christ's second coming as if it were just around the corner, and so should we, as we sing,

> The strife will not be long;
> This day the noise of battle,
> The next the victor's song.[27]

B. A Motivation for the Believer

It is sometimes said such an emphasis on the coming of Christ has a detrimental effect on the life of Christians. The admonition to "be watchful" is understood as mere star-gazing. People become so busy looking up to the heavens for Jesus to return that they are no earthly good.[28] Life on this side of Christ's coming becomes almost frivolous and without significance.

But such an understanding could not be further from the truth. Being watchful does not mean that we should sit out on the porch like a lonely dog, pining away until our master returns. Instead, we are to live with the certainty that Christ is coming, and when he does we will be held accountable for how we have lived. Jesus compared our situation to that of stewards responsible for the master's estate (Matt. 24:45-51) or to financial managers entrusted with the master's money (Matt. 25:14-30). We have a job to do, and when our Master returns, he will

---

27 From the hymn "Stand Up, Stand Up for Jesus" by George Duffield, Jr. (1858).

28 It is sometimes argued that Paul's warnings against idleness in 2 Thess. 2:6-15 are directed against those who had taken this approach.

reward his servants for their faithfulness.

Living with a sense of expectancy of the coming of Christ ought not to draw us away from earthly responsibilities but make us more faithful to them. Lord Shaftesbury, the nineteenth-century English social reformer who worked tirelessly to improve conditions in the London slums, said near the end of his life, "I do not think that in the last forty years I have lived one conscious hour that was not influenced by the thought of our Lord's return."[29] The coming of Christ ought to motivate the believer to godly living, sacrificial service and energetic mission. "For what comes," wrote C. S. Lewis, "is judgment." Lewis continues:

> [H]appy are those whom [the Lord] finds laboring in their vocation, whether we're merely going out to feed the pigs or laying good plans to deliver humanity a hundred years hence from some great evil. Perhaps the curtain *will* fall—those pigs will *never* in fact be fed, the great campaign against slavery or governmental tyranny will never in fact proceed to victory. No matter; you were at your post when the inspection came.[30]

Regardless of how much time is left before our Lord returns, we must live each day with an eager hope to hear his words of commendation, "Well done, good and faithful servant" (Matt. 25:21). Blessed will be that servant whose Master finds him living faithfully when he returns (Matt. 24:46).

"The night is nearly over; the day is almost here" (Rom. 13:12). We wait for the day when our Lord will come to fulfill all that has been promised by the prophets (cf. Acts 3:21), when Christ "will appear a second time, not to bear sin, but to bring salvation to those who are waiting for him" (Heb. 9:28). The gospel's promise of redemption will be fulfilled when Christ comes again in glory. This hope of the final consummation of what was begun in Jesus' resurrection from the dead is essential, for as one writer put it, "Faith in Jesus, faith in his life, and his death, and his resurrection from the grave, without the expectation of his [return] is a cheque that is never cashed, a promise that is not made in earnest. A faith in Christ without the expectation of a [return] is like a flight of

---

29 Quoted in James Montgomery Boice, *Foundations of the Christian Faith* (Downers Grove: InterVarsity, 1986), 707.

30 C.S. Lewis, *The World's Last Night, And Other Essays* (San Diego, CA: Harcourt, 1960), 111-112.

stairs that leads nowhere, but ends in the void."[31]

Jesus Christ is coming again, and until then we must "continue in him, so that when he appears we may be confident and unashamed before him at his coming" (1 John 2:28). "We wait for the blessed hope—the glorious appearing of our great God and Savior, Jesus Christ" (Titus 2:13). So we pray in the words preserved in the Aramaic language of the first Jewish Christians, *marana tha*, which means "Come, O Lord!" (1 Cor. 16:22).

---

31 Emil Brunner, *The Christian Doctrine of the Church, Faith and the Consummation: Dogmatics,* vol. 3 (Eng. trans., London: Lutterworth, 1966), 396, cited in Stephen H. Travis, *I Believe in the Second Coming of Jesus* (Grand Rapids: Eerdmans, 1982), 105.

Evangelical Convictions

A THEOLOGICAL EXPOSITION OF THE STATEMENT OF FAITH
OF THE EVANGELICAL FREE CHURCH OF AMERICA

Article 10

RESPONSE AND ETERNAL DESTINY

10. We believe that God commands everyone everywhere to believe the gospel by turning to Him in repentance and receiving the Lord Jesus Christ. We believe that God will raise the dead bodily and judge the world, assigning the unbeliever to condemnation and eternal conscious punishment and the believer to eternal blessedness and joy with the Lord in the new heaven and the new earth, to the praise of His glorious grace. Amen.

God's gospel requires a response that has eternal consequences.

The Statement of Faith of the Evangelical Free Church of America is an exposition of the gospel—God's gospel, the gospel of Jesus Christ. And what is the gospel? It is the *evangel*, the good news that God has acted graciously to save a people for himself through his Son Jesus Christ. The gospel is the simple message that Jesus died for our sins and rose again so that we might have eternal life. This message of good news can be stated as concisely as this: "God so loved the world that he gave his one and only Son so that whoever believes in him may not perish but have eternal life" (John 3:16). Our Statement seeks to unpack this gospel by organizing the essential doctrines of our faith—our critical Evangelical convictions—around this central theme.

Our final article brings the entire document to a fitting conclusion. The gospel, and our Statement, begins with God and his saving purpose, which flows out of the wondrous perfections of his nature. He is the Creator of all things and is holy, infinitely perfect, and eternally existing in a loving unity of three equally divine Persons: the Father, the Son, and the Holy Spirit. This one God, all-knowing and all-powerful, has, in love and grace, purposed from eternity to redeem a people for himself and to restore his fallen creation for His own glory.

But how do we know this good news? We know it only because God himself has revealed it to us. Our second Article affirms that God's gospel is authoritatively announced in the Scriptures. Through the words of its human authors, God has spoken in his Word, the Bible, without error. The Scriptures are the complete revelation of his will for salvation, and the ultimate authority that stands over every realm of human knowledge and endeavor. Therefore, the Bible is to be believed in all that it teaches, obeyed in all that it requires, and trusted in all that it promises.

This gospel revealed in the Bible is important to us because it alone addresses our deepest human need. Our central problem is not a lack of education, inadequate healthcare or a terrorist threat. It is our alienation from God. We have sinned, all of us, beginning with our first ancestors. We are fallen in our nature before we take our first breath. By our own volition we go our own way in defiance of God's rightful rule, refusing to allow God to be God in our lives. This cosmic rebellion is evil, and God will not stand for it. As a result we now stand under his wrath, and we can be rescued, reconciled and restored only through God's gracious work in Jesus Christ.

In the Person of Jesus Christ the gospel is revealed in history. As Israel's promised Messiah, Jesus Christ is God incarnate, fully God and fully man. He was born of the virgin Mary, lived a sinless life, was crucified under Pontius Pilate. He was buried and arose bodily from the dead, and ascended into heaven, where, at the right hand of God the Father, he is now our High Priest and Advocate.

God's gospel is not only revealed in Jesus Christ, it is also accomplished through his work. For when he died on the cross, Jesus acted as our representative and substitute as the perfect, all-sufficient sacrifice for our sins. He was raised from the dead as a foretaste of his victory over all the forces of sin and death.

What Jesus did then, two thousand years ago, is now applied to our lives by the Holy Spirit. The Spirit glorifies Christ as he works within us to convict us of our guilt and to grant us new spiritual life as we are born again into a new union with Christ. We are joined to him in his death and resurrection. The indwelling Holy Spirit now empowers us to live in a new way, so that we might become like Christ.

When we are joined to Christ by faith, we become a part of a new family, the family of God, and we become a part of a new body, the body of Christ. God's gospel is now embodied in a new community, the church, which is manifest in local churches. In the fellowship of the church and through its ordinances, our faith is nourished and strengthened.

In the grace of the gospel, God justifies us, accepting us just as we are. But in his grace, he does not leave us just as we are. This gospel also changes us; it sanctifies us, compelling us to Christ-like living and witness to the world. We are to grow in our love for God and for other people who are created in his image. We are to show the same compassion we have received toward others who are in need. We are to do battle with the forces of evil in this world, in fellowship with one another, in dependence on him, using all the resources he has given us. And in all that we do, in word and deed, we are to bear witness to this glorious gospel among all people.

We believe that one day God will bring his saving purpose in the gospel to fulfillment, when Jesus Christ comes in glory with his holy angels to establish his kingdom fully and completely and to exercise his role as Judge of all. Jesus Christ is coming again, and that is our blessed hope—a hope that spurs us on to remain faithful to our Lord to the end.

This is the gospel—God's saving purpose in Jesus Christ. We might well ask, does the saving work of Christ apply to everyone whether they want it to or not? Is everybody automatically forgiven and reconciled to God simply because Jesus died and rose again? Will everyone be saved in the end?

But what does it mean to be saved? Doesn't it mean that we are rescued from the self-centeredness of our sin and brought into a relationship with God in which he is worshiped and adored and given all glory and honor? Do all people really *want* this kind of salvation? They may want to be free from pain or sickness or death, but do they really want to enter into a realm in which God rules supreme? Would God force such people into his kingdom against their will?

I. God's Gospel Requires a Response

The gospel is a declaration of what God has done to rescue us, but it does not benefit us whether we want it to or not. No, God's gospel requires a response. The gospel certainly proclaims something God has accomplished outside of us, without our help, but God's saving work is not effective apart from our personal involvement. In any biblical understanding of the gospel, the objective work of God in Christ requires a subjective response, a response of faith.[1] We are called, indeed we are commanded, to believe the gospel. By faith in Christ, and by faith alone, this gospel becomes ours. By faith we become recipients of God's saving work.

A. God Commands Us to Respond

The gospel message comes to us as a declaration of fact—God has acted to save us through Jesus Christ's death and resurrection. But that declaration also issues in a command—we must repent and believe that good news. The New Testament presents the gospel not simply as a helpful suggestion to implement or even an invitation to accept, but as a command to obey (cf. 2 Thess. 1:8; Rom. 10:16-21; also Acts 5:32; 6:7; 17:30; Rom. 6:17; Heb. 5:9; 1 Pet. 1:22; 4:17). The proper response to this command, however, is faith, the sole means of receiving God's saving grace (cf. John 6:29).

---

1 We do not specify to what extent our response of faith is enabled by God through the Holy Spirit. Here, as throughout our Statement, our intention is to include a spectrum of Evangelical views, including, in particular, both Arminian/Wesleyan and Reformed understandings. On the notions of effective and prevenient grace, see Article 3, sec. III.A.2, n. 40.

B. The Gospel Addresses Everyone Everywhere

In reference to the Athenians' altar to "an unknown god," the Apostle Paul declared to the pagan philosophers of Mars Hill, "In the past God overlooked such ignorance, but now he commands all people everywhere to repent" (Acts 17:30). The call of the gospel message is not limited to Jews or even to God-fearing Gentiles. It is universal in its scope, addressing everyone, everywhere. Jesus had authorized this world-wide reach of the gospel when he commissioned his followers to "make disciples of all nations" (Matt. 28:19; cf. also Luke 24:46-47), acting as his witnesses "to the ends of the earth" (Acts 1:8). The Book of Acts documents the extension of the gospel from the Jews of Jerusalem (Acts 2), to the Samaritans (Acts 8), and finally to the Gentile world (Acts 10). The gospel "is the power of God for the salvation of everyone who believes: first for the Jew, then for the Gentile" (Rom. 1:16). "Here there is no Greek or Jew, circumcised or uncircumcised, barbarian, Scythian, slave or free, but Christ is all, and is in all" (Col. 3:11; cf. Gal. 3:28).

Regardless of the various views on the nature of God's election, we affirm that it is not within our power to know who will respond to the gospel. We do know, however, that Christ has purchased people for God "from every tribe and language and people and nation" (Rev. 5:9). Therefore, we are to proclaim the good news of God's saving grace far and wide, calling everyone everywhere to respond. We now turn to look more closely at the response the gospel requires.

C. We Are to Believe the Gospel

As we have affirmed already,[2] the one essential response to which we are called is faith—we are to believe in Jesus Christ as he is revealed in the gospel. The notion of faith, however, is often misunderstood. One skeptic described faith as "the illogical belief in the occurrence of the impossible." Others see it as a vague positive attitude toward life, a form of "positive thinking." But in considering the biblical conception of faith, it is important to notice the definite connection that Paul makes between faith and truth. He speaks, for example, of the Colossians' faith in "the word of truth, the gospel," that had come to them (Col. 1:5). This gospel, he says, was bearing fruit in them since the day they heard of it and "understood God's grace in all its truth" (v. 6). Faith, in Paul's mind

---

2 See Article 7, sec. I.A.1.

was not just a feeling; it involved a comprehension, an understanding, of truth.[3]

Faith has content; it is faith *in* something. To believe, in a biblical sense, we must first understand the *content* of the gospel. This first aspect of faith is what the Reformers called in Latin *notitia*. It consists of the notions, the ideas, the conceptions that are to be believed. The early Christians sometimes called this "the faith"—the doctrines taught in the Bible about God and man and the revelation of God in a man, Jesus Christ. Paul speaks of the content of our faith in a passage like 1 Corinthians 15:3-4 (cf. also, e.g., 1 Tim. 3:9; 4:6; Titus 1:13). In this sense, faith involves knowledge—we must know who Christ is and what he has done before we can believe in him. "Faith comes from hearing the message, and the message is heard through the word of Christ" (Rom. 10:17).

A second aspect of biblical faith is what the Reformers called *assensus*. We must not only understand the message, we must assent to it. To believe, in a biblical sense, we must come to a conviction about the truth of the gospel. Is there truly a God who created the universe? Did he really enter into our world in Jesus Christ? Did Jesus actually die on a cross for our sins? And did he rise from the dead? Is it true? Biblical faith involves an understanding of certain content—a body of claims about reality; and it involves a conviction about the truth of those claims.

But these two dimensions of faith are not enough. Understanding the message is crucial, believing that it is true is essential, but without a third dimension that faith is still deficient. James can speak of such faith as merely the faith of demons (cf. James 2:19). Faith, to be real, must pass from understanding, and even conviction, to personal commitment. This third dimension of faith is what the Reformers called *fiducia*. Christian faith requires a personal element of trust, reliance and allegiance.

Consider the analogy of marriage. A man and a woman may be attracted to one another and may get to know the content of each other's character. They may become convinced that they would make good marriage partners. But marriage requires more than that. One's faith must be put on the line; they must make a commitment to one another—a very personal commitment. Real faith comes only when they forsake all others and say, "I do." For that reason the marriage vow is called "a pledge of faith." The gospel calls us to make just such a "pledge of faith" to Jesus Christ. Such faith unites us to Christ, and in that union

---

3 cf. also 2 Thess. 2:10,12-13; 1 Tim. 2:4; James 1:18; 1 Pet. 1:22.

his saving work flows into our lives. Faith is not our contribution to the saving work of God any more than accepting a marriage proposal earns the love of the one who proposes. Faith is simply the means of receiving God's saving grace in Christ.

God commands everyone everywhere to believe the gospel, and our Statement expounds what this believing means in two ways: it is both moral and personal.

1. We Are to Turn to God in Repentance

First, believing the gospel entails turning to God in repentance. Repentance is not something that is done in addition to faith, as if it were some human work that merits God's favor. It is an inherent part of what it means to believe the gospel, for it reflects the moral reality which the gospel declares.

The gospel message only has meaning within a moral framework. It assumes that God has the right to command our obedience and that we have rebelled against his authority. We are now sinners before God in need of a Savior. To believe the gospel one must agree with this basic truth. Faith in Christ implies that a person no longer wants to remain in this state of rebellion but desires rescue from sin and reconciliation with God. Repentance is simply a description of that "change of mind" intrinsic to this turning toward God. It is a recognition of the moral order which God has established, and repentance is a desire to align oneself within that order. As Paul declares, to worship God one must forsake all idols (cf. 1 Thess. 1:8-10). Turning toward God implies turning away from sin.

Our repentance does not save us—faith is the sole means of receiving God's grace. Faith is what joins us to Christ and enables us to enjoy his riches. Repentance can be understood as a logical prerequisite of faith, putting faith within the moral context in which it must be understood.

Repentance was a prominent theme of Jesus' preaching. Mark introduces Jesus' message in this way: "After John was put in prison, Jesus went into Galilee, proclaiming the good news of God. 'The time has come,' he said. 'The kingdom of God is near. Repent and believe the good news!'" (Mark 1:14-15; cf. also Matt. 11:20-21; 12:41; Luke 13:3,5,7; 16:30). And after his resurrection Jesus instructed his disciples: "This is what is written: The Christ will suffer and rise from the dead on the third day, and repentance and forgiveness of sins will be preached in his name to all nations, beginning at Jerusalem" (Luke 24:46-47).

Peter echoed that emphasis on the day of Pentecost, closing his first sermon with this appeal: "Repent and be baptized, every one of you, in the name of Jesus Christ for the forgiveness of your sins" (Acts 2:38; cf. also 2 Pet. 3:9). Paul also emphasized the need for repentance, summarizing his message this way: "I have declared to both Jews and Greeks that they must turn to God in repentance and have faith in our Lord Jesus" (Acts 20:21). And again, "First to those in Damascus, then to those in Jerusalem and in all Judea, and to the Gentiles also, I preached that they should repent and turn to God and prove their repentance by their deeds" (Acts 26:20; cf. also 3:19; 14:15; 17:30; 26:17-18; Rom. 2:4; 2 Cor. 7:10; Isa. 55:6-7) We are saved by faith alone, but true faith includes repentance.

Repentance is a turning away from sin, but we must be clear. This turning from sin must be a desire of the heart, but it does not mean that our lives must be without sin before we can put our faith in Christ. The requirement of repentance simply means that one desires both to be rescued from one's sin by God's power and to submit to God's authority, however weak that desire may be. People may come to God for many reasons, but if they do not acknowledge their moral obligation to love and obey God and if they do not embrace Jesus Christ as God's gracious provision for their failure to fulfill that obligation, then they have not rightly understood the gospel. Believing the gospel means, first, turning toward God in repentance.[4]

2. We Are to Receive the Lord Jesus Christ

A second aspect of believing the gospel is found in the phrase "receiving the Lord Jesus Christ." Here we emphasize the personal nature of faith. The gospel is not just a set of facts to be believed (though, as we have said, the content of our faith is important); it is also a Person to be trusted. When Jesus Christ came into the world, he was largely rejected by his own people, but John writes, "Yet to all who received him, to those who believed in his name, he gave the right to become children of God" (John 1:12; cf. also Col. 2:6). The personal nature of our response

---

4 Like faith, repentance is to be constantly present in the life of the Christian. So long as sin remains within us, we will need a broken and contrite heart before God as we continue to turn to Christ as our only hope of salvation. This truth was at the heart of the Reformation. In the first of his Ninety-Five Theses, Martin Luther stated, "When our Lord and Master, Jesus Christ, said 'Repent,' he called for the entire life of believers to be one of repentance."

is such that Paul can speak of "knowing Christ my Lord" (Phil. 3:8) and of Christ living "in us" (Col. 1:27).[5] This language of "receiving Christ" also expresses the divine initiative in this relationship—God gives, and we can only receive (cf. 1 Cor. 4:7; Rom. 5:17).[6]

Further, we affirm that the One whom we receive not only saves us from our sin, he is also the ruler of the universe. He is the *Lord* Jesus Christ. He is the Lord of heaven and earth, the One who is now on the throne at the right hand of the Father. "Jesus is Lord" is the affirmation that rings from the heart of the believer (Rom. 10:8-13; 1 Cor. 12:3), and it gives us hope in the efficacy of his work and in his power to save.[7]

Jesus said, "Come, follow me" (e.g., Matt. 4:19). The Lord calls, and we must personally respond to that call in an act of faith, entrusting our lives into his care. Just as in marriage, faith only becomes real when you actually commit yourself to the other person. So in our relationship with Christ, our faith becomes real when we *receive* him—personally committing our lives to him in faith.[8]

II. Our Eternal Destiny

Contrary to the opinion of some, the gospel is not simply a self-help strategy for finding peace and happiness in this life. The Bible presents the gospel as a matter of eternal significance. In fact, it is a matter of heaven and hell, for our eternal destiny hinges on our response to Jesus Christ (cf. John 3:36; 5:24; 8:24).

Jesus himself spoke in stark terms of the two ways set before every human being. "Enter through the narrow gate," he said. "For wide is the gate and broad is the road that leads to destruction, and many enter through it. But small is the gate and narrow the road that leads to life, and only a few find it" (Matt. 7:13-14). Or "When the Son of Man comes in his glory, . . . he will sit on his throne in heavenly glory. . . . and he will

---

5 The personal nature of this relationship is often expressed using Jesus' words of invitation to the church in Laodicea: "Here I am! I stand at the door and knock. If anyone hears my voice and opens the door, I will come in and eat with him, and he with me" (Rev. 3:20).

6 Cf. also the notion of receiving "the gift of the Holy Spirit" (Acts 2:38).

7 The term "Lord" was used in the Greek Old Testament (LXX) to translate the divine name, and the New Testament writers applied that same term to Jesus (cf., e.g., Phil. 2:9-11, referring to Isa. 45:21-23).

8 Again we emphasize, it is Christ who saves us, not our faith. The Reformers put it this way: "Faith justifies not because of itself, insofar as it is a quality in man, but on account of Christ, of whom faith lays hold."

separate the people one from another as a shepherd separates the sheep from the goats. He will put the sheep on his right and the goats on his left" (Matt. 25:31-33). One is either on a road to life or on a road to death, among the sheep or among the goats, a believer or an unbeliever—there is no middle ground.[9]

The theological truths that have been set forth throughout our Statement concerning God's nature, the human condition, the Person and work of Christ, the missionary mandate given to all believers, and the need for a response of repentance and faith naturally raise two common questions, which we must pause to address before proceeding. First, what is the destiny of those who die in infancy or who may be mentally incompetent and unable to respond to the message of the gospel in conscious faith? Some difference of opinion exists among us on this issue. Almost all would contend that God can accept such people into his eternal presence, though the grounds on which this is possible differ. Some believe that even though all are sinful by nature in Adam, those who die in infancy or who may be mentally incompetent are incapable of conscious and deliberate sin, and, therefore, their sinful nature has not been personally ratified. Consequently, Adam's guilt is not attributed to them.[10] (All, however, would agree that both infants and the mentally incompetent are still subject to a corruption of nature flowing from the fall and that Christ's saving work of restoration is still necessary.) Others believe that though all humans at any stage of development or level of mental capability are guilty by virtue of their union with Adam, God can apply the saving work of Christ to them without conscious and deliberate faith through the regenerating work of the Spirit.[11] How many God may choose to save in this way, we

---

9 The Bible affirms that God will reward believers in heaven for their faithfulness and appears to promise reward in various degrees (cf. Matt. 5:12; 6:1-6; 10:42; 25:14-30; 1 Cor. 3:8, 12-15; Eph. 6:8), just as it suggests degrees of suffering in hell (Matt. 11:21-24; Luke 12:47-48). We affirm this biblical teaching while confessing that it is difficult to conceive of gradations of blessedness or suffering, since the two states (heaven and hell) are themselves described in the Bible so often in such absolute terms.

10 The fact that judgment in the Bible is "according to works" is cited in support of this view. Cf. Millard J. Erickson, *Christian Theology*, 2nd ed. (Grand Rapids: Baker, 1998), 656. Because of their emphasis on faith flowing from the freedom of the human will, this position is more often associated with Arminians and Wesleyans.

11 The work of the Spirit in the John the Baptist's life even while in the womb is offered in support (Luke 1:15). This view is more often associated with those with a Reformed understanding of salvation, and it is captured in the Westminster Confession of Faith: "Elect infants, dying in infancy, are regenerated and saved by Christ through the Spirit, who works when, and where, and how He pleases. So also are all other elect persons, who are incapable of

cannot know, but we do have confidence that God is gracious, especially to those who are the weakest and most vulnerable.[12]

Second, we ask, what then is the destiny of those who have not heard of God's saving work in Jesus Christ, that is, the unevangelized—can they be saved? Since the coming of God's final work in Jesus Christ, Scripture speaks clearly of the need to hear and to believe the gospel (cf. Rom. 10:13-15; Acts 4:12; John 14:6; Luke 24:46-47; Acts 26:16-18). And among those capable of understanding the gospel, we affirm that we have no clear biblical warrant for believing that, since the coming of Christ, God has saved anyone apart from conscious faith in Jesus.[13] Paul's statement referring to the Christian Ephesians' previous state as pagans without a faith in Jesus is straightforward and comprehensive: "remember that at that time you were separate from Christ, excluded from citizenship in Israel and foreigners to the covenants of the promise, without hope and without God in the world" (Eph. 2:12). Further, we find nothing in Scripture that suggests that the nations may find God somehow present in a redemptive way within their own religious practices, theological outlooks, or cultural structures.

And again, while God could reveal Christ to some apart from the normal means of the ministry of the Word (e.g., through dreams or

---

being outwardly called by the ministry of the Word" (10.3).

12 Cf., e.g., Deut. 10:18; Pss. 10:14; 146:9. In support of this view, many take comfort also in the statement of King David after the death of his first child through Bathsheba: "I will go to him, but he will not return to me" (2 Sam. 12:23). They contend that David is confident that he would again be with his child in the presence of the Lord.

13 We recognize, however, that some concede it may be theoretically possible for God to save some through Christ's work without them hearing the name of Jesus. This possibility has been acknowledged by some Evangelicals through history, including John Wesley in the eighteenth century, W. G. T. Shedd in the nineteenth and D. Martyn Lloyd-Jones in the twentieth. Millard Erickson writes, "Paul [referring to Rom. 2:1-16] seems to be laying open this theoretical possibility." He then adds, " Yet we have no indication from Scripture how many, if any, actually experience salvation without having special revelation. Paul suggests in Romans 3 that no one does." (*Christian Theology*, 2nd ed. [Grand Rapids: Baker, 1998], 197). Harold Netland, Professor at Trinity Evangelical Divinity School, in his extensive study concludes, "It seems to me that the wisest response to this perplexing issue is to recognize that we cannot rule out the possibility [of some being saved without hearing the name of Jesus]. . . . But to go beyond this and to speculate about how many, if any, are saved this way is to move beyond what the Scriptures allow" (*Encountering Religious Pluralism: The Challenge to Christian Faith and Mission*, [Downers Grove: InterVarsity, 2001], 323). J. I. Packer also acknowledges this view, but affirms that, because of its lack of biblical warrant in any particular case, "our missionary obligation is not one whit diminished by our entertaining this possibility" ("What Happens to People Who Die Without Hearing the Gospel?" *Decision Magazine*, Jan. 2002, 11).

visions[14]), we have no biblical warrant for believing that he will reveal himself in that way to anyone.[15] The Bible speaks instead of the mandate given to Christ's followers to preach the gospel to all nations (cf., esp., Rom. 10:14-15), and we are woefully remiss if we fail to engage in that great task when so much is at stake.

The "benevolent impulse" in Christian believers that desires and seeks eternal life for as many as possible is good and right. Abraham pleaded with God for the salvation of the city of Sodom (Gen. 18:23-24), and Jesus' disciples were rebuked for being more zealous to punish evildoers than their Lord (Luke 9:54-55). As we humbly consider this question of the unevangelized we are confident that God's ways are always just and right, and in the end they will be seen to be so. As Abraham reflected, "Will not the Judge of all the earth do right?" (Gen. 18:25). At the same time, we must remain faithful to the clear and insistent message of the Bible—Jesus Christ is the Savior of the whole world, and the whole world needs to hear about his saving work.[16] Because all have sinned and are deserving of God's condemnation, we believe that we can be saved only by the atoning work of Christ, and we believe that we can be sure that people can be saved by that work only if they are told about it.

A. God Will Raise the Dead Bodily

The eternal nature of our destiny is affirmed in our conviction that physical death is not the end of our existence. Our lives are not simply absorbed as a drop into "the eternal ocean of being," nor do we simply "live on in the hearts of those we love," as many suppose. The Bible affirms that every human being will assume an eternal form in which we maintain our unique personal and bodily existence. This is described as our resurrection from the dead.

In the Old Testament the doctrine of the resurrection was most clearly articulated in the Book of Daniel: "Multitudes who sleep in the dust of the earth will awake: some to everlasting life, others to shame and everlasting contempt" (Dan. 12:2; cf. also Job. 19:25-27; Isa. 26:19). Jesus, too, affirmed that all will rise from the dead: "Do not be amazed at

14 The Westminster Confession suggests this possibility when it declares that the gift of saving faith is "*ordinarily* wrought by the ministry of the Word" (14.1; italics added).

15 The biblical pattern is that dreams are confirmed by God's Word—as when, e.g., God sent Peter to Cornelius in Acts 10.

16 Cf. Matt. 28:19-20; Acts 1:8; Rom. 1:16; 1 Tim. 2:3-6; 1 John 2:2.

this, for a time is coming when all who are in their graves will hear [the Son's] voice and come out—those who have done good will rise to live, and those who have done evil will rise to be condemned" (John 5:28-29; also Matt. 22:23-32). Paul echoed this conviction: "there will be a resurrection of both the righteous and the wicked" (Acts 24:15).

The nature of the resurrection body is a great mystery, and Paul's teaching on the subject is focused on the new bodies of those united to Christ, leaving us with less clarity regarding those raised apart from Christ. For believers, the resurrection body will be like that of Jesus (Phil. 3:20-21), with a significant physical discontinuity with our present body of flesh (cf. 1 Cor. 15:50) but maintaining a continuity of personal identity. Paul uses the image of a seed that is buried and then re-emerges from the ground in a new form, becoming a "spiritual body," glorious and imperishable (1 Cor. 15:35-49).

The Bible describes our future state as the resurrection of the body rather than simply the immortality of the soul. This recognizes that God the Creator is not abandoning his creation, but redeeming it. In addition, as bodily creatures we will maintain our ability to represent God in his redeemed created order, displaying his glory. Though death cannot separate the believer from Christ (Rom. 8:38-39), and after death we can be assured of being in his presence (cf. Phil. 1:21-23),[17] our salvation will not be complete until we are raised bodily when Christ returns.[18] Human beings are created as embodied souls, and Christ's own incarnation demonstrates the dignity of our embodied existence. Our future bodily resurrection further affirms this reality.

Physical death is not the end of our existence, for all human beings will be raised bodily.[19] Yet physical death does mark the end of our ability to make a response to God in faith. At death our eternal destiny is fixed, for, as we read in Hebrews, "man is destined to die once, and after that to face judgment" (Heb. 9:27; cf. also Luke 16:26).

---

17 We consider the notion of "soul sleep" (in which the believer has no conscious experience of Christ between death and the resurrection) a doctrinal aberration.

18 Note that Paul describes those who are first to rise when Christ appears as "the *dead* in Christ" (1 Thess. 4:16). Thus, in this "intermediate state" between death and resurrection, the body and soul can be separate in a temporary and unnatural disembodied condition (cf. also 2 Cor. 5:1-10).

19 Paul, in 1 Thess. 4:15-17, referring to believers, puts the resurrection at the time of Christ's return (though some understand this as referring only to the pretribulational rapture). The Book of Revelation separates the time of the resurrection of believers from that of unbelievers, with the latter coming after Christ's earthly millennial reign (Rev. 20:4-5,13).

B. God Will Judge the World

Though God sometimes acts in judgment in the course of human history, the Bible affirms that there will come a day when he will act to judge the world in what we call the last or final judgment.[20] Paul stated it clearly to the Athenians: God "commands all people everywhere to repent. For he has set a day when he will judge the world with justice" (Acts 17:30-31). Jesus spoke frequently of this "day of judgment": "For the Son of Man is going to come in his Father's glory with his angels, and then he will reward each person according to what he has done" (Matt. 16:27; cf. 10:15; 11:22,24; 12:36, 41-42; 25:31-32).[21] We are assured that this judgment will be perfectly just (cf. Gen. 18:25; Ps. 145:17; Acts 17:31; Rom. 2:11), for nothing will be hidden and all will be made known (Heb. 4:13; Rom. 2:16; 1 Cor. 4:5).

The prospect of divine judgment is certainly mortifying, but we must appreciate the broader significance of our ultimate accountability to God. First, far from degrading us, God's judgment actually gives great dignity to our lives. Unlike all other earthly creatures, God treats us as responsible moral agents, conferring value to our choices by bringing them before his bar of judgment. If we are not held accountable for our actions, why not eat, drink, and be merry, for tomorrow we die? But because we will be judged by God, our choices have eternal consequences.

Second, the judgment of God is necessary for the existence of a real moral order in the universe. It provides the ultimate sanction which underlies all moral demands, without which law breakers would go unpunished. In an age of moral relativism, the judgment of God provides the absolute objective standard to which all other moral judgments must conform.

Further, the judgment of God is necessary if divine goodness is to be victorious over evil. Because God will judge the world, his will will be done on earth as it is in heaven; justice will prevail; and the good will be seen to be good, finally and fully. Judgment brings glory to God by

---

20 cf. Eccl. 12:14; Matt. 12:36; 25:31-32; John 5:28-29; Acts 17:31; Rom. 14:10; 2 Cor. 5:10; 2 Tim. 4:1; Rev. 20:12.

21 Sometimes God is the Judge (cf., e.g., Eccles. 12:14; Rom. 3:6; 1 Cor. 5:13; Heb. 12:23), but often the divine Judge is more specifically designated as Jesus (cf., e.g., John 5:22,27; Acts 10:42; 17:31; 2 Cor. 5:10; 2 Tim. 4:1). Paul also refers to believers as participating in the judgment (1 Cor. 6:2-3). Some distinguish various judgments depicted in the Bible (e.g., the "judgment seat of Christ" [2 Cor. 5:10]; "the judgment seat of God" [Rom. 14:10]; the "great white throne" [Rev. 20:11]; the royal judgment of the Son of man [Matt. 25:31-46]), while others see these as different ways of describing the same great reality.

displaying his holy nature.

God will judge the world, and that reality gives meaning to all that we do in this life. It provides an assurance that no good will go unrewarded (cf. Matt. 10:42) and no evil will be left unpunished (cf. Matt. 12:36), and it gives us the hope that righteousness will rule in the kingdom of God (2 Pet. 3:13).

The Bible affirms that each person will be judged "according to what he has done" (Rev. 20:13; Matt. 16:27; Rom. 2:6; 2 Cor. 5:10). In light of what we have already declared concerning the universality of sin,[22] such a standard might lead us to despair. But the Bible makes it clear that "there is now no condemnation for those who are in Christ Jesus" (Rom. 8:1), for Jesus has taken our judgment upon himself (cf. Rom. 3:21-26).[23] This judgment "according to works" will really be a judgment about faith—faith as attested through the fruit of our lives. That is, our works will not be the *basis* of our salvation but the evidence of our faith in our Savior, Jesus Christ, who alone can save.[24]

The Book of Revelation speaks of "the dead, both great and small, standing before the throne, and the books were opened. . . . The dead were judged according to what they had done as recorded in the books" (Rev. 20:12). But if we are left to the justice of God, who of us could stand? But the good news is that John says another book will be opened. He calls it "the book of life" (20:12). In the ancient world the names of the citizens of a city were written on a scroll. So the names written in this book are those who are citizens of heaven, the people of God. Later John calls it the "Lamb's book of life" (21:27). It inscribes the names of those who have looked in faith to the Lamb who was slain as their Savior (cf. 7:14; 13:8). Though people are judged according to their deeds, they are saved according to God's grace. Only those whose names are written in this book will enter the Holy City. Our faith in Christ alone provides the basis for our names being written there.

The judgment of God will result in a great separation, for there are but two roads on which all people are traveling which lead to but two destinations (Matt. 7:13-14). On that day, the Judge will separate the sheep from the goats (Matt. 25:32). Some will enter into the Holy City,

---

22 On the human condition, see Article 3.

23 On the saving work of Christ, see Article 5.

24 The Bible does speak of rewards for the faithfulness of believers as an additional aspect of judgment (see n. 9 above).

and some will be thrown into the lake of fire (Rev. 20:15; 21:27). Some will go away to eternal punishment, and some to eternal life (Matt. 25:46). We turn now to consider these two final destinies.

1. The Destiny of the Unbeliever: Condemnation and Eternal Conscious Punishment

It is Jesus above all who forces us to affirm the dreadful truth that those who stand alone before God as sinners on the day of judgment will face condemnation into a state of eternal punishment called hell.[25] To the religious hypocrites he declared, "You snakes! You brood of vipers! How will you escape being condemned to hell?" (Matt. 23:33). Those rejected as subjects of the kingdom, Jesus said, "will be thrown outside, into the darkness, where there will be weeping and gnashing of teeth" (Matt. 8:12; cf. 13:42,50; 22:13; 25:30). Stressing the seriousness of sin, Jesus urged, "If your hand causes you to sin, cut it off. It is better for you to enter life maimed than with two hands to go into hell, where the fire never goes out" (Mark 9:43; cf. Matt. 18:8), a place where "their worm does not die, and the fire is not quenched" (Mark 9:48). On that day of judgment, those who failed to respond to Jesus through his humble brothers "will go away to eternal punishment, but the righteous to eternal life" (Matt. 25:46). We cannot be faithful to our Lord and not speak of this stark reality. Though it is often ridiculed as a primitive remnant of a medieval age, this doctrine of eternal punishment of sinners is rooted in the teaching of Jesus himself.

The apostolic witness of the New Testament echoes Jesus' weighty words on this topic. Paul speaks of a time of "wrath and anger" awaiting those who reject the truth (Rom. 2:8). Those who do not obey the gospel "will be punished with everlasting destruction and shut out from the presence of the Lord" (2 Thess. 1:9). Jude offers the inhabitants of Sodom and Gomorrah "as an example of those who suffer the punishment of eternal fire" (Jude 7). Finally, the Book of Revelation speaks in these harrowing tones:

> If anyone worships the beast and his image and
> receives his mark on the forehead or on the hand, he,
> too, will drink of the wine of God's fury, which has

---

25 Various terms are used in the Bible to convey this reality with slightly different shades of meaning—e.g., Sheol, Hades, Gehenna, the lake of fire and the Abyss.

> been poured full strength into the cup of his wrath. He
> will be tormented with burning sulfur in the presence
> of the holy angels and of the Lamb. And the smoke of
> their torment rises for ever and ever.
>
> (Rev. 14:9-11)

With our meager understanding of the utter purity of God's holiness and of his absolute abhorrence of evil, we may find it difficult to conceive of such punishment, but it is real, and only God's grace can rescue us from it.

The Bible offers various images to seek to convey something of the nature of hell's terror. First, hell is pictured as a place of burning fire, emphasizing its physical torment (Mark 9:43,48; Jude 7; cf. Rev. 21:8— "a fiery lake of burning sulfur"). In hell, the wrath of God is poured out as a punishment for sin.

Second, hell is described as a place of darkness— "outer darkness" (Matt. 8:12; 22:13; 25:30) or "blackest darkness" (2 Pet. 2:17; Jude 13), emphasizing a banishment from God's presence (1 Thess. 1:9). The foolish bridesmaids are shut outside the door (Matt. 25:10-12); the wicked servant is assigned a place with the hypocrites (Matt. 24:51); those improperly dressed for the wedding banquet are thrown outside into the darkness (Matt. 22:13). In some of the most dreaded words of the Bible, Jesus says to evil doers who assumed they would be welcomed by him, "Depart from me. I never knew you" (Matt. 7:23). Nothing is left but loneliness and despair, for it is a place of "weeping and gnashing of teeth," full of the hopeless remorse of self-condemnation.

Finally, hell is characterized by death and destruction. John in the Revelation refers to the lake of fire as "the second death" (Rev. 20:14; 21:8; cf. 2:11; 20:6). Destruction is where the wide road leads (Matt. 7:13); it is what happens to the house built on sand (Luke 6:49); it is what is prepared for the objects of God's wrath (Rom. 9:22); and it is the destiny of the enemies of the cross of Christ (Phil. 3:19).

Some, especially in recent years, have taken this language of death and destruction in a more literal sense and have argued that though God's punishment of the wicked is real, it is not eternal. This view, known as "annihilationism" (or "conditional immortality"[26]), holds that

---

26 This expression derives from the view that immortality is not inherent in human nature but is a gift given to those joined to Christ. Those holding this position believe that those who die apart from Christ will be judged and then not enter into the immortal state but will cease to exist.

the unrighteous will cease to exist after they are judged. In this sense, the punishment for sin is eternal in its effect (that is, it is irreversible), but not eternal in the experience of the one judged. Our Statement denies such a view, contending that the Scripture teaches the continuing existence of persons—both believers and unbelievers—after the judgment, and that the experience of hell is eternal. Hence, we include the expression "eternal *conscious* punishment."

Though the term "conscious" is not commonly used in historic confessions, what it expresses has been the almost universal view of the church through history, with, until very recently, only a few theologians and smaller sects standing in opposition.[27] The church has held that the language of Scripture assumes that the destinies of believers and unbelievers, though very different, stand in parallel, and both will continue to experience the consequences of their choice through eternity.

Jesus himself established this connection when he spoke of the Son of Man separating two classes of human beings on the day of judgment as sheep and goats and saying to the goats on his left hand, "Depart from me, you who are cursed, into the eternal fire prepared for the devil and his angels... Then they will go away to eternal punishment, but the righteous to eternal life" (Matt. 25:41,46). It is true that the word translated "eternal" here (*aiōnios*) means "pertaining to the age to come." But it is precisely because the age to come was perceived to be without end that the word is most commonly translated in this way. Because this verse uses precisely the same word to describe both the blessedness of the righteous and the punishment of the wicked, we must affirm that both enter into an unending conscious state.

But what are we to make of the language of destruction? The Greek verb for "destroy" (*apollymi*, cf. also the related noun *apōleia*) need not mean "cease to exist" but is commonly used to describe the ruining of something such that it becomes useless for its intended purpose. So, for example, this word is used of wineskins that are burst (Matt. 9:17),

---

27 Annihilationism was defended by one fourth-century apologist (Arnobius of Sicca [d. 330]), but it was condemned by the Second Council of Constantinople (553) and the Fifth Lateran Council (1513). It was rare, if non-existent, during the Middle Ages through the Reformation period. It is now held by both Jehovah's Witnesses and Seventh-Day Adventists. This view was even held by one early Free Church Leader, J. G. Princell (1845-1915), but it was repudiated explicitly in the 1950 EFCA Statement of Faith. It has been embraced more recently by a number of Evangelicals, particularly in British circles.

of a coin that is lost (Luke 15:9), of food that spoils (John 6:27), of perfume that is poured out (Mark 14:4), of Jews that were not following the Lord ("lost sheep"—Matt. 15:24), or of Christian brothers adversely affected by the freedom of others (Rom. 14:15; 1 Cor. 8:11). All of these are impaired to the point of ruin, unable to function properly, but they do not disappear.

A related word (*olethron*) is used in a similar way.[28] Paul speaks of those who oppose the gospel as being "punished with everlasting destruction (*olethron*) and shut out from the presence of the Lord" (2 Thess. 1:9). The second expression, qualifying "everlasting destruction," supports the notion that Paul is referring to a continuing state.[29] As one commentator has observed, "It makes little sense to describe people who have been annihilated as being separate from the presence of God."[30] Paul's words imply an ongoing conscious existence, but one in which persons have been so corrupted that they almost cease to function as human beings created in the image of God.[31]

But does "the second death" refer to total extinction? Here again the apostles can speak of death as a state of being rather than an event resulting in annihilation. We were all once "dead in our transgressions," Paul says (Eph. 2:1). The Book of Revelation most commonly uses this language, and the fact that in that book the "first death" does not require the cessation of existence leads one to believe that the "second death" need not either. Furthermore, that book repeatedly stresses the unceasing duration of God's punishment (cf. Rev. 14:11; 19:3; 20:10). It is significant that the most extensive description of the eternal state in the Bible (Revelation 21-22) contains a contrast between those who enter the heavenly city (22:14) and those who remain outside (22:15). Some drink from the "spring of the water of life" (Rev. 21:6), while others

---

28 These two words occur together in 1 Tim. 6:9: "People who want to get rich fall into temptation and a trap and into many foolish and harmful desires that plunge men into ruin (*olethron*) and destruction (*apōleia*)."

29 The intertestamental Jewish book *4 Maccabees* also uses the term *olethron* in a similar context of divine judgment which supports enduring existence in a state of punishment (4 Macc. 10:15; cf. 9:9; 12:12; 13:15).

30 Douglas J. Moo, "Paul on Hell," in *Hell Under Fire*, Christopher W. Morgan and Robert A. Peterson, eds. (Grand Rapids: Zondervan, 2004), 108.

31 Moo uses the helpful illustration of the meaning of "destroy" in the expression, "The tornado destroyed the house." The house is ruined in that it ceases to function as a human dwelling, though its material components continue to exist ("Paul on Hell", 105). The similar term *diaphtheirō* can also mean "destroy" as well as "corrupt, ruin" and both senses are found in Rev. 11:18.

are consigned to the "fiery lake of burning sulfur" (21:8). The "second death" (21:8) is a condition, a state of existence, rather than an event, and this is supported by the description of this "lake of burning sulfur" in Revelation 20:10, which is "the second death," as a place of torment "day and night for ever and ever." In John's view, the continuing punishment of evil in the eternal state does not mar the joy and harmony of the new heaven and the new earth, nor does it diminish the victory of God over evil. God is glorified even in the display of his wrath (cf. Rev. 6:9-11; also, e.g., Pss. 58:10-11; 59:13).

Hell may be understood as a culmination of the effects of sin and the confirmation of God's opposition to it. It is both the inexorable result of human choice and the active and deliberate judgment of God. The three-fold description of hell as wrath, alienation and corruption is illustrated in the effects of the first sin. Adam and Eve incurred the wrath of God through the curse which resulted in physical suffering (strenuous work and painful childbearing), they were alienated from God (cast from the garden), and their nature was corrupted (through the spread of sin and death to all their descendants). Fallen humanity continues to experience these effects unless they are rescued by God's grace in the gospel. Apart from that rescue, that state of wrath, alienation and corruption will be confirmed, intensified and made permanent when at the judgment God's verdict of condemnation is pronounced and the sentence is executed in the on-going reality the Bible calls hell.[32]

Eternal conscious punishment is a sobering subject, but faithfulness to our Lord Jesus obliges us to speak of it, for he certainly did. God is just, and the Judge of all the earth shall do what is right—of that we can be absolutely certain. One day his glory will be wonderfully displayed even in his judgment. Until then, compassion toward those traveling on that road to destruction[33] must compel us to reach out in love with the good news of God's means of rescue and new life in the gospel of Jesus Christ.

---

32 This present experience of wrath, alienation and corruption is sometimes referred to as an "inaugurated eschatology" of judgment, comparable to the inaugurated experience of salvation—with both a "now" and "not yet" dimension (cf., e.g., Moo, "Paul on Hell," 93-94).

33 Cf. the compassion of both Jesus and Paul in Luke 19:41-44; 23:28-31; Rom. 9:2-3; 10:1.

2. The Destiny of the Believer

a. Eternal Blessedness and Joy with the Lord

If the biblical language depicting the eternal state of the unbeliever is as bad as it can be, the language regarding the future for the believer is better than can be imagined. Where once we were alienated from God as his enemies and banished from his presence, we shall be with him forever. Where once we suffered the painful consequences of God's wrath in this fallen world, we will be filled with an inexpressible joy. And where once we experienced the corruption of sin resulting in death, we shall enjoy a state of eternal blessedness, fully pleasing to God in a restored, and even glorified, state of righteousness.

Heaven is the place where God dwells,[34] where his presence is manifest, and its contrast with hell could not be more complete. Hell is a place of pain and suffering; heaven will be one of unceasing joy, like that of a wedding banquet (Rev. 19:7; Matt. 22:2; 25:1-13). Hell is a place of destruction and death; heaven will be one of everlasting life. Hell is a place of darkness and lonely despair; heaven will be one of glorious light and overwhelming love. There "the righteous will shine like the sun in the kingdom of their Father" (Matt. 13:43). It will have no need of sun or moon to illumine it, for "the glory of God is its light, and its lamp is the Lamb" (Rev. 21:23; also 22:5). It will be a place of unimaginable splendor, greatness, excellence, and beauty, as that new Jerusalem, which comes down from heaven, is pictured as a place of pure gold and decorated with precious jewels (Rev. 21:18-21).

The nature of this glorious future may best be captured in the theme of holy love. Jonathan Edwards in the conclusion of his exposition of 1 Corinthians 13 speaks of heaven as "a world of love."[35] There God manifests himself gloriously for all eternity. And what does God make known when he reveals himself? What is the essence of his nature, the very substance of his character? It is love. Writes Edwards: "And this renders heaven a world of love; for God is the fountain of love, as the sun is the fountain of light. And therefore the glorious presence of God in heaven, fills heaven

---

34 Jesus often spoke of his Father in heaven (e.g., Matt. 5:16,45; 6:1) and he taught us to pray to him there (Matt. 6:9). Heaven is the place of God's throne (Matt. 5:35; Pss. 14:2; 103:19). Cf. also Solomon's emphasis of this in 2 Chron. 6:21,30,39.

35 Jonathan Edwards [1749], "Sermon Fifteen: Heaven Is a World of Love," in *Ethical Writings,* ed. Paul Ramsey, *The Works of Jonathan Edwards,* vol. 8 (New Haven: Yale University Press, 1989), 366-397.

with love, as the sun, placed in the midst of the visible heavens on a clear day, fills the world with light."[36] There this infinite fountain of love flows out forever. "There this glorious God is manifested, and shines forth, in full glory, in beams of love."[37] In heaven love reigns—it reigns in every heart allowed to dwell there. It is a holy and divine love. The saints in heaven love God for His own sake, and each other for God's sake, wholly and completely devoted to God's glory and the good of others. This love is perfect in every way, without any taint of selfishness or pride or sinful desire—always sincere, never self-seeking. It delights in the happiness of others, without a hint of envy or jealousy, abounding in perfect peace and harmony—without malice or revenge or selfish ambition. It is a love that results in the sweetest of all joys.

Edwards continues:

> Every saint in heaven is as a flower in that garden of
> God, and holy love is the fragrance and sweet odor
> that they all send forth, and with which they fill the
> [arbors] of that paradise above. Every soul there, is as a
> note in some concert of delightful music, that sweetly
> harmonizes with every other note, and all together
> blend in the most rapturous strains in praising God
> and the Lamb for ever. And so all help each other, to
> their utmost, to express the love of the whole society
> to its glorious Father and Head, and to pour back
> love into the great fountain of love whence they are
> supplied and filled with love, and blessedness, and
> glory. And thus they will love, and reign in love, and in
> that godlike joy that is its blessed fruit, such as eye hath
> not seen, nor ear heard, nor hath ever entered into the
> heart of man in this world to conceive; and thus in the
> full sunlight of the throne, enraptured with joys that
> are for ever increasing, and yet for ever full, they shall
> live and reign with God and Christ for ever and ever![38]

---

36 *Ibid.*, 369.

37 *Ibid.*, 370.

38 *Ibid.*, 386.

b. In the New Heaven and the New Earth

We often speak of heaven as the destiny of the believer, and that way of speaking is not wrong. As those united with Christ, we know that nothing, not even death, can separate us from our Savior (Rom. 8:38-39), and that when we die we will "depart and be with Christ" (Phil. 1:23), who is himself seated in heavenly glory. But the redemptive purposes of God are greater still. As we have seen,[39] our salvation will not be complete until our bodies are resurrected and we share the glory of Christ when he returns triumphantly to this earth (cf. Phil. 3:21). And the Bible declares that his victory over sin and death will be so complete that his return will result in the transformation of the creation itself[40]—making all things new (Rev. 21:5). God will restore his people and overcome the effects of sin in this fallen world, bringing about a new heaven and new earth in which the separation that now exists between heaven and earth will be overcome (2 Pet. 3:13; Rev. 21:1-4; Rom. 8:21-23; also Isa. 65:17-25; 66:22-23). In that Holy City, the New Jerusalem, "the dwelling of God is with men, and he will live with them. . . . There will be no more death or mourning or crying or pain, for the old order of things has passed away" (Rev. 21:2-4).[41]

Evil will have no place in this new existence. In that Holy City John envisions, "nothing that is impure will enter" (Rev 21:27). We will be secure in "the city with permanent foundations," a "kingdom that cannot be shaken" (Heb. 11:10; 12:28). The curse of God upon life in this world will be rescinded (Rev. 22:3), and our work will no longer be toilsome. We will discover the true Sabbath rest of God, even as we actively serve the Lamb upon the throne (Rev. 22:3), reigning over God's created order (Rev. 22:5; cf. Gen. 1:28). The communal life of God's people there will be like a great banquet or wedding feast where God himself is the host (cf. Matt. 22:1-10). As Augustine wrote at the conclusion of his magisterial treatise *City of God*: "On that day we shall rest and we shall see; we shall see and we shall love; we shall love and we shall praise; this is what will be at the end without end."[42] Would that all believers meditated on this

---

39 See section II.A above.

40 There is some debate as to whether the notion of the renewal of the present created order or its obliteration best fits the biblical data (cf., e.g., Rom. 8:20-21; Heb. 12:25-29; 2 Pet. 3:10). Both have elements of truth in that the future state will represent both continuity and discontinuity with the present world, not unlike that of our own physical bodies.

41 Cf. Graham A. Cole, *God the Peacemaker: How Atonement Brings Shalom*, NSBT 25 (Downers Grove: InterVarsity, 2009), 231, n. 4: "Ruin through Adam, redemption through Christ, regeneration through the Spirit and restoration of creation through the triune God."

42 *City of God*, 22.30.

glorious state as did the Puritan Richard Baxter in his wonderful treatise, *The Saints' Everlasting Rest*, published in 1649. He concludes:

> Be acquainted with this heavenly work, and thou wilt, in some degree, be acquainted with God; thy joys will be spiritual, prevalent, and lasting, according to the nature of their blessed object; thou wilt have comfort in life and death. . . . Thy graces will be mighty, active, and victorious; and the daily joy, which is thus fetched from heaven, will be thy strength.[43]

III. God's Final Purpose: To the Praise of His Glorious Grace

When God's saving purposes have been fulfilled and his people are redeemed, reconciled and restored in the transformed creation, they will gather in joyful celebration and adoration as a great multitude that no one can count. Coming from every nation, tribe, people and language, they will stand before the throne and in front of the Lamb and exclaim: "Salvation belongs to our God, who sits on the throne, and to the Lamb" (Rev. 7:10). Because salvation is all a gift of God's grace, no one will have cause to boast and God alone will be exalted. The unfolding of God's saving purpose in the gospel of Jesus Christ will be "to the praise of his glorious grace" (Eph. 1:6).

IV. Our Final Response: Amen

All theology, because it is truth about God, is to be doxological, a prayerful profession, a joyful declaration, an act of worship. In the end, all that we can do is offer our hearty and heart-felt affirmation of God's glorious gospel revealed in Jesus Christ—So be it! We began our Statement by declaring that in all that God does, he acts "for His own glory" (Article 1). We now close with the word which ends the Bible itself: Amen.[44]

---

43 *Practical Works of Richard Baxter, Select Treatises* (Grand Rapids: Baker, 1981), 120.

44 Rev. 22:21. For other biblical doxologies, see, e.g., Rom. 11:36; Eph. 3:21; 1 Tim. 1:17; Heb. 13:20-21; 2 Pet. 3:17-18; Jude 24-25.

APPENDIX ONE
Statements of Faith in the Free Church Movement in America

I. The Swedish Evangelical Free Church (1884)

This organization accepts the Bible, both Old and New Testaments, as the Word of God, containing the Gospel of salvation for all men and the only perfect rule for teaching, faith and life.

II. The Norwegian-Danish Evangelical Free Church Association (1912)

1. We believe, that the Bible, the Old and New Testament, is the Word of God and is the only infallible rule and guide for faith, life, and doctrine.
2. We believe in the triune God: Father, Son and Holy Spirit, one God in three persons, in accordance with the apostolic faith.
3. We believe that all men by nature are sinners, aliens and strangers to God, and as a result thereof under condemnation.
4. We believe that Jesus Christ gave Himself as a Redeemer for all mankind, and those who repent from their sins and believe on Him shall be granted forgiveness and be adopted as children of God.
5. We believe that as many as by faith receive Jesus Christ as their Savior and Lord are born again and are given the witness of the Holy Spirit, and become children and heirs of God, and joint-heirs with Christ.
6. We believe that Christian churches should be organized in conformity with the teachings of the New Testament, and only those who have the witness of the Holy Spirit that they are children of God, and live accordingly, should be considered eligible to church membership.
7. We believe that Jesus Christ is the Lord and head of the Church, and that every local church has the right, under Christ, to decide and govern its own affairs.
8. We believe that the Lord has given His Church two sacraments: baptism and communion. (1) Baptism in the name of the Father, Son, and Holy Spirit. Freedom of conscience is given as to age and mode. (2) Communion should be administrated only to true believers, in accordance with the Word of God.

9. We believe that Jesus Christ who ascended into heaven, shall come again in great power and glory.

10. We believe in the resurrection of the dead, both the righteous and the unrighteous, and that every one shall give an account to a righteous God for his life and conduct on earth.

11. We believe that there is eternal glory for those who believe on Jesus Christ and faithfully endure to the end, and eternal condemnation for those who die in impenitence and unbelief.

12. We believe that the sole duty of the Christian Church is to proclaim the Gospel to the whole world, and to assist charitable institutions, to work for righteousness and temperance, for unity and cooperation with all believers, and for peace among all people and nations on the whole earth.

III. The (Swedish) Evangelical Free Church Ministerial Association (1947)

1. We believe the Scriptures, both Old and New Testaments, to be the inspired Word of God without error in the original writings, the complete revelation of His will for the salvation of men, and the Divine and final authority for Christian faith and life.

2. We believe in one God, creator of all things, infinitely perfect, and eternally existing in three persons, Father, Son and Holy Spirit.

3. We believe that Jesus Christ is true God and man, having been conceived of the Holy Ghost and born of the Virgin Mary. He died on the cross a sacrifice for our sins according to the Scriptures. Further, He arose bodily from the dead, ascended into heaven, where, at the right hand of the Majesty on High, He now is our High Priest and Advocate.

4. We believe that the ministry of the Holy Spirit is to glorify the Lord Jesus Christ, and during this age to convict men of sin, regenerate the unbelieving sinner, indwell, guide, instruct and empower the believer for godly living and service.

5. We believe that man was created in the image of God but fell into sin and is therefore lost, and only through regeneration by the Holy Spirit can salvation and spiritual life be obtained.

6. We believe that the shed blood of Jesus Christ and His resurrection provide the only ground for the salvation and justification of all who believe, and that only such as receive Jesus Christ are born of the

Holy Spirit, and thus become the children of God.

7. We believe in the personal, pre-millennial, and imminent return of our Lord Jesus Christ, and that this "blessed hope" has a vital bearing on the personal life and service of the believer.

8. We believe in the bodily resurrection of all the dead; of the believer to everlasting blessedness with his Lord, and of the unbeliever to judgment and everlasting, conscious punishment.

9. We believe that the true church is composed of all such persons, who, through saving faith in Jesus Christ have been regenerated by the Holy Spirit and are united together in the body of Christ of which He is the head.

10. We believe that water baptism and the Lord's Supper are ordinances to be observed by the Church during the present age. They are, however, not to be regarded as means of salvation. [This article was adopted as an amendment by the Ministerial Association on June 13, 1950, two days prior to the adoption of the EFCA Statement of Faith.]

IV. The Evangelical Free Church of America (1950)

The Evangelical Free Church of America Believes –

1. The Scriptures, both Old and New Testaments, to be the inspired Word of God, without error in the original writings, the complete revelation of His will for the salvation of men, and the Divine and final authority for Christian faith and life.

2. In one God, Creator of all things, infinitely perfect and eternally existing in three persons, Father, Son and Holy Spirit.

3. That Jesus Christ is true God and true man, having been conceived of the Holy Ghost and born of the Virgin Mary. He died on the cross a sacrifice for our sins according to the Scriptures. Further, He arose bodily from the dead, ascended into heaven, where at the right hand of the Majesty on High, He is now our High Priest and Advocate.

4. That the ministry of the Holy Spirit is to glorify the Lord Jesus Christ, and during this age to convict men, regenerate the believing sinner, indwell, guide, instruct, and empower the believer for godly living and service.

5. That man was created in the image of God but fell into sin and is therefore lost and only through regeneration by the Holy Spirit can salvation and spiritual life be obtained.

6. That the shed blood of Jesus Christ and His resurrection provide the only ground for justification and salvation for all who believe, and only such as receive Jesus Christ are born of the Holy Spirit, and thus become children of God.

7. That water baptism and the Lord's Supper are ordinances to be observed by the Church during the present age. They are, however, not to be regarded as means of salvation.

8. That the true Church is composed of all such persons who through saving faith in Jesus Christ have been regenerated by the Holy Spirit and are united together in the body of Christ, of which He is the head.

9. That only those who are thus members of the true Church shall be eligible for membership in the local church.

10. That Jesus Christ is the Lord and Head of the Church, and that every local church has the right under Christ to decide and govern its own affairs.

11. In the personal and premillennial and imminent coming of our Lord Jesus Christ and that this "Blessed Hope" has a vital bearing on the personal life and service of the believer.

12. In the bodily resurrection of the dead; of the believer to everlasting blessedness and joy with the Lord, of the unbeliever to judgment and everlasting conscious punishment.

APPENDIX TWO
Congregationalism and the EFCA

Though not included among our central doctrinal convictions, the Evangelical Free Church of America is congregational. That is, Evangelical Free churches are autonomous and self-governing.[1] We hold this as an integral part of our history and tradition, and on the basis of our understanding of biblical teaching.

Jesus is the lone Head of the Church (Eph. 1:22; Col. 1:18). This means the church is governed preeminently as a Christocracy not a democracy. Based on the priesthood of all believers (1 Pet. 2:9; Rev. 1:6; 5:9), we believe that the will of Christ for his church is best discerned through the collective understanding of the congregation. Therefore, the congregation is the highest governing authority under Christ for the local church (cf. Matt. 18:15-18; 1 Cor. 5:4).

With Christ as the Head of this priesthood of believers, he has also given spiritual gifts to each one to be used to glorify him and build up the body (Rom. 12:3-8; 1 Cor. 12:4-7, 28-30; Eph. 4:11-13; 1 Pet. 4:10-11). Some of these gifts are to be used for positions of leadership in the local church, specifically elders/overseers/pastors (Phil. 1:1; 1 Tim. 3:1-7; Titus 1:5-9)[2] and deacons (Phil. 1:1; 1 Tim. 3:8-13). These servant-leaders are to be affirmed/chosen by the people they serve (cf. Acts 6:5). This addresses an internal call of God and gifting by God and an external recognition and acknowledgment of this by the people in the local church.

What does congregational church government look like? In 2000 the District Superintendents and other national leaders (composing what was then called the National Ministries Team) created a statement (updated in 2008) seeking to provide some guidance to local churches on this issue. Here is what they wrote:

1. An EFC [Evangelical Free church] has the freedom under the guidance of the Holy Spirit to govern its own affairs in accordance with both the mind of Christ and the Word of God.

---

1   The Articles of Incorporation of the Evangelical Free Church of America mandate that the EFCA "shall be an association and fellowship of autonomous but interdependent congregations of like faith and congregational government" (II.A).

2   Note that these terms are used synonymously: Acts 20:28; Eph. 4:11; Phil. 1:1; 1 Tim. 3:2; 1 Pet. 5:2.

2. An EFC develops a local church polity that fits within the following parameters of congregationalism:

   a. The membership includes only those who have a personal faith in Christ (a believers' church).

   b. The collective membership in a duly called meeting is the highest authority, under Christ, in the local church, exhibiting both a willingness to be scripturally accountable to the elected leadership and encouraging elected leadership to be mutually accountable to them as the ultimate authority in the local context. Moreover, members and leaders unitedly subscribe to a relationship covenant based on Matthew 18, giving priority to biblical patterns of conflict resolution and exercising biblical discipline within the context of Christian love and cultural sensitivity.

   c. Congregationalism is that form of government wherein the highest authority under Christ in a local church resides in the corporate understanding of the mind of Christ and in which a realistic process and reasonable opportunity exists by which that understanding is determined and carried out, especially as it affects such matters as:

      1) Determination of membership.
      2) Selection or appointment of the principal governing board (elder, deacon, etc.).
      3) Selection of the senior pastor or senior directional leader(s).
      4) Approval or alteration of constitution/bylaws.
      5) Approval of an annual church budget.
      6) Approval of any major purchase or dissolution.

3. An EFC has as its local polity a form of congregationalism that fits the size and demographics of the congregation.

4. An EFC teaches that congregationalism includes the involvement of the entire body in ministry.

5. An EFC entrusts much of the decision-making to godly leaders who are trained, trusted and allowed to lead.

SCRIPTURE INDEX
Old Testament

SCRIPTURE INDEX

New Testament